CAMBRIDGE TEXTS IN THE
HISTORY OF PHILOSOPHY

PHILIP MELANCHTHON
Orations on Philosophy and Education

CAMBRIDGE TEXTS IN THE
HISTORY OF PHILOSOPHY

Series editors
KARL AMERIKS
Professor of Philosophy at the University of Notre Dame
DESMOND M. CLARKE
Professor of Philosophy at University College Cork

The main objective of Cambridge Texts in the History of Philosophy is to expand the range, variety and quality of texts in the history of philosophy which are available in English. The series includes texts by familiar names (such as Descartes and Kant) and also by less well-known authors. Wherever possible, texts are published in complete and unabridged form, and translations are specially commissioned for the series. Each volume contains a critical introduction together with a guide to further reading and any necessary glossaries and textual apparatus. The volumes are designed for student use at undergraduate and post-graduate level and will be of interest not only to students of philosophy, but also to a wider audience of readers in the history of science, the history of theology and the history of ideas.

For a list of titles published in the series, please see end of book.

PHILIP MELANCHTHON

Orations on Philosophy and Education

EDITED BY

SACHIKO KUSUKAWA
University of Cambridge

TRANSLATED BY

CHRISTINE F. SALAZAR

CAMBRIDGE
UNIVERSITY PRESS

CAMBRIDGE UNIVERSITY PRESS
Cambridge, New York, Melbourne, Madrid, Cape Town, Singapore, São Paulo

Cambridge University Press
The Edinburgh Building, Cambridge CB2 2RU, UK

Published in the United States of America by Cambridge University Press, New York

www.cambridge.org
Information on this title: www.cambridge.org/9780521583503

First published 1999

A catalogue record for this publication is available from the British Library

Library of Congress Cataloguing in Publication data
Melanchthon, Philip, 1497–1560.
[Selections. English. 1999]
Philip Melanchthon : orations on philosophy and education / edited by Sachiko Kusukawa:
translated by Christine F. Salazar.
p.   cm. – (Cambridge texts in the history of philosophy)
Includes bibliographical references and index.
ISBN 0 521 58350 0 (hardback). – ISBN 0 521 58677 1 (paperback)
1. Philosophy – Early works to 1800. 2. Education – Philosophy – Early works to 1800.
I. Kusukawa, Sachiko. II. Title. III. Series.
B785.M41 1999
193–dc21 98-8077 CIP

ISBN-13 978-0-521-58350-3 hardback
ISBN-10 0-521-58350-0 hardback

ISBN-13 978-0-521-58677-1 paperback
ISBN-10 0-521-58677-1 paperback

Transferred to digital printing 2006

In amicitiam

Contents

Acknowledgements

We wish to thank Professor Desmond Clarke for his encouragement, generosity and helpful suggestions. Dr Hilary Gaskin wisely and efficiently guided us to the completion of this project. We are grateful to Mr I. M. LeM. DuQuesnay for granting us access to the CD-ROM facilities in the Classics Faculty Library, University of Cambridge, and to the staff there for their help.

Introduction

Philip Melanchthon is today remembered primarily as the colleague and ally who stood alongside Martin Luther. It is well known that with his humanist skills Melanchthon helped Luther to interpret Greek passages, and assisted him in supporting justification by faith alone as the true message of the Gospel. It was Melanchthon who composed the first systematic treatise of Reformed theology, the *Loci communes*, which underwent several editions and revisions. He proved to be a formidable exegete, despite not taking a doctorate in divinity. He took part in numerous visitations across German lands to ensure that Luther's message of the Gospel was taught correctly, travelled to diets and colloquies to defend Luther's cause, and undertook various diplomatic missions on behalf of the Electors of Saxony. In 1530 he penned the *Augsburg Confession*, the first Protestant manifesto. He reformed the arts curriculum of the University of Wittenberg, and revived classical learning in schools and universities across Germany. He wrote textbooks on most of the subjects in the arts curriculum: Latin and Greek grammar, rhetoric, dialectics, moral philosophy and natural philosophy. For subjects on which he did not write, such as geometry, arithmetic, astronomy and astrology, he wrote commendatory prefaces to textbooks by others. For classroom use, he edited and commented upon texts of numerous classical authors such as Cicero, Demosthenes, Virgil, Ovid, Hesiod and Ptolemy. These texts and textbooks were used well into the seventeenth century, and he trained and inspired a vast number of students who in their turn passed on the message of their teacher to the next generation. For his educational reforms, Melanchthon was accorded the title of Praeceptor Germaniae, the teacher of Germany.

Despite the major rôle he played in the Reformation, and despite the lasting influence he exerted on German schools and universities, Melanchthon's philosophical views have remained curiously unfamiliar to those in the English-speaking world, though recent translations of his work have begun to redress the balance. In particular, Ralph Keen's *Melanchthon Reader* (New York, 1988), a selection of his writing aimed at presenting several different aspects of his life, has included some extracts from Melanchthon's philosophy textbooks and a few orations on philosophical topics, amongst others.[1] However, there has been no attempt to translate and present systematically Melanchthon's philosophical views. The aim of this volume, therefore, is to supplement and augment earlier efforts to make Melanchthon's work available to the English-speaking world, but to concentrate, at the same time, on presenting the breadth and scope of Melanchthon's philosophy as a whole.

Melanchthon's philosophy, however, cannot be studied in isolation from his career as a teacher of classics or as a Reformer. It is difficult to appreciate his passion for Homer without acknowledging his vocation as a Professor of Greek. It is impossible to understand his use of moral philosophy without his concerns with the claims of the radical evangelicals. And his natural philosophy is inconceivable without recognising that the natural world and the universe meant God's Creation for Melanchthon. Most importantly, he expressed his philosophical views within the context of his teaching – in his textbooks and academic orations. Thus, all the writings presented in this volume were composed by Melanchthon in an academic and didactic context, and as such reflect the concerns of the Praeceptor. Since Melanchthon understood all branches of the arts to be connected to each other and to serve one another (orations 1 and 2), it seemed more appropriate to present, so far as was possible, the broad range and scope of what Melanchthon considered as philosophy, rather than to concentrate on translating just one edition of his philosophy textbook out of several other, equally important, textbooks. I have therefore chosen shorter pieces – the orations, prefaces and disputations – on a variety of topics, disciplines and authorities. These orations help illustrate the scope of Melanchthon's philosophy and the interrelationship of the various parts of philosophy education he considered essential. It is through these orations that he promoted the importance of studying philosophy and it is in this form of writing that students in German schools would have

---

[1] Three of my selected orations ('On philosophy', 'On Aristotle' and 'At Luther's funeral') overlap with those selected by Keen; such an overlap, however, was inevitable in order to ensure a representative coverage of topics. For English translations of Melanchthon's texts, see 'Further Reading'.

first come across his ideas. Orations were, in fact, the most influential form of his writings.

Through his offices of teacher, rector or dean, Melanchthon composed a vast number of orations which were often delivered by others, as was customary at the time.[2] From the many orations and prefaces of Melanchthon that are extant, those that illustrate the breadth and depth of Melanchthon's thought have been chosen and arranged in order to resemble closely the structure of the arts curriculum Melanchthon promoted. The first section, 'the scope of education', contains orations which elucidate the relationship between philosophy and religion as well as the importance of philosophical education. In the second section, 'the arts course', virtually all of the disciplines taught in the arts curriculum are discussed so that the scope and rôle of philosophy in the arts faculty could be properly understood. The relevance of philosophy to the higher disciplines of medicine, law and theology was the theme for the next section, 'the higher faculties'. The last section, 'authorities', is intended to show the relative merits of classical and contemporary authors for Melanchthon. I have chosen three classical figures (Plato, Aristotle and Galen), one Arabic commentator (Avicenna), and four contemporaries of Melanchthon: the astronomer and mathematician Johannes Regiomontanus, the humanists Rudolf Agricola and Desiderius Erasmus, and his colleague Martin Luther.

Melanchthon's career

Just over 500 years ago, in 1497, Philip Schwarzerd was born in the town of Bretten to an armourer, Georg Schwarzerd, and Barbara Reuter, the niece of the renowned humanist, Johann Reuchlin. It was this great-uncle who in 1509 hellenised the surname Schwarzerd ('black earth') into 'Melanchthon' for the boy who had shown proficiency in Latin and Greek. Melanchthon went on to obtain his BA from the University of Heidelberg in 1511 and his MA from the University of Tübingen in 1514. While at Tübingen, he learnt Aristotelian dialectics from Franciscus Stadianus, astronomy from Johannes Stöffler and read Rudolf Agricola's *Dialectics*. He worked as corrector for the Tübingen printer Thomas Anshelm who published Melanchthon's edition of Terence's *Comedies* (1516) in which he

---

[2] For Melanchthon's authorship of the orations, see H. Koehn, 'Philipp Melanchthons Reden. Verzeichnis der im 16. Jahrhundert erschienenen Drucke', *Archiv für Geschichte des Buchwesens* 25 (1984),1289–92.

praised Erasmus. Erasmus, in turn, recognised and publicly praised Melanchthon's talents. The two humanists never met, but kept up a cordial correspondence. Each held great respect for the other's works on the classics, but disagreed on matters of religion.

In 1518, at the age of twenty-one and on the recommendation of his great-uncle, Melanchthon was appointed to the Greek professorship at the University of Wittenberg which had been founded by Frederick the Wise in 1502. The inaugural speech, 'On correcting the studies of youth', in which Melanchthon declared his commitment to restore pure, classical learning, impressed Luther, the professor of theology there who had just begun his battle to purify the teaching of Christ. Melanchthon was soon co-operating wholeheartedly with Luther to abolish scholastic teachings at Wittenberg, and writing pamphlets and treatises against Luther's opponents. His *Loci communes* and biblical commentaries were clear and powerful expositions which underpinned Luther's doctrine of justification by faith alone.

When Luther went into hiding on the way back from the Diet of Worms, Melanchthon was expected to assume the leadership of reform in Wittenberg. However, he was unnerved at the speed with which the movement for reform was gathering momentum. Riots and iconoclasm by those impatient for reform followed in Wittenberg, and attendance at the university plummeted. Luther returned to Wittenberg to quell the rioters and resume control.

Meanwhile, more radical and even seditious messages began to be advocated amongst Luther's erstwhile followers, such as Thomas Müntzer and Andreas Carlstadt, while others, such as the peasants in Swabia, Thuringia and the Black Forest, saw in Luther's opposition to the Pope an inspiration for relieving their own grievances. In the spring of 1525 the peasants took up arms, only to be quashed cruelly. Thomas Müntzer, who took part in the uprising, was captured, tortured and executed. Luther publicly distanced himself from the series of insurrections with a tract, *Against the Heavenly Prophets and Against the Robbing and Murdering Hordes of the Peasants*. This was the series of tumultuous events which led both Luther and Melanchthon to turn towards the 'Magisterial Reformation' – from then on, they argued that the initiative for Reform had to come from the ruling princes and governments, not from the populace.

Melanchthon saw an answer to these troubles in education, and he began to rebuild university learning with the arts curriculum at its foundation. His curricular reforms reflect his humanist values: students first had to attain a good grasp of Latin, Greek, dialectics and rhetoric. Twice a month, declamations took place: one by the teacher of rhetoric or grammar, another by a student whose declamation had been checked and authorised by the teacher. Students then learnt mathematics: first from Euclid's *Elements*, arithmetic and Sacrobosco's *De Sphaera*, followed by the *Theorica planetarum* and the *Almagest*. The students were also introduced to elements of natural philosophy through the second book of Pliny's *Natural History*. They then learnt Aristotelian natural philosophy and moral philosophy. Twice a month, disputations by the teacher of natural philosophy or mathematics were held. The teaching of Aristotle's *Metaphysics* was dropped at Wittenberg, since it was considered primarily as the 'divine science' which studied the various modes of God's being and thus formed the bulwark of scholastic theology.

Melanchthon also wrote textbooks on several arts subjects for use in the classroom: Latin grammar, Greek grammar, rhetoric, dialectics, moral philosophy and natural philosophy. These works were influential in spreading the format of the textbook, designed specifically for classroom use, which paraphrased and summarised several works of Aristotle and other authors into a small quarto or octavo booklet.[3] Instead of the traditional *quaestio* method by which all seeming inconsistencies within the texts of Aristotle and amongst authorities were resolved through logical distinctions, Melanchthon adopted in his textbook a topical method, dealing with principal topics (*loci*) which were mainly explicated in a question-and-answer form. Thus, Melanchthon designed a new arts curriculum for the University of Wittenberg, wrote new textbooks for it, and taught them himself. He also advised on educational reforms for the universities of Tübingen, Leipzig and Heidelberg, as well as other secondary schools.

On 18 February 1546 Luther died, and soon afterwards the Elector John Frederick was defeated by Charles V in the Schmalkaldic War, and Wittenberg fell into the hands of Maurice of Saxony. Melanchthon persuaded Maurice to re-open the university, and negotiated the Leipzig Interim which allowed Saxony to retain Protestant doctrine under conservative rites. For the remaining years of his life Melanchthon sought dialogue with Roman Catholics and other evangelicals. He was, however, dogged with attacks from his previous colleagues and students such as Nicholas

---

[3] For the development of the philosophical textbook, including Melanchthon's contribution, see C. B. Schmitt, 'The Rise of the Philosophical Textbook', *The Cambridge History of Renaissance Philosophy*, ed. C. B. Schmitt *et al.* (Cambridge, 1988), pp. 792–804.

Amsdorff and Matthias Flaccius Illyricus (the 'gnesio-Lutherans'), for having departed too far from Luther's original message and for having conceded too much to the opposition. Yet even those who turned against him on doctrinal matters could not shake off the humanist education he had instilled in them. His students, both friends and foes alike, owed him a great debt for their classical heritage.

Melanchthon's use of Aristotelian philosophy

One of the puzzling issues in the scholarship on Melanchthon and Luther has been the seeming contradiction between the two in their attitudes towards the use of Aristotelian philosophy. As is well known, Aristotle's works comprised a substantial and essential part of the arts curricula in late medieval universities. The *Categories*, the *Prior Analytics* and the *Posterior Analytics* were the basis of logical training; the *Nicomachean Ethics* was used for moral philosophy; and for the mastery of natural philosophy, the *Physics*, *On the Soul*, the *Meteorology* and *On Generation and Corruption* were essential. Natural philosophy was an important subject in which the nature of being, insofar as it was natural, was studied. This was a necessary preparation for studying Aristotle's *Metaphysics*, which was regarded as the study of being *qua* being, which led to the study of the modes of being of the divinity. Natural philosophy was thus often called a 'handmaiden' to theology. Hence natural philosophy had little to do with observing nature and performing experiments in this period. Rather, it was based on reading and understanding Aristotle's texts and was studied with rigorous logical reasoning, reconciling on the way seeming inconsistencies within Aristotle's texts, amongst scholastic commentators of Aristotle, and between philosophy and the doctrine of the Church.[4]

Luther's famous attack on Aristotle was levelled at such scholastic uses of Aristotle for theology and at the underlying assumption that human reason on its own could scrutinise essential modes of the divinity – as Luther thundered, 'the whole of Aristotle is to theology as darkness is to light'.[5]

---

[4] For the study of metaphysics, see Charles Lohr, 'Metaphysics', in *The Cambridge History of Renaissance Philosophy*, ed. C. B. Schmitt *et al.* (Cambridge, 1988), pp. 537–638, and for the nature of medieval natural philosophy see John Murdoch, 'The Analytical Character of Late Medieval Learning: Natural Philosophy without Nature', in *Approaches to Nature in the Middle Ages*, ed. L. D. Roberts (New York, 1982), pp. 171–213.

[5] Martin Luther, 'Disputation against Scholastic Theology', trans. H. J. Grimm, in *Luther's Works*, ed. J. Pelikan and H. T. Lehman (55 vols., St Louis, 1955–76), vol. 31, p. 12.

Melanchthon, fourteen years junior to Luther, initially supported his move at the University of Wittenberg to abolish the teaching of Aristotle.

Historical circumstances, however, forced Melanchthon to re-evaluate the importance of Aristotle. He began to feel keenly the threat of evangelical radicals who advocated (among other things) the right to disobey civil governments. During the riots in Wittenberg in 1521 and 1522 he had come across the 'Zwickau Prophets', who claimed to hold direct colloquies with the Holy Spirit, and who interpreted the Bible freely. Thomas Müntzer preached evangelical and seditious messages, and perished with the peasants in 1525. In 1527 and 1528 Melanchthon had a first-hand encounter with the Anabaptists in Thuringia. All these people seemed to claim some special access to the Holy Spirit or sacred knowledge, imposed arbitrary human interpretations on the Bible, and drew out radical messages of action which would have resulted in resisting or overturning the existing political order. Melanchthon saw poor education and confusion of philosophy and theology as the root of the problem. And this is when he turned to Aristotelian philosophy for a solution to the problem of the evangelical radicals. He needed to establish the distinction between theological truths and truths attainable through human reason alone. He needed to establish proper ways of philosophical demonstration. Above all, he needed to prove that everybody, both believers and unbelievers alike, had to obey civil authority. To this end, Melanchthon was to find Aristotle's philosophy, especially his teleology, a powerful tool. Melanchthon's revaluation of philosophy and of Aristotelian philosophy was therefore not undertaken in defiance of Luther's programme for Reform. Rather, Melanchthon's was a reform of philosophy carried out in order to defend Luther's cause.

Philosophy as knowledge of law

In order to appreciate the transformation Melanchthon effected on Aristotelian philosophy as it was traditionally taught in universities, it is important to heed the distinction he himself employed time and again between Law and Gospel. Melanchthon explained that, at best, philosophy was knowledge of Law, and could never prove or teach the central saving message of the Gospel, justification by faith alone (oration 3). Philosophy may indeed *confirm* certain theological ideas, such as the providential care of God towards humans, but it would never prove or *affirm* the truth of such concepts. This was an important distinction to maintain in the face of

Luther's distrust of human reasoning in understanding God's will. Melanchthon's definition of philosophy as knowledge of Law is particularly apposite, as he was intent on demonstrating the moral philosophical point that civil magistrates and rules had to be obeyed.

There are three areas of philosophy Melanchthon developed in order to render it a proper knowledge of Law: dialectics, moral philosophy and natural philosophy. In his dialectics textbooks (*Four Books on Dialectics*; *Questions on Dialectics*), Melanchthon affirmed, in opposition to Aristotle, that there was innate knowledge given by God to all human beings, namely natural light. Drawing on Stoic ideas, Melanchthon explained that there were three criteria of certainty. Moral principles (e.g. killing one's parents is wrong) and scientific principles (e.g. two plus two equals four); universal experience (e.g. fire is hot), the opposite of which would lead to destruction of the thing concerned; and understanding of the procedures of syllogism. A fourth criterion of certainty was available for believers only, namely divine revelation.[6] The first three criteria, divinely endowed innate knowledge, guaranteed the validity of demonstrative knowledge in philosophy. Such innate knowledge would ensure the certainty needed to compel every human being, regardless of their faith, to acquiesce to philosophically derived consequences, such as the rightness of obeying civil governments. Proper dialectical procedures would thus force all people to agree to demonstrated conclusions, and this is why Melanchthon calls dialectics a 'chain of concord' (oration 9).

For moral philosophy, Melanchthon used parts of Aristotle's *Nicomachean Ethics* (especially book V) in order to argue that humans were created for a purpose and that that purpose was to obey the divinely instituted order, such as civil governments. Indeed, Melanchthon was adamant that, even at times of war, laws had to be upheld (orations 17 and 22). Following the Aristotelian definitions of demonstrative science, however, Melanchthon explained that the first principle of moral philosophy – that humans were created for a definite purpose – could *not* be demonstrated within moral philosophy itself.[7] This first principle had to be demonstrated elsewhere, and he allotted this rôle to natural philosophy.

Melanchthon's immediate aim was to prove this principle by using Aristotle's *On the Soul*, and he produced a commentary on it in 1540

[6] *Liber de anima*, in Philip Melanchthon, *Corpus Reformatorum Philippi Melanthonis Opera quae supersunt omnia*, ed. C. B. Bretschneider and H. E. Bindseil (28 vols., Halle, 1834–52, Brunswick, 1853–60) (CR hereafter), vol. 13, 150f.

[7] Ibid., 650.

(*Commentary on the Soul*), and a revised edition in 1552 (*Book on the Soul*). He then gradually expanded the scope of natural philosophy by drawing on Aristotle's other books on nature (such as the *Physics*, *On the Heavens* and *Meteorology*), so that he could prove that the entire universe, with the earth and humans at its centre, was created by God with wonderful providential care. This culminated in his textbook, the *Elements of Natural Philosophy* (1549).

These textbooks on natural philosophy are well known to historians of science because they incorporate findings from the two most famous books in the history of science, printed in 1543 – *On Fabric of the Human Body* of Andreas Vesalius, and *On the Revolutions* of Nicholas Copernicus. Melanchthon's references to Vesalius may be found in his *Book on the Soul*, and those to Copernicus in the *Elements of Natural Philosophy*. Rather than singling out these cases as 'progressive' moments in Melanchthon's thought, they should be understood in the light of an ethically orientated natural philosophy designed to address the political problems faced by Luther.

Melanchthon's aim in his natural philosophy was to demonstrate that absolutely everything in this world was created by God. His belief, which was shared by Luther, that God's providence was at work in this physical world led to his promotion of two important areas of natural philosophy – human anatomy and astrology. The importance of human anatomy was underlined in the *Commentary on the Soul* (oration 18). At the outset Melanchthon explains that his commentary is about the human soul, rather than about a generic definition of the soul for all 'ensouled' beings, which was Aristotle's original programme. Melanchthon explains, furthermore, that by the human soul he means both the human body and soul. This is consistent with Luther's position that the entire human being, both body and soul, rather than the rational soul alone, is the object of grace.[8] Melanchthon therefore devotes almost two-thirds of his textbook on the soul to human anatomy based on Galen before tackling the standard topics of the nutritive, sensitive and rational souls. He explained that one should examine the human body as if one were in a 'temple or sacred place' in order to praise the wondrous care and skill of the Maker.[9] By showing that every single part of the human body is designed to fulfil a specific purpose, Melanchthon argues that the study of human anatomy reveals the

---

[8] Martin Luther, *Dr. Martin Luthers Werke, kritische Gesamtausgabe* (63 vols. Weimar, 1883–1987), vol. 2, p. 415.

[9] Philip Melanchthon, *Commentarius de anima* (Wittenberg, 1540), sigs. 44^v – 45^r.

admirable skill, foresight and care of the Creator. It is similarly for the unravelling of the teleological structure of the human body that Melanchthon found Vesalius' findings[10] important and worth including in the revised edition of 1552, the *Book on the Soul* (oration 19).

Alongside the praise of the skill of the Creator, Melanchthon presented a view of the human body which was strikingly passive in the section on medical spirits. Medical sprits were considered to be very fine vapours squeezed out of the blood, and were believed in standard medical theories to be the instrument by which heat was conveyed throughout the body and by which knowledge was transmitted in the ventricles of the brain. Melanchthon argued that the Holy Spirit or the Devil could mix with these medical spirits. In pious men, the Holy Spirit would mix with the medical spirits and render knowledge of God clearer; evil spirits on the other hand could also mix with the medical spirits and impede judgement and cause the limbs to perform the cruellest of deeds, such as when Medea killed her own children.[11] The presence of the Holy Spirit as well as the Devil thus became a physical reality for Melanchthon, but the human body itself was a mere passive recipient unable to control these spirits.[12] The best one could do was pray for help. The human anatomy which praised the skill of the Creator thus also taught that, in stark contrast, humans were incapacitated in controlling their spiritual welfare (oration 20).

The second part of Melanchthon's commentary on the soul dealt with the traditional topics of Aristotle's *On the Soul*. What is noticeable in Melanchthon's commentary, however, is the preponderance of biblical quotations in the discussion of the human will and the image of God in man. When defining the object of the human will, Melanchthon points out that had knowledge of humans *not* been clouded by Original Sin, then we would know that the object of our will was God. But Fallen Man does not have perfect knowledge, so Fallen Man cannot know the true object of his will. That is, philosophical arguments cannot define the true object of the human will. Thus, Melanchthon had recourse to the Bible: Deuteronomy 6:5: 'you shall love the lord your God with all your heart'. This quotation is the basis on which Melanchthon affirms that the object of will should be God. Similarly, when discussing the immortality of the soul it is simply

---

[10] For Vesalius' teleology, see Nancy Siraisi, 'Vesalius and the Reading of Galen's Teleology', *Renaissance Quarterly*, 50 (1997), 1–33.

[11] Melanchthon, *Liber de anima*, CR XIII, 88f.

[12] D. P. Walker, 'Medical Spirits and God and the Soul', in *Spiritus*, ed. M. Fattori and M. Bianchi (Rome, 1984), p. 228.

treated as given and unproblematic by Melanchthon.[13] He shows no interest in dealing with the extensive and sophisticated philosophical arguments brought to bear on the subject by the Italian philosophers, such as Pomponazzi, of a generation earlier. In fact, Melanchthon's strategy here is a deliberate one: to use biblical arguments whenever defining or discussing spiritual issues or theological truths. This, of course, is consistent with the Lutheran position that human reason cannot discover theological truths unaided. Such truths have to be found in the Bible. It thus indicates the limit of philosophy as knowledge of Law.

In the textbook *The Elements of Natural Philosophy* Melanchthon taught how the entire physical universe was created by God's providential design. Astronomy and astrology showed the orderliness of Creation. The studies of astronomy and astrology were inseparable for him, since the one taught how the planets moved and what positions they would take, and the other what effects the planets in certain positions would have. Melanchthon believed that God was at work physically through the planets and that astrology would yield knowledge about the physical effects of planets (oration 14). Geography also became a study in which traces of the providence of God could be investigated, rather than a study of the process of God's creation (orations 12 and 13). These areas of study were all considered part of natural philosophy. According to Melanchthon, astrology was useful for another reason, because it provided moral guidance. By consulting horoscopes, individual humans could become aware of their weaknesses and thus could better avoid temptation and the devil. It is particularly important to note that Melanchthon's use of Copernicus' findings was restricted to the data that offered improved predictions of planetary positions (such as the apogees of the sun and of the three superior planets). They therefore improved astrological knowledge.

The ways in which Melanchthon incorporated the findings of Vesalius and of Copernicus thus illustrate well the nature of Melanchthon's natural philosophy. They were integrated into a natural philosophy that demonstrated that God's providence was at work in this universe. This reformed philosophy became the core of the arts curriculum for Melanchthon, and other humanistic studies were promoted as necessary preparations for studying this reformed philosophy. The classical languages, rhetoric and dialectic were all essential for the good citizen as well as for the good theologian (orations 4–9). Compared to earlier humanists who had promoted

[13] Melanchthon, *Liber de anima*, CR XIII, 154, 172–8.

the mathematical arts as useful for sharpening one's natural intelligence, Melanchthon provided a much stronger reason for studying them. For Melanchthon the studies of both arithmetic and geometry were necessary preparations for his kind of natural philosophy (orations 10 and 11), while the studies of astronomy and astrology were integral parts of natural philosophy. For Melanchthon, therefore, to study philosophy meant to study the whole of the arts curriculum, and such a study was necessary for all good Christians, be they statesmen or theologians (oration 2). In essence, Melanchthon's philosophy was Aristotelian in that he saw in Aristotle's works a coherent method of philosophising, whereas he found Plato's style of writing rather obscure and unhelpful (orations 24 and 25).

A Lutheran philosophy

Melanchthon thus reformed traditional Aristotelian philosophy in order to provide a world-view in which civil disobedience had to be refuted conclusively. In the sense that this reform was instigated by the need to defend Luther's cause against the threat of the evangelical radicals, one can interpret Melanchthon as trying to create a Lutheran philosophy. Melanchthon's philosophy may be understood as Lutheran in another sense in that it was reformed according to the principle of the Lutheran distrust of human reason. By drawing on traditional concepts from logic, philosophy and medicine and providing them with new emphases and distinctions, Melanchthon redefined the scope of philosophy so that human reason on its own could not discover theological truths.

For instance, Melanchthon preserved the scholastic distinction between intuitive and abstract cognition: intuitive knowledge was knowledge of an object which was present in front of oneself and perceived by the senses and the mind simultaneously. Melanchthon explained that the ancients called it 'intuitive definition', and he illustrated this point by saying that there was no better way of knowing the plant called wormwood than by having one shown to you directly. Intuitive cognition was such a direct apprehension of the singular, while abstract cognition was knowledge of things which were not necessarily present, such as absent friends, universals or thoughts which cannot be perceived by the senses.

Of these two kinds of knowledge, Melanchthon indicated that intuitive knowledge of God was not available to humans any more. Due to the Fall, he pointed out that humans now have less knowledge of God, as well as of spiritual natures and of substances of other bodies, and that at best one recognised these things rather obscurely and tenuously. This is an obvious reference to the passage in 1 Corinthians 13:12: 'for now we see through a glass, darkly; but then face to face'. A 'face-to-face' knowledge of God, Melanchthon is quite clear, is something which is allowed only when one enters heaven. As he explained, we may hear his Word in this life, but we may see him only in the life after.[14] Intuitive cognition of God, which was often considered possible by scholastic thinkers as beatific visions by holy men, is a path now firmly closed by Melanchthon to every Fallen Man.[15]

Thus only abstract cognition of God, which was at best dark and tenuous, was now available to humans. This obscure and tenuous, abstract knowledge of God, spirits and substances was, Melanchthon further explained, acquired through *a posteriori* reasoning, namely by tracing causes from their effects. This form of reasoning is best observed in Melanchthon's natural philosophy: the beautiful orderliness of nature proves that it cannot have come into existence by chance, but that it came into being because of a skilful creator who cared for humankind (oration 16). The limitation placed on human knowledge of God in this life also explains why, at Luther's funeral, Melanchthon so enviously refers to the state of Luther's knowledge: what beautiful vision he must be beholding, face to face with God (oration 31).

The fact that Fallen Man was now restricted to an abstract knowledge of God also meant for Melanchthon that Fallen Man necessarily needed his internal senses. Internal senses were considered the faculties of the sensitive soul, such as common sense, imagination and memory, which functioned in the ventricles of the brain: They were the functions that retained and manipulated the sensible species received from the five external senses. These sensible species were then abstracted into intelligible species, which could then in turn be manipulated by the intellect. The concept of internal senses was fully developed by Arabic commentators of Aristotle who found his explanations somewhat vague and unsystematic. The humanist tendency of the Renaissance was to concentrate on the Greek text of Aristotle and therefore to gloss over the extensive medieval

---

[14] *Ibid,.* 145, 172.
[15] For the scholastic treatment of intuitive and abstract cognition, see Leen Spruit, *Species Intelligibilis* (2 vols., Leiden, 1994–6); S. J. Day, *Intuitive Cognition: a Key to the Significance of the Later Scholastics* (New York, 1947).

discussions on these interior senses of Arabic origin.[16] Indeed, there are some humanist commentaries on the *On the Soul* of this period, such as the one by Johannes Lonicer, which refused even to mention the internal senses (*On Aristotle's Physics ... On the Soul*, Marburg, 1540). In spite of his humanist training, Melanchthon went against this trend and retained the concept of internal senses, because it was a corollary to the limited scope of human rational knowledge.

In addition to the traditional concept of intuitive cognition, Melanchthon closed another traditional path of attaining knowledge of God by reason, namely analogy. As is well known, 'analogy' was considered to be the third mode of supposition, half way between univocation and equivocation, mentioned by Aristotle in the opening passage of the *Categories*. The original term used there by Aristotle, namely 'amphibolous', did not carry the sense of transferring the meaning of a predicate in a manner proportionate to the relation of the two subjects involved. For Aristotle, the term in fact meant 'ambiguous' supposition. It was the Arabic and Jewish commentators who reinterpreted the section of the *Categories* and developed the concept of 'analogy' as something between univocation and equivocation. The medieval scholastic commentators, especially Aquinas, considered analogy an important and powerful way to infer something about the Creator from his Creation.[17] Melanchthon completely ignores this sense of the term 'analogy'. For Melanchthon, analogy instead meant proportionality, namely similarity of two proportions, which in turn are ratios between two quantities. In other words, for Melanchthon analogy was now restricted to mean an *arithmetic* relation. And meanwhile Melanchthon uses the term 'amphibolous' to mean an error generated by ambiguous phrases or syntax (rather than an error generated by ambiguity of a single word, which is classed under 'equivocation'), and it occurs in a discussion of how to refute *false* arguments.[18]

[16] Melanchthon, *Liber de anima*, CR XIII, 145. For the medieval commentary tradition on the internal senses, see H. A. Wolfson, 'The Internal Senses in Latin, Arabic and Hebrew Philosophic Texts', *Harvard Theological Review* 27 (1935), 69–133, and for Renaissance trends, see K. Park, 'The Organic Soul' in *The Cambridge History of Renaissance Philosophy*, ed. Quentin Skinner *et al.* (Cambridge, 1988), pp. 464–84.

[17] Something close to analogy is Aristotle's use of paradigm, for which see G. E. R. Lloyd, 'Metaphor and the Language of Science', in his *The Revolutions of Wisdom: Studies in the Claims and Practice of Ancient Greek Science* (Berkeley, Los Angeles and London, 1987), pp. 172–214. For Arabic commentators, see H. A. Wolfson, 'The Amphibolous Terms in Aristotle, Arabic Philosophy and Maimonides', in his *Studies in the History of Philosophy and Religion*, ed. I. Tuersky and G. H. Williams (Cambridge, MA, 1973), vol. 1, pp. 455–77.

[18] Melanchthon, *Erotemata dialectices*, CR XIII, 696, 727–9.

Melanchthon's use of the term 'amphibolous' may at first sight seem to indicate his humanist leanings to be faithful to the original Greek text of Aristotle, but, as we have seen earlier, he was equally happy to retain medieval concepts such as the internal senses. It is important to note, therefore, his effort to incorporate the Lutheran distrust for human reason if we are to establish a coherent strategy behind what seems like a mixture of humanist and non-humanist tendencies in his philosophy. Analogy, for Melanchthon, now cannot be a path by which essential modes of the Creator may be inferred from his Creation. Significantly, neither Calvin nor Luther found use for analogy in their theology either.[19]

Such modifications of traditional scholastic concepts based on the Lutheran distrust of human reason meant that Melanchthon indeed had transformed the character of philosophy. And this transformation is nowhere seen more clearly than in his natural philosophy, which can be characterised by the Aristotelian, *a posteriori* arguments of tracing causes from the effects in nature, and an almost obsessive reiteration that such arguments *confirmed* God's providence in this creation. *A posteriori* arguments for the providence of God in nature using Aristotle's teleology were not new, and indeed they remind us of one of Thomas Aquinas' proofs for the existence of God. Melanchthon's natural philosophy, however, is narrower than that of Aquinas in the sense that Melanchthon's aim was to confirm one point only: the providence of God in nature. Moreover, this point was confirmed with only one kind of causality, an *a posteriori* one. That is, Melanchthon's natural philosophy narrowed down the range of arguments that may be validly employed therein and focused on just one aspect of the divinity which was knowable even to the pagans. These characteristics were the results of Melanchthon's reorganisation of philosophy based on the Lutheran distrust of human reason.

It may seem that confirming one theological truth with one kind of causal argument was a weak *raison d'être* for a natural philosophy; especially once demonstrated, such a natural philosophy would only have a function as a theoretical justification for moral philosophy and not much else. Melanchthon, however, explained that there was a point in repeatedly confirming the providence of God in this world. And this was for times of adverse conditions and hardship: a knowledge of the providence of

---

[19] The scholastic idea of 'analogia entis' is not found either in Luther or Calvin; see B. Mondin, *The Principle of Analogy in Protestant and Catholic Theology* (The Hague, 1968, 2nd edn originally published 1963).

God in such circumstances built trust and hope that one day the wicked will be punished by God and the just saved. Indeed, as Robert Kolb has argued, a proclamation of the providence of God became one of the most important marks of martyrdom and witnesses to faith among Lutherans.[20] Melanchthon often called nature a theatre of God, a theatre which men were created to watch. Humans, in their wretched spiritual incapacity, are here passive onlookers, but at least they can watch and what they watch is the plan of God unfolding in the universe. To trace the providential design of God in nature was essentially a tracing of the footprints of God, and it became the most prominent theme running through the studies of nature pursued by Melanchthon and his followers.

Not only did Melanchthon transform traditional philosophy into an inspirational, Lutheran one, but he also provided further ways in which philosophical studies could be enriched. Particularly important in this context is his view on non-essential predication. Traditionally, a definition was constructed with a genus and attribute which was essential to or part of the essence of the substance in question, such as 'man is a rational animal.' A mode of definition by listing non-essential accidents, such as 'a crow is a bird with black feathers, yellow beak and so on', was considered the weakest form of definition and more useful for rhetorical purposes. Specifying such accidental attributes was considered a weak form of definition because the attributes were related to substances in a non-essential way and could be shared by other substances. Hence this definition was often called 'description'.

Melanchthon nevertheless pointed out that this description was useful when, for instance, one could indicate what sort of a person Thersites (*Iliad* I. 225–45) was by defining him as a man who was squint-eyed, pointy-headed, hump-backed, garrulous and scurrilous. More importantly, Melanchthon said that it is with such description that one often had to content oneself, because Fallen Man could have knowledge of substances *only* through their accidents.[21] By allowing inferences from non-essential accidents, Melanchthon broadened the ways in which one may attain understandings of substances. This was a dialectical and epistemological

---

[20] Melanchthon, *Initia doctrinae physicae*, CR XIII, 339. R. Kolb, *For All the Saints: Changing Perceptions of Martyrdom and Sainthood in the Lutheran Reformation* (Macon, GA, 1987).

[21] Melanchthon, *Erotemata dialectices*, CR XIII, 522–9; note that Melanchthon was aware of the shortage of *propria*, as was Agricola, for whom see Peter Mack, *Renaissance Argument: Valla and Agricola in the Traditions of Rhetoric and Dialectic* (Leiden, 1993).

position that had important implications for his followers. For instance, it enabled the Professor of Medicine at the University of Tübingen, Leonhard Fuchs, to justify his use of pictures in his commentary on plants.[22]

Fallen Man for Melanchthon was thus a human being who needed the internal senses and the intelligible species generated by them in order to gain some knowledge, albeit obscure, of God. There was now no direct way that human reason could catch even a glimpse of divine truth in this life. As knowledge by abstraction, philosophy started with the effects of nature or accidents of substances and sought to establish the cause or the nature of a substance. This and only this type of cognition was available to humans for gaining an understanding of God, spirits or substances. Although this knowledge may be obscure and limited, philosophy was an important and positive knowledge for Fallen Man. It could demonstrate the rightness of civil obedience; it could demonstrate that the whole of nature was created by God; it could prove God's providence for humans; and above all it was necessary for a true Christian (oration 15).

Melanchthon's legacy

Melanchthon's philosophical legacy was vast: his Aristotelian philosophy was taught and re-taught in numerous universities and schools across Protestant Germany. This tradition has sometimes unfortunately been characterised as the 'Second Scholastic', due to its reliance on the Aristotelian corpus, but it is a legacy which was neither rigid nor monolithic. Indeed, during the last quarter of the sixteenth century several of his followers found ways to forge a fertile synthesis with the works of Petrus Ramus (the 'Philippo-Ramists'), whilst other Lutherans, such as Nicholas Taurellus, saw that metaphysics could be used profitably in their controversy with the Calvinists. Natural philosophy as a study of God's providential plan was taken into new areas by his followers. A large number of botanists were associated with the teaching at Wittenberg; a new tradition of studying geography was established at Wittenberg; astrology and anatomy were studied by students in the arts faculty who did not necessarily become medics; while astronomy, as part of a natural philosophy of

---

[22] See my 'Leonhard Fuchs on the Importance of Pictures', *Journal of the History of Ideas*, 58:3 (1997), 403–27.

Creation, was an important element in the teaching at the University of Tübingen, which Kepler attended.[23]

Melanchthon's commentary on the soul was also influential. His way of reading Aristotle's *On the Soul* for a Christian knowledge of the human body and soul was taught at Jena by Johannes Stigelius (*Commentaries on the Soul*, Wittenberg, 1570) and Victorinus Strigelius (*On Philip Melanchthon's Booklet on the Soul*, Leipzig,1590). Strigelius and Stigelius, both students of Melanchthon, argued that only abstract knowledge of God was possible. At the turn of the century, Melanchthon's commentary on the *On the Soul* also attracted much attention amongst mainly Calvinist teachers associated with the Marburg professor, Rudolph Goclenius Sr: Bruno Seidel, *Instructive Commentary on the Body and Soul of Man* (Hanau, 1594); Rudolph Snell, *On Philip Melanchthon's On the Soul* (Frankfurt, 1596); and Otto Casmannus, *Psychological Anthropology* (Frankfurt, 1594) and *Anthropology, the Second Part* (Frankfurt, 1596). Casmannus called Melanchthon's doctrine of the human soul and body an 'anthropologia', which was to be subdivided into a study of the soul ('psychologia'), and a study of the human body ('somatologia'). The term 'anthropologia' was also used in the same vein by Johannes Magirus, another Marburg professor (1560–96), to refer to his commentary on Melanchthon's *On the Soul* (*Anthropology, that is, a Commentary on Melanchthon's Booklet on the Soul*, Frankfurt, 1603). It is in this context of studying Melanchthon's commentary on *On the Soul* that Goclenius and his circle are credited with the promotion of the term 'psychology'.[24]

The Calvinist philosopher Goclenius himself, following Strigelius (who in turn was drawing on Melanchthon), explained in his *Philosophical Lexicon* that only abstract knowledge of the divine was available in this life. Goclenius then gave his famous tripartite distinction of abstraction: physical, mathematical and transnatural. Physical abstraction was abstraction from individuals, as one extracted the signified from this or that body. Mathematical abstraction abstracted from both individual and universal things, such as simple or mixed bodies. Finally, transnatural abstraction was abstraction from all things. The second abstraction, the mathematical

---

[23] For the 'Philippo-Ramists', see Joseph S. Freedman, 'The Diffusion of the Writings of Petrus Ramus in Central Europe, c. 1570–c. 1630', *Renaissance Quarterly* 46 (1993), 98–152. For Nicholas Taurellus, see Charles Lohr, 'Metaphysics', pp. 623f. For Melanchthon's legacy in other fields of inquiry, see 'Further Reading'.

[24] F. H. Lapionte, 'The Origin and Evolution of the Term "Psychology"', *Rivista Critica di Storia della Filosofia*, 28 (1973), 138–60.

one, which was also defined as a study of being and transcendental things, Goclenius named, for the first time, *ontological*.[25] Thus new philosophical concepts developed out of Melanchthon's philosophical legacy, which eventually formed the philosophical background to important philosophers such as Gottfried Wilhelm Leibniz.

By the time Melanchthon died, the emphasis on the proper grasp of Latin and Greek, the promotion of the mathematical arts, and the extensive use of dialectical and rhetorical methods – the humanistic values he extolled repeatedly in his orations – were taking root in schools and universities across German Protestant lands. Melanchthon had been instrumental in introducing these values into Germany, just as the Jesuits elsewhere were similarly engaged in establishing those humanistic values as the bedrock of university education. It is important to note, however, that philosophy was the core of Melanchthon's humanistic curriculum. The way he reformed philosophy also indicates how his Lutheran beliefs affected the way he utilised his humanistic, as well as scholastic, heritage. He saw the works of classical authors as excellent models for reforming the arts curriculum and scholastic philosophy, but he was also prepared to draw on contemporary authors, such as Copernicus or Vesalius, so long as they provided useful improvements to his reformed philosophy. His attitude towards Erasmus (oration 30) sums up well his attitude to the studies of the humanists; he has the highest respect for the scholarly achievements of Erasmus in the classics, and in some ways Erasmus even anticipates Luther; yet he is no Luther.

It would, of course, be misleading to associate any particular philosophy or ideology with humanism itself, but the new humanist attitude towards the text, the author and the past in some ways gave rise to, it seems, a renewed way of philosophising. With the passionate zeal of the first generation of humanists to recover the texts of classical authors, the range of philosophical authors and sects in classical antiquity one could draw upon had expanded dramatically. The humanist paraphrases, summaries, topical treatments and philological analyses in fact approached statements by classical authors in a way fundamentally different from the traditional *quaestio* method, by which inconsistencies within the same author or amongst established authorities were resolved through logical distinctions. The humanist approach, as argued by Kessler, eventually relativised the

[25] Rudolph Goclenius, *Lexicon Philosophicum* (Frankfurt 1613), pp. 770, 16.

importance of the words of a single philosophical authority.[26] The question of how humanism affected the history of Western European philosophy is still open and requires further research. I hope nevertheless that with this volume we are now in a position to appreciate the historical context in which at least one humanist, Philip Melanchthon, found the need and positive use for philosophy.

Melanchthon's style of writing: the demonstrative oration

Most of Melanchthon's orations and prefaces follow the style of demonstrative speeches. As is well known, classical rhetoricians and their followers distinguished three kinds of rhetorical speeches according to the attitude of the listeners (Aristotle, *Rhetoric* I.iii.9). The deliberative speech urges the listener to make a decision about a future action. The forensic speech, attacking or defending somebody as in legal cases, urges the listener to make judgements on past events. The demonstrative speech praises or censures somebody, and is concerned to present a case to listeners as if they were spectators. Speeches eulogising various disciplines and persons thus follow the style of the demonstrative genre of praise and blame. As many historians have pointed out, the sixteenth century saw the rise of the use of the demonstrative speech to unprecedented scales: from papal courts to student classrooms, demonstrative orations were written and delivered frequently.

Melanchthon himself made the demonstrative genre the central format of his teaching. In his *Three Books on Rhetoric* (1519), he explained how the demonstrative speech was the fundamental type of speech: it gave rise to topics of invention and the entire method of judgement, and ensured the way to the other genre of speeches. The first function of demonstrative speeches was to teach, and the second to praise or blame. According to Melanchthon, many rhetoricians had dealt amply with the second function, but hardly with the first; the first function of teaching by demonstrative speech was explained properly in his dialectics. As Schneider has pointed out, the demonstrative genre is what united Melanchthon's rhetoric and dialectics.[27]

[26] Eckhard Kessler, 'Introducing Aristotle to the 16th Century: the Lefèvre Enterprise', in *Conversations with Aristotle*, ed. Constance Blackwell and Sachiko Kusukawa, forthcoming.

[27] 'Nos a genere demonstrativo vel hoc maxime ordimur, quod ex ipso loci omnes inventionis, iudicandi ratio tota nascitur, et ad reliqua genera viam munit.' *De rhetorica libri tres* (Cologne, 1523), a2^r. R. Schneider, *Philip Melanchthon's Rhetorical Construal of Biblical Authority: Oratio Sacra*, Text and Studies in Religion 5 (Lewiston, NY and Lampeter, Wales, 1990), pp. 65–85.

By 1529, in his *Elements of Rhetoric*, Melanchthon had made this first function of demonstrative speech into an independent, fourth kind of speech alongside the traditional three, and called it the didactic genre. The didactic speech was considered particularly useful for his time, for suasory meetings of the Church and to teach dogma correctly. It was centred on a dialectical definition, which was then further amplified by rhetoric in order to teach effectively to the uninitiated. Demonstrative speech as praise or blame still closely resembled the didactic genre: if somebody wished to praise the laws or to speak on the authority of laws, he should define the laws and amplify on their definition.[28]

Melanchthon further explained in his rhetorical manuals what an exemplary oration should contain. For instance, when praising or blaming a person, the entire *narratio* should be devoted to relating a person's entire history in order: the person's native country, sex, family, talent, education, learning, teaching, deeds, distinctions in such deeds, death, and reputation after death. When praising something like philosophy, eloquence or peace, the reputation of the thing may be taken from its efficient causes or inventors, for example, philosophy is the gift of God; and the utility of the thing from its purpose, for example, philosophy shows important things about life, civil behaviour, law and medicine.[29]

In practice, Melanchthon taught rhetoric by analysing numerous Ciceronian orations as well as central biblical texts such as Romans. Rhetorical study of these texts was important because he believed that a methodical analysis of a text by uncovering its logical coherence was to reconstruct the actual process of creating a text and thus to disclose the author's intention. As Meerhoff has argued, rhetorical analysis of a text was for Melanchthon tantamount to composing the text.[30] Melanchthon's own rhetorical manuals are thus excellent keys to understanding how his orations were composed and structured.

During the course of the sixteenth century Melanchthon's orations themselves became examples by which students learnt rhetoric. The following collection therefore presents Melanchthon's philosophy in his most influential form of writing and in his most inspirational office as a teacher.

---

[28] CR XIII, 421.
[29] *Ibid.*, 449f.
[30] For Melanchthon's rhetoric, see Kees Meerhoff, 'The Significance of Philip Melanchthon's Rhetoric in the Renaissance' in *Renaissance Rhetoric*, ed. Paul Mack (Basingstoke, 1994), pp. 46–62.

Chronology

1524–5	Controversy over freedom of will between Luther and Erasmus
1525	Peasants' War
1527–9	Went on church and school visitations in Thuringia, where Anabaptist practices were discovered; disputation 'on the distinction between Law and Gospel'; published his *Four Books on Dialectics* in 1528
1529	The Marburg Colloquy; published *Elements of Rhetoric*
1530	Attended the Diet of Augsburg; composed the *Augsburg Confession* and its *Apologia*
1535	Fall of Münster in Westphalia, which had been taken over by Anabaptists
1536	Re-foundation of the University of Wittenberg along Protestant principles; The Wittenberg Concord; Melanchthon helped with the reorganisation of the University of Tübingen; composed the oration, 'On Philosophy'
1538	Published his *Epitome of Moral Philosophy*
1539	Helped the reorganisation of the University of Leipzig
1540	Published his *Commentary on the Soul*
1540–1	Colloquy of Worms
1543	Nicholas Copernicus published *On the Revolutions*; Andreas Vesalius published *On the Fabric of the Human Body*
1545	Council of Trent begins
1546	18 February, Luther died; composed the oration 'At Luther's funeral'
1546–7	Schmalkaldic War; John Frederick of Saxony defeated by Charles V and his territory, including Wittenberg and the University, fell to Maurice of Saxony
1548	Leipzig Interim (continuation of Protestant doctrine, but clergy had to wear surplices) adopted; criticised by gnesio-Lutherans such as Matthias Flaccius Illyricus
1549	Published the *Elements of Natural Philosophy*
1552	Published the *Book on the Soul*. He also composed the *Saxon Confession* in preparation for the Council of Trent, but his journey was interrupted by the Princes' War
1555	Religious Peace of Augsburg
1557	Melanchthon reorganised the University of Heidelberg
1560	19 April, Melanchthon died

Further reading

The standard text for most (but by no means all) of Melanchthon's writings is still the *Corpus Reformatorum Philippi Melanthonis Opera Quae Supersunt Omnia*, ed. C. B. Bretschneider and H. E. Bindseil, 28 vols, Halle, 1834–52, Brunswick, 1853–60. Fortunately, a new edition of his correspondence is now in progress: *Melanchthons Briefwechsel: kritische und kommentierte Gesamtausgabe, im Auftrag der Heidelberger Akademie der Wissenschaften*, ed. H. Scheible, Stuttgart, 1977– (in progress) (with text, index and summary of content). For information on editions and the printing history of his works, see *A Checklist of Melanchthon Imprints Through 1560*, ed. R. A. Keen, St Louis, 1988. Particularly useful for Melanchthon's orations is H. Koehn, 'Philipp Melanchthons Reden. Verzeichnis der im 16. Jahrhundert erschienenen Drucke' *Archiv für Geschichte des Buchwesens* 25, 1984, 1277–1486.

A good selection of Melanchthon's philosophical and theological writings is *A Melanchthon Reader*, trans. R. Keen, New York, 1988. An English translation of the first edition of the *Loci Communes* is available in *Melanchthon and Bucer*, trans. L. J. Satre and rev. W. Pauck, London, 1969. For the 1555 edition, see *Melanchthon on Christian Doctrine: Loci Communes of 1555*, trans. C. L. Manschreck, New York, 1965. For the *Augsburg Confession*, see W. Maurer, *Historical Commentary on the Augsburg Confession*, trans. H. George Anderson, Philadelphia, 1986. Melanchthon's commentary on Colossians is translated in Melanchthon, *Paul's Letter to the Colossians*, trans. D. C. Parker, Sheffield, 1989. For other English translations, see the list in L. C. Green and C. D. Froehlich, *Melanchthon in English – New Translations into English with a Registry of Previous Translations*, Sixteenth-Century Bibliography, vol. 22, St Louis, 1982.

The most comprehensive biography is by Karl Hartfelder, *Philipp Melanchthon als Praeceptor Germaniae*, Berlin, 1889. In English, there are: R. Stupperich, *Melanchthon*, trans. R. H. Fischer, London, 1966, and C. L. Manschreck, *Melanchthon: The Quiet Reformer*, New York, 1958. L. C. Green, *How Melanchthon Helped Luther Discover the Gospel: the Doctrine of Justification in the Reformation*, Fallbrook, CA, 1980, concentrates specifically on Melanchthon's role in developing the doctrine of justification. For the relationship between the two reformers, see the collection of essays in *Luther und Melanchthon*, ed. V. Vajta, Göttingen, 1961. For an excellent summary of the relationship between Erasmus and Melanchthon, see the entry by Heinz Scheible in *Contemporaries of Erasmus*, Toronto 1986, vol. 2. pp. 424–9 and now T. J. Wengert, *Human Freedom, Christian Righteousness: Philip Melanchthon's Exegetical Dispute with Erasmus of Rotterdam*, Oxford, 1998. For Melanchthon's reaction to the evangelical radicals, see J. S. Oyer, *Lutheran Reformers against Anabaptists: Luther, Melanchthon and Menius and the Anabaptists of Central Germany*, The Hague, 1964. For the claims of the radical evangelicals, see *The Radical Reformation*, ed. Michael G. Baylor, Cambridge, 1991 and T. Scott, *Thomas Müntzer: Theology and Revolution in Reformation Germany*, London, 1989. For iconography of Melanchthon, O. Thulin, 'Melanchthons Bildnis und Werk im zeitgenössischer Kunst', in *Philipp Melanchthon*, ed. W. Ellinger, Göttingen, 1961, pp. 180–93, is an excellent starting-point.

For a study of his natural philosophy, see S. Kusukawa, *The Transformation of Natural Philosophy: the Case of Philip Melanchthon*, Cambridge, 1991, and C. Methuen, 'The Role of the Heavens in the Thought of Philip Melanchthon', *Journal of the History of Ideas*, 56–3 (1996), 385–403. For his moral and political philosophy, see Ralph Keen, *Divine and Human Authority in Reformation Thought: German Theologians on Political Order 1520–1555*, Nieuwkoop, 1997.

Several studies look at his exegetical methods: T. J. Wengert, *Philip Melanchthon's Annotationes in Johannem in Relation to Its Predecessors and Contemporaries*, Geneva, 1987; T. H. L. Parker, *Commentaries on the Epistle to the Romans 1532–1542*, Edinburgh, 1986; A. Williams, *The Common Expositor: an Account of the Commentaries of Genesis 1527–1633*, Chapel Hill, 1948.

Recent studies have focused on the importance of rhetoric in Renaissance thought, such as Peter Mack, *Renaissance Argument: Valla and Agricola in the Traditions of Rhetoric and Dialectic*, Leiden, 1993; Brian Vickers,

'Epideictic and Epic in the Renaissance', *New Literary History*, 14 (1983), 497–537 and John W. O'Malley, *Praise and Blame in Renaissance Rome: Rhetoric, Doctrine and Reform in the Sacred Orators of the Papal Court, c.1450–1521*, Durham, NC, 1979. For Melanchthon's rhetoric specifically, see Kees Meerhoff, 'The Significance of Philip Melanchthon's Rhetoric in the Renaissance' in *Renaissance Rhetoric*, ed. Paul Mack, Basingstoke, 1994, pp. 46–62 and *idem*, 'Logique et Création selon Philippe Mélanchthon: à la recherche du lieu commun', in *Logique et Littérature à la Renaissance, Actes du Colloque de la Baume-les-Aix, Université de Provence, 16–18 septembre 1991*, Paris, pp. 51–68; R. Schneider, *Philip Melanchthon's Rhetorical Construal of Biblical Authority: Oratio Sacra*, Text and Studies in Religion 5, Lewiston and Lampeter, 1990; T. J. Wengert, 'Philip Melanchthon's 1522 Annotations on Romans and the Lutheran Origins of Rhetorical Criticism', *Biblical Interpretation in the Era of the Reformation*, ed. R. A. Muller and J. L. Thompson, Grand Rapids, MI and Cambridge, 1996, pp. 118–40.

For the reception of humanism in educational institutions, see Erika Rummel, *The Humanist–Scholastic Debate in the Renaissance and Reformation*, Cambridge, MA and London, 1995; A. Grafton and L. Jardine, *From Humanism to the Humanities: Education and the Liberal Arts in Fifteenth- and Sixteenth-Century Europe*, London, 1986; *L'Humanisme allemand, 1480–1540*, XVIIIe Colloque International de Tours, Munich, Fink and Paris, 1979; Peter Dear, *Mersenne and the Learning of the Schools*, Ithaca and London, 1988. For studies on the humanist influences at the University of Wittenberg, see Maria Grossmann, *Humanism in Wittenberg 1485–1517*, Nieuwkoop, 1975 and *Humanismus und Wittenberger Reformation: Festgabe anlässlich des 500. Geburtstages des Praeceptor Germaniae Philipp Melanchthon am 16. Februar 1997: Helmar Junghans gewidmet*, ed. Michael Beyer and Gunther Wartenberg with Hans-Peter Hasse, Leipzig, 1996.

For an important and extensive study of Melanchthon's Aristotelian legacy, see Peter Petersen, *Geschichte der Aristotelischen Philosophie im Protestantischen Deutschland*, Leipzig, 1921; and for his students, see *Melanchthon in seinen Schülern*, ed. Heinz Scheible, Wolfenbuetteler Forschungen, Wiesbaden, 1997. For Melanchthon's influence in various areas, see the following: R. S. Westman, 'The Melanchthon Circle, Rheticus and the Wittenberg Interpretation of the Copernican Theory', *Isis*, 56, 1975, 165–93; V. Nutton, 'Wittenberg Anatomy', and S. Kusukawa, '*Aspectio divinorum operum*: Melanchthon and Astrology for Lutheran

Medics', in *Medicine and the Reformation*, ed. O. P. Grell and A. R. Cunningham, London, 1993, pp. 11–56; H. Dannenfeldt, 'Wittenberg Botanists During the Sixteenth Century', in *The Social History of the Reformation*, ed. L. P. Buck and J. W. Zophy, Columbus, 1972, pp. 223–48; Charlotte Methuen, 'Kepler's Tübingen: Stimulus to a Theological Mathematics', Ph.D. dissertation, Edinburgh, 1995; M. Büttner, 'The Significance of the Reformation for the Reorientation of Geography in Lutheran Germany', *History of Science*, 17, 1979, 151–69; F. H. Lapionte, 'The Origin and Evolution of the Term "Psychology"', *Rivista Critica di Storia della Filosofia*, 28, 1973, 138–60; for 'Philippo-Ramism', see Joseph S. Freedman, 'The Diffusion of the Writings of Petrus Ramus in Central Europe, c. 1570–c. 1630', *Renaissance Quarterly* 46 (1993), 98–152; Robert Kolb, 'Philipp's Foes, but Followers Nonetheless: Late Humanism among the Gnesio-Lutherans', in his *Luther's Heirs Define His Legacy*, Aldershot, 1996.

Note on the text

The translation for this volume was based mainly on the Latin texts from the *Corpus Reformatorum Philippi Melanthonis Opera quae supersunt omnia*, ed. C. B. Bretschneider and H. E. Bindseil, 28 vols., Halle, 1834–52, Brunswick, 1853–60 (abbreviated as CR, followed by volume number and column numbers). The Latin text was then collated against the following: *Melanchthons Werke in Auswahl*, ed. R. Stupperich, 5 vols., Gutersloher, 1963 (StA in notes). These texts have been further collated with those in *Selectarum declamationum Philippi Melanthonis, quas conscripsit et partim ipse in schola Vitebergensi recitavit, partim alijs recitandas exhibuit*, 3 vols, Strasburg: S. Emmel *et al.*, 1558–9 and *Declamationum Philippi Melanthonis, quae ab ipso et alijs in Academia Witebergensi recitatae ac editae sunt*, ed. Johannes Richardius, 3 vols., Strasburg: T. Rihel, 1560.

This English translation is not a word-for-word translation from the Latin, although we have endeavoured to stay close to the original so that readers wishing to follow the Latin with the English translation may be able to do so with little difficulty. We have, however, taken the liberty of punctuating lengthy sentences, transposing clauses, spelling out pronouns and supplying extra words in order to render the English translation more intelligible.

Melanchthon interspersed his orations with quotations, phrases and terms in Greek, whose meanings he often (though not always) supplied in Latin immediately after. In order to preserve the original sense of Melanchthon's use of Greek, transliterated Greek words have been retained in the text in round brackets ( ), except for very long quotations, which have been reproduced in the notes.

Sources of biblical, patristic and classical citations have been supplied in the main text in square brackets [ ]. For Latin and Greek verse, if the text in Melanchthon's orations corresponded to the modern established text, standard English translations of these works were supplied and indicated in the notes. Biblical quotations are taken from the Revised Standard Version. Unless otherwise stated, all translations were done by Christine F. Salazar, with minor corrections by Sachiko Kusukawa. Where Melanchthon's citation does not match the corresponding passages in the modern established texts, this has been pointed out in the notes. Reasons for this may be various: Melanchthon may have made deliberate alterations; he may have been quoting from memory; he may have made mistakes; or the original texts of Melanchthon as we know them may have been corrupted. Moreover, the case may be that the established text of a classical author in the sixteenth century was different from that of a twentieth-century edition. It is of course difficult to determine or distinguish these various causes, and we have made some limited suggestions in the notes, which should not be taken as final or definitive.

All other editorial comments and textual corrections have been kept in the notes so that the main text may be read as smoothly as a public oration would have been read, without interruption. All references to Erasmus' *Adages* are based on the translation in the series Collected Works of Erasmus, 31–34 (Toronto 1982–93).

For the form of personal names, the principles suggested in the *Contemporaries of Erasmus* have been adopted. That is, first and second names are given in the appropriate vernacular, where predominant forms could be established; Latin forms have been retained for less well-known persons where the vernacular counterparts were uncertain; humanist forms of names in Latin or Greek were preferred wherever they were deemed to be more widely known, hence Melanchthon, Camerarius and Regiomontanus.

The scope of education

1 On the order of learning (1531)

CR XI, 209–14

Oration of Caspar Cruciger on the order of learning, given at the graduation of Masters, in the year 1531[1]

At this point one would often speak of the whole of philosophy and of the excellence of all those arts that are taught in the schools, because they are considered necessary for living well and happily. Nevertheless – having passed over these declarations on the higher disciplines, which I consider to be most commendable for all because of their obvious usefulness – I have (because of the mediocrity of my wit) set about saying a few things about the kind of disciplines in which we lecture, and by which the young are prepared for grasping the greater arts. Although the teachers also repeat their usefulness to you daily in the schools, still something has to be said here of that matter, so that we may serve tradition.

Since the oration is given by me in the name of all, attribute as much authority to it, young men, as you esteem being in this society of the best and most learned men, your teachers, who have conferred this rôle upon me. For the thoughts of all of them are conveyed to you by my voice; as they want the best plan for you, they do not desist from urging you in this place to cherish those studies which they judge becoming and useful to you in private, as well as necessary for the upkeep of the state. If, on the other hand, anyone should spurn the importance of this order and scorn the judgement of men who are not only experts, but also wish the best for the entire state, humanity will be lacking in such a judgement.

I believe, however, that you have to be urged not to neglect the study of the lower arts, which, even if they have little outward appeal for the crowds, nevertheless pave the way for knowing the higher arts, which sustain the administration of the state. And so let us add a few things also about the order of learning, which is very important in all things, as Xenophon has said so delightfully: 'Nothing is as useful and nothing as beautiful for men as order' [*Household Management* VIII.3].

And if I may take my beginning from here, you know that there is a close relationship between the arts. Therefore, even if some of them appear to excel and to be pre-eminent in life, they nevertheless stand in need of the

---

[1] Caspar Cruciger (1504–48) was the Dean of the arts faculty and presided over the promotion of Masters on 31 January 1531.

resources of the others. For this reason those act foolishly, who – be it spurred by ambition or by the hope for gain – rush on to the higher arts, the fruits of which are constantly visible even to the inexperienced, and neglect and scorn the remaining disciplines as though useless for life.

But when I think about it, it seems to me that there is a similarity to that relationship in the very elements of the alphabet, where, even if the vowels excel by their dignity, there can be no speech without consonants. And since all arts are brought forth by letters, we are able to notice some traces in the very elements – in the seeds, so to speak – of the differences between the arts. The vowels excel among the others by far, having a life and spirit of their own, because they produce a perfect sound, not helped by the others. The remaining letters receive the sound like pipes blown by these vowels.

Thus the vowels signify the most distinguished of all arts, the doctrine of religion, which is placed high above the other arts and rules all of life's deliberations, business and studies. And, indeed, it is not possible to uphold civil discipline without religion, and the science of law is influenced to the greatest extent by religious doctrine. But just as the semi-vowels – even if they have a somewhat obscure sound – cannot perform their task without the vowels, so in political discipline religion adds its voice to the civil precepts, protects human law by its authority and, when necessary, reforms it.

The silent letters signify more or less the private life, which is indeed mute, i.e. rustic and wild, without religion and civil conventions. Therefore, just as speech is woven together out of dissimilar letters, likewise various kinds of arts and activities are necessary in life.

Although I have been afraid for some time that the learned men in this assembly would not bear these ineptitudes with patience, I nevertheless hope that – because the oration is given for the young – they will bear with me in this game by which we have wanted to depict society as well as the ranking of the arts. And it has been seen in the elements of letters themselves that – given that they are daily present to the eyes – they often come to the scholars' minds, and it seems to us at any rate that by thinking about them the judgement on the usefulness of the arts is sharpened and formed. And I, professor of grammar in this school, have gladly borrowed this oration from this occupation which I practise.

But consider, young men, what would happen if someone, having left out all the consonants, wanted to use only vowels in speaking. Undoubtedly he would be fighting against the entire nature of things. That is to say, letters are called elements for the reason that, just as in nature the elements of which bodies consist are necessary, so letters are necessary for composing speech. Therefore, just as that divine order in the totality of things is perturbed if one element is removed, so there can be no articulated sound if the consonants are discarded. And in the same way, just as there is a natural relationship of the various letters with each other, the various arts are associated and yet separated. And those who feel that the lower disciplines are useless for life, because their benefit is not so visible, disturb this chorus of the arts.

If some admirer of the sky and the stars – and what can one think of that is more beautiful than these bodies? – wanted to remove water from the nature of things, because it is no match for the brightness of the stars, would we not say that he is mad? If someone, out of admiration for the teachings of religion, ordered us to remove from our lives all laws and precepts of the state and all links of domestic life, would not all sane men judge it necessary for him to be suppressed by force and by the use of weapons?

And in these recent years we have seen some who were practising theology in an unholy way, madmen with fanatical opinions, punished for their errors. For you will remember Müntzer and the Anabaptists[2] and other monsters of that kind. Consider those mad in the same way, who disturb the chorus and the harmony of the arts by neglect of, and contempt for, the lower arts. Therefore, just as when you think of the elements of writing you believe that the entire alphabet is necessary for discourse, so you will consider all the disciplines that are taught in the schools necessary for life.

For only he can have the right feelings about the arts, who, when he has noticed their order, understands that each art has been devised because of its certain usefulness.

I have said this to remind young men of it, many of whom we see rushing unrestrainedly towards the higher disciplines, not only to their own detriment, but also to that of the state. For your studies do not concern only you, but also the state.

---

[2] Thomas Müntzer (*c.* 1489–1525), an erstwhile follower of Luther, soon developed his own radical and seditious message, and perished in the Peasants' War in 1525. Those who believed that infant baptism was inefficacious and who thus practised re-baptism of adults were called Anabaptists. Melanchthon associated them with illiteracy, civil unrest and sedition: see J. S. Oyer, *Lutheran Reformers against Anabaptists: Luther, Melanchthon and Menius and the Anabaptists of Central Germany* (The Hague, 1964).

5

And you ought to keep in view the purpose of your studies, and decide that they are provided for giving of advice for the state, for teaching in the churches and for upholding the doctrine of religion. You will not be able to excel in any of those without perfect doctrine, and perfect doctrine is not granted to anyone without the lower disciplines.

When the mind is shaped by this thought, one needs next to deliberate on the order of learning. And I am not going to say here how great the power of order is in general, as this fact is well known and covers a wider field than can be explained here. If the farmer wants to sow first and to plough later, or if he wants to sow under the Dog Star and plough at the winter solstice, his labour and expenditure will go to waste. In the same way, if the correct order is not preserved in grasping the disciplines in one's mind, one will have to despair of any success.

A good thing brings forth a bad one, they say,[3] if it is not given at the right time. Accordingly even the study of the best and greatest things are harmful if they are not undertaken at the appropriate time. Therefore our ancestors – when they established the sequence of learning – thought out certain steps like grades, by which the young would be led in order from the lower arts to the higher ones. Now, as if these restraints had been broken, the matter is done without order. Suddenly, like mushrooms, theologians, lawyers and doctors are brought forth, without dialectics, without knowledge of speaking, without the cradle-bands of natural and moral philosophy. The knowledge of these was once taught to all alike, before they were admitted to the higher disciplines, not only because this makes for very good education, but also because it sharpens the judgement and prepares one for the acquisition of greater things. However, now it is sufficient to take a large felt cap[4] to these most venerable disciplines, and to show great contempt for all humanities teaching.

If the laws and the magistrates do not restrain this temerity, there will soon be no erudition in the state, no teaching of anything. For these theologians, lawyers and doctors who spring forth suddenly, not endowed with any decent teaching, not only allow the other arts to perish, but they cannot preserve their own professions either. And it is not the case that these concerns for the preservation of scholarship are not the business of the magistrates, for they are called gods by the Holy Spirit, so that they would preserve and

---

[3] For sources of this saying, see Erasmus, *Adages*, IV.iii.2.

[4] *Pilleus* is a cap of liberty worn by manumitted slaves and it was also worn at the feast of Saturnalia as a licence to do anything; Martial, *Epigrams*, XIV.i.2, cf. Erasmus, *Adages*, II.i.27.

retain the divine gifts on earth – religion, civil order and all the honourable arts. Because of that responsibility for divine things they bear the solemn title, and the magistrates have no greater and more venerable distinction than that.

Therefore it is appropriate that they keep watch on them, so that the honourable disciplines do not fall into oblivion, the order of learning having been upset. Plato said [*Republic* IV, 424c] that the state changes if it comes about that the music changes; and this is not said uselessly. But it is much truer that the state changes if studies are changed. And indeed, all changes of the state are of concern to the magistrates. An overturned order of studies brings with it the downfall of the greatest and best things; therefore the magistrates need to be more watchful about this than about anything else. And I do not doubt that one day new laws will be established concerning these things, once the current disorder and commotion of the state have calmed down. May an effortless and easy overturning be granted to them by the favour of God!

In the mean time, however, we shall make an effort – as much as we can achieve by authority, enthusiasm and diligence – that the young learn in the correct order.

But in large part this depends on you, too; for we both admonish you diligently on this matter and make available excellent lectures in all disciplines. In the best faith the arts that contain the method of speaking are passed on; the elements of philosophy and mathematics are made clearly available. In which other school is the second book of Pliny[5] expounded as clearly as it is here? And then there remains the fact that you yourself do not wish to be wanting, but you wish to avail yourselves of the present advantages.

Assuredly, to induce you to do so must be the very pleasantness of study, as well as its usefulness. For eloquence procures incredible delight; and the history of past exploits gives pleasure to men in a wonderful way – history itself is taught, as well as its exploits set up as rhetorical exercises. And nothing is sweeter than to understand in one's mind those things that are passed on to us in philosophy – about the size of the heavenly bodies and the Earth, the movements of the various stars, and how the heavenly lights, variously mixed and blended among themselves, create differing effects in

---

[5] By 1531, the second book of Pliny's *Historia Naturalis* had become an elementary textbook on geocentric cosmology and astrology at the University of Wittenberg: see S. Kusukawa, *The Transformation of Natural Philosophy: the Case of Philip Melanchthon* (Cambridge 1995), pp. 136f.

this sublunar nature, like voices mingled now in one way, now in another, articulating varied songs. It is also profitable to see the causes of civil duties inscribed in nature by divine agency, and observed by learned men with marvellous sagacity.

Already the usefulness deriving from these studies can be apprehended to a great extent, for they are, as the Greeks say, further on the way [*Iliad* IV.382; *De caelo* 292b9] towards the higher arts, which certainly require knowledge of speaking. For what progress could anyone make, if he were unable to judge the style of a speech? And everywhere many things are taken from natural and moral philosophy, on which those who do not see the origins sometimes hallucinate in an improper manner.

And because it is of importance for the state to preserve the good arts, you should all feel that the state requests this of you that you apply yourselves, so that the arts do not perish through your negligence. Since we all reap greater benefits from the state than from any private persons, be they parents or friends, it is right that we in our turn express our gratitude for this and keep and defend the arts by our toil.

Therefore I admonish you, young men, to convince yourselves that you first need to know the elements of philosophy, before you advance to the higher disciplines, and that you diligently devote zeal and effort to them.

The beginning, they said, is half of the whole.[6] Who makes a good start, has obtained half the result [Horace, *Letters* I.2.40]. Everything will be easier in the other disciplines for those who have started in the right way, who bring to the other arts the knowledge of those arts, without which these can neither be perceived nor considered nor understood.

Think of me as giving this speech by public authority, and if anyone scorns it, may he know that God will be the avenger of this insult. And the state has provided these our studies with privileges and honours, which we now willingly bestow upon these young men, because – in these times and among such wrong-headedness of judgements – those deserve outstanding praise who have engaged in these general studies of philosophy. I have spoken.

---

[6] For classical sources for this saying, see further Erasmus, *Adages*, I.ii.29.

2 On the rôle of the schools (1543)

CR XI, 606–18

Oration on the necessity of joining together the schools and the ministry of the Gospel, recited by Doctor Bernhard Ziegler.[1]

At this point custom imposes on me the need to speak of an ecclesiastical topic, and the choice is difficult for many reasons amidst such a multitude of things of the greatest importance; but in the end I have chosen a most ordinary subject-matter, the consideration of which should nevertheless lead to stimulating the study of literature, and confirm us in loving this kind of life more, and in bearing with greater strength the toil of this task. For I wish to speak of the schools of Scriptures, and to show that the schools have always, by God's counsel, been joined to the churches, and that they need to be joined.

Indeed, it is of great delight to me, when I recall to mind all the ages of the Church and the entire chain of history, to see, as if before my eyes, so many luminaries of humankind – Adam, Noah, Shem, Abraham, Joseph, Elias, Elijah and the Apostles. I believe that for you, too, the recalling to mind both of such great men and of the excellent things that they have accomplished is highly enjoyable. And even if, consequently, in the choice of argument I was swayed by the pleasantness of these things, nevertheless the following was the more important reason.

I know that we scholars are not only despised, but also hated. Many believe that our labours are not something necessary for life, but slothful leisure. In fact, they even curse the theologians as 'outcasts' (*katharmata*) and a plague of the state.[2] And I am not as uncouth and inexperienced in human affairs as to believe that by anybody's oration all those who feel that way can be brought to reason. But, nevertheless, that error has to be censured, so that we may understand better the kind of life to which we are called by divine agency, and that we may confirm our minds in this our course, and instil into some good minds, within this gathering of young men listening to us, honourable and, indeed, useful opinions. What more glorious thing can one imagine than that we (although we are by far inferior in teaching, wisdom and virtue) uphold in truth the same duty in the Church of God that those most illustrious men – Noah,

---

[1] Bernard Ziegler (1496–1556) was then the Professor of Hebrew at the University of Leipzig.
[2] Reading *Rerum* for *Rerem*.

Shem, Abraham, Isaiah, Jeremiah, John the Baptist and the Apostles – upheld?

I do not detract anything from the dignity of any hierarchy, but rather I strive to honour them all, and I recall the saying of Aristotle, who said (with the meaning that many classes and arts are necessary for life): a state is not made up from doctors and doctors, but from doctors and farmers,[3] i.e. from a union of all the arts that God has shown us, so that they may be a protection for life. The glory of those who rule the government is great in every aspect, and that of the soldiers who protect the state by their weapons is no less. Then the farmers, the craftsmen and also the merchants have their own place. God wanted men to be united among themselves by this variety of duties.

But what purpose do all these duties serve? Perhaps some pig from the herd of Epicurus [Horace, *Letters* 1.4.16] may say: so that, in a quiet life, we may pleasurably enjoy its delights, and decay gradually without the hope of immortality, as the innate heat gradually abates. In truth this utterance is full of indecency and villainy. More correctly, men are formed for fellowship to such a degree that the knowledge of God shines in this gathering, and God is praised and invoked, and one is imbued by the other with that doctrine that opens access to eternal joy and to the presence of God. Consider this fellowship of men similar to a school, in which men have to occupy their minds with God and with virtue more than with anything else. The homes of that assembly are the states. And we hold the view that the government – the leaders, the army, the farmers, the craftsmen, in short all the ranks of life – serves this highest work, that is the propagation of doctrine.

Why did David fight his wars abroad? Not in order to be carried into the town on elephants in triumph, but so that, at home, at the temple and in schools, the boys and girls might study the Scriptures, read Moses and hear those who interpret the law and the promises by which God has made Himself manifest. By the weapons of strong men these assemblies in the temples and in the schools are protected, so that the knowledge of God may not be extinguished utterly among men. And yet, few rulers strive for that aim. Julius Caesar fights so that he be not divested of his dignity by the envious, and Anthony wages war so that he can squander other people's money.

---

[3] This seems to be a paraphrase of the beginning passages of Aristotle's *Politics*, IV.iii: 'every state contains many elements. ... of the common people, some are farmers, traders and some artisans'.

However, in the Church it is proper for all those of good sense to make provision for that most exalted purpose: to establish, to build and to protect states, so that the knowledge of God be spread in them.

Let me add an image, perhaps foolishly taken from a trifling thing – but, on the other hand, there are many small but manifest images of the greatest things. Often when I think about the communal life, when by night the servant goes in front carrying a lantern, it comes to my mind that states are similar to the lantern, and the heavenly teaching to the light. And just as the lantern is of no use in the dark without light, thus the city is a useless mass, if the knowledge of God and the teaching of what is good are destroyed.

Therefore it has to be acknowledged that it is necessary that there be churches and assemblies which praise God and which spread the teaching of His nature and His will far and wide. Only the Cyclopes will dare to deny this. Therefore, even if many – illiterate men – think that, by the guidance of nature, they can comprehend the will of God, nevertheless we in the Church know that God, in His infinite goodness, has disclosed Himself to humankind by certain and manifest evidence, so that He might make plain His hidden will concerning our salvation. He thundered forth the law from heaven, He sent His son and He added evidence – the resurrection of the dead and other acts, of which it is manifest that they are the work of God alone. He also ordered us with a loud voice to listen to His son, saying: 'This is my beloved son, hear him' [Luke 9:35]. Therefore the doctrine necessary for the Church is not a wisdom that is understood by the cunning of human wit, but it is the secret will of God, brought forth by His son from the bosom of the eternal Father. God wanted it to be committed to writing right from the beginning, so that its memory could be preserved for all times.

The creation of things is a great and admirable work. However, it is no smaller favour that He disclosed Himself, made Himself known to men and has spoken to us in friendly terms, so as to show that He is moved by concern for humankind. As far as I am concerned, I am moved to think of the goodness of God when I consider the nature of things, adorned by wonderful variety, and suitable for our enjoyment. I am much more strongly moved, though, every time I think of God's conversations with the Church Fathers and prophets, of the friendly companionship of Christ with the entire people, of the light of the Holy Spirit spread from heaven, and of the conversations of Christ with many after His resurrection. All minds need to be turned assiduously to the thought of these most excellent things. For, indeed, it is not in vain or without reason that God has disclosed Himself so many times, in such manifest evidence. We do not judge these to be empty spectres, or illusions or games. God performed great and serious things; he wanted to show that He was truly moved by solicitude for our salvation. He wished to pass on to us testimonies both of His voice and of His teaching, in which He bestows upon us the heavenly gifts and the fellowship of His felicity. He did not want the Fathers, the Prophets and the Apostles to rejoice in these friendly conversations any more than He wants all men of all times to rejoice in the doctrine itself. Just as Moses, standing on the rock, saw God before his very eyes in the clear light, thus you should know that, with certainty, He converses with you every time you read those very books of the law, of the Prophets and of the Apostles, which God has consigned to the Church, so that it may hear His voice in perpetuity.

Now I reach the topic that I chose. If God wanted the prophetic and apostolic book to exist forever in the Church, and our minds to be guided by that document, and the understanding of Himself to be intensified, then it is always necessary for schools to be attached to the churches. They would teach the elements of education, and explain and interpret the Word of God. Even though the matter of which I am speaking is hardly doubtful, one still has to speak about it in greater detail, given that education is held in such contempt.

First let us consider the history of all ages and the sequence of all the eras of the Church. You know that in Moses' community the classes of the priests and the Levites were placed by the tabernacle, as it was called, not only in order to sacrifice animals, but much more in order to explain the law to the people, to answer doubting minds and to judge on dogmatic quarrels. Chapter seventeen of Deuteronomy demonstrates this clearly, ordering that all quarrels be taken to the priests, the Levites and to the place of the tabernacle, and that cases be adjudicated not by the whims of those in power, but by divine law [Deuteronomy 17:8–12].

You must not think that these groups of priests were idle, or occupied only with sacrifices. An altogether greater responsibility and a greater burden were imposed on them, namely to be the keepers and interpreters of doctrine, and the judges of the most serious disputes. Their profession comprised education, divine law, history, the classification of time periods, the pattern of the year, by establishing the turning-points from the observation of the movements of the heavens, the investigation of nature, the medical art and finally music. It was among their foremost duties to report, in good faith, in the public records also the deeds accomplished among God's people, so that a continuous sequence of history existed in the Church. For God wanted all the past times to be known to posterity, so that they might have certain evidence of His doctrine. For God did not want our minds to waver, without knowing of the beginning of the world, the beginning of religion, its spread, its perversions and renewal. Therefore, He wanted a history of all times – short, but containing the highest things – to be always present in the Church, and He preserved it.

What then was that assembly of priests other than a school or an academy, set up in an excellent way? In the approximately 1,500 years until Christ it was the interpreter and keeper of divine teaching. For although often the popes wielded a tyrannical rule, and there were great periods of darkness in regard to doctrine because of the ignorance of priests, nevertheless thereupon, having roused the prophets, God has rekindled the study of virtue and the light of teaching in that school. Indeed, because God promised that He would always be present at that assembly, there have always been some pious and serviceable teachers, who educated the elite of the people. In this matter the succession of great men is worthy of consideration. Just as in the line of battle the next soldier follows in the footsteps of the one before him when he is slain, so the succession not only of high priests but also of prophets has been continuous in that school.

After Samuel Nathan flourished, then Ahijah the Shilonite, under Solomon, and Jeroboam. [1 Kings 1:11–15] Then Ananias followed at the time of Asa. Then Elias was roused to prophesy. After having performed many great deeds during a long time, he chose Elijah as his successor before being transported to Heaven by God. For about seventy years Elijah not only directed the principal councils of the realm, but also upheld the task of teaching, when crowds of disciples followed him about in great numbers and with great assiduity. The young Isaiah saw Elijah, who was then in his old age, just as Jeremiah saw Isaiah, Daniel Jeremiah, Zacharias Daniel, Ezra and Nehemiah saw Zacharias, and Onias, celebrated in Ecclesiastes, saw Nehemiah.

Some time later there followed the wars of the Maccabees; at that time the priests had already been struggling ambitiously for some time for leadership – after the fashion of the pagans – and they had been scandalously neglecting teaching and discipline. Nevertheless, the priest Mathatias arose, an upholder of divine law, and many pious men took his side. Some time later there were Simeon and Zacharias, who are mentioned in Luke's Gospel. Then there was John the Baptist and after him Christ, who had the assiduous assembly of the Apostles, began his teaching.

I have discussed a long period of time, in which there is not only the pleasure of remembering so many excellent men, but there are many other things, too, which can delight pious minds. We can see that God cares for His Church, since He later gave it such excellent leaders and made His presence clear by manifest evidence. We can see that the authority of His teaching is confirmed by heavenly deeds. It is most useful to consider these things. Those excellent men of whom I have spoken not only gave judgement in the law-court, but many of them had assemblies of avid listeners, to whom they explained the law and the divine promises – shown clearly by the stories of Elias, Elijah, John the Baptist and Christ.

The Jews uphold the institution of Moses by choosing seventy elders (as it is written in chapter eleven of Numbers [Numbers 11:16]) to remain for all posterity. Later this became the assembly of most learned men that they call the Sanhedrin, having adopted the Greek word *synedrion* [assembly]. Whatever kind of assembly it was, it is obvious that the prophets were surrounded by assiduous crowds of listeners. The Apostles, who had seen this custom preserved by John the Baptist and by Christ, also continued it themselves. It is certain that John the Apostle had his own disciples in Ephesus, who consecrated themselves wholly to teaching. Polycarpus was among them, who went on, for about fifty years, to spread the teaching received from John with success in the Church of Smyrna. His disciple Irenaeus diverted the streams of teaching into Pannonia and Gaul.

It seems that there were such schools wherever there was a larger number of churches – the famous ones of Antioch, Alexandria (where Origen used to teach) and Byzantium (Gregory of Nazianzen writes that Basil taught there). It is certain that in the beginning the seminaries of the clergy were nothing other than assemblies of teachers and students. I believe that even in Germany, before Attila, medium-sized schools were attached to the churches, for Irenaeus and Epiphanius cite evidence for the German churches. This shows that the Gospel was quickly spread in Germany and that some study of the Scriptures was going on in this country. We can also read that Lucius of Cyrene, a disciple of Paul's, first taught the Gospel by the Danube in Augusta Tiberina (which is now called Regensburg). It seems that he arrived there with the Roman troops who were occupying

Raetia. The Gospel illuminated the people of Strasburg and Cologne through the teacher Maternus, a disciple of Peter. Eusebius witnesses that the former was brought up at Arles; Clement of Metz called him to the knowledge of Christ. They say that Marcus, a disciple of Paul, came to Mainz as a young man.[4] The ancient monuments of the church at Passau by the Danube give testimony that he delivered public speeches at Vienna, which was the seat of the bishop of Nuremberg before the foundation of the seminary at Passau.

When such great and wise men came to Germany and Gaul, they undoubtedly had great concern for studies, so that the Gospel would be transmitted to later generations by men who were correctly appointed and properly taught. Later, in barbarous times, when the wars between the Vandals, the Huns and the Franks gave rise to great devastations, the old schools were overturned. Nevertheless, what remnants of the Church there were could not make do without writings.

Therefore seminaries and monasteries were founded again, and when learning was neglected in the seminaries, because they were occupied with affairs of kings and courts, the task of teaching was transferred to the monasteries. When these were burdened with ceremonies, they could not at the same time sustain the tedious and difficult task of teaching. Therefore the universities originated, in which the study of the Scriptures was stimulated as far as possible, but the restraints of discipline were greatly relaxed.

It is sufficiently clear from this historical recollection both that the schools were always joined to the churches, and that the light of the Gospel is extinguished without erudition. For that purpose, it is proper that wise rulers unite the churches and the universities by their care. Without any doubt it is the ruler's highest duty to retain the knowledge of God among men. Our erudition serves this great task. Therefore let the ruler take care that the universities flourish with their true ornaments – with teachers who are intelligent, erudite and distinguished by virtue and sagacity, who both understand the method useful for rhetoric and perform their duty faithfully. These the princes shall support in safeguarding discipline – for without the authority of those above, discipline cannot be upheld.

---

[4] Lucius of Cyrene is recorded as one of the members of the Church of Antioch in Acts 13.1. Maternus, first bishop of Cologne, is known to have attended the Council of Arles: Eusebius, *Ecclesiastic History*, x.18 . Clement of Metz, first bishop of Metz, probably sent from Rome in the third century. Irenaeus refers to a Christian community in Mainz in his *Against the Heretics*, IV.2.

The faithful teachers should also be given decent wages. Excessive opulence is not to be desired, because the attachment to wealth obstructs studying and fosters extravagant living in the idle. Moderate means are called for, because teachers cannot have time to spare for their task if they are forced to look for a living for themselves and their families elsewhere, and also because poor students have to be fostered, so that the Church may not be lacking in ministers.

It is a great mistake to imagine that ministers can be carved from any wood, and that the teaching of religion can be grasped without erudition and without long training. First, the mode of prophetic and apostolic speech has to be known. Consequently the ancient languages have to be learnt, and the entire method of composing a speech has to be known. For this purpose good teachers need the reading of the ancient writings, literary exercises and also time. After that greater toil follows.

The Church has its own wisdom, placed above human judgement. It has the devil as its enemy, who attempts to smother the truth, and there are many small minds who, out of effrontery, ambition or envy (*philoneikeiai*), corrupt the true ideas. Therefore in all ages there have been the most violent disputes in the Church. However, for the explanation of the major controversies one needs not only a ready mind and a certain knowledge of the sacred books, but also the art of disputation, fluent speech and a knowledge of history, antiquity and judgements of the past. He who upholds the propagation of the truth needs to have investigated and discussed all these things at length and to a great extent. And it is not sufficient for someone to occupy his mind with them on his own; ideas need to be compared, the judgements of many others need to be heard, and errors have to be corrected, for at times *deuterai phrontides* (second thoughts) that are more accurate bring us back to the right path. On the other hand, nothing is worse, or more pernicious, than to argue hotly against the truth – like some who are less ashamed to persevere in their error than to correct and change their erroneous opinion.

Well then, we have investigated the truth by these studies to a great extent and at length, in our own mind and, by discussion, with others, because the opinions that we intend to reveal to the people – just like oracles or laws – have to be chosen with long and careful deliberation. For this reason the ancients wanted there to be assiduous performance in the schools, and they established disputations, so that the students would become used to this organising of opinions, and also, by this exercise, would acquire the art of discussing and the ability to explain. By what method could this possibly be done in a more delightful way? (And I do not even mention its usefulness.) What is more pleasant than to hear from a learned man what he thinks about the greatest things, and with what relevance and propriety and finally with what modesty he relates them? For impropriety in discourse is to be avoided, and so are obscurity and confusion; and, finally, one also has to steer clear of untimely humour.

We are born for the mutual communication of speech – and why? Is it only for reciting love stories, or for disputing with other guests at a banquet, or for talking about contracts, buying, selling and similar things for the accumulation of money? No, but without doubt so that one may teach others about God and the duty to be virtuous. Therefore the debate on these excellent things should be the most agreeable to good minds. Certainly this our assembly, which has to be prepared for leading the Church, should love that comparison of excellent things most.

No one hands an oar to someone in a small boat if that man has not learnt to row. No one can cultivate[5] fields without a guide – not to speak of other, more complicated, skills. How much less could one who has not learnt to do so be an interpreter of heavenly teaching and a leader of the Church? It is necessary that every child and every old man know the general sense of the heavenly teaching, and it can be grasped in a short time, but not for nothing do we read in Dionysius that the Apostle Bartholomew said that the Gospel is both long and short. The general sense can be communicated in brief, but the knowledge of divine things must become clearer little by little, through meditation on, and comparison of, the words of the Prophets and the Apostles, for all the pious, whether they have erudition or not. This cannot be done without reading and interpretation and, as I said above, extensive and varied teaching is necessary for interpretation.

Christ orders the learned scribe to disclose the new and the old. He does not want the scribe, i.e. the teacher, to be uncouth and untrained, but He wants him to be educated and developed in advance in the Church, and steeped in the true and salutary teaching.

Furthermore, Paul often repeats the following precept: he enjoins us not to disregard reading, and to choose one who is apt not only for teaching, but also for the defence of doctrine. How many things do these two tasks involve? What erudition, what industry, what sagacity, what moderation and what intelligence are required for teaching with lucidity, for uncovering what is

---

[5] Reading *colere* for *colore*.

concealed, for casting light on what is obscure, for adjusting the method of teaching to the grasp of the inexperienced and the experienced, and for being of use – as Paul says [Romans 1:14] – to the wise as well as to the foolish?

Then even more difficult is the defence of religion, in which it is necessary to bear in mind the quarrels of all ages, to reveal snares, to refute sophisms, to remove the disguise of false convictions and to make clear and fortify the true opinions. No one can do these things without a great variety of skills and without erudition.

It is even more astonishing that, as Paul says, we can find hope from the consolation of the Scriptures [Romans 15:4]. Does hope shine then in the letters and in these written records? Some Anabaptists say that this utterance is truly absurd, but Paul says so with great discernment: hope shines in the everlasting God Himself. Paul links us to God, who made Himself manifest in His voice, which he wanted to be recorded in writing by the Prophets and the Apostles, so that the testimony may exist forever. In this He wanted us to recognise the concealed will for reconciliation, which cannot be understood by the keenness of human wit.

There are many reasons why God made a link between us and this testimony. So whenever the mind begins a prayer and seeks God it should not only think of Heaven and of the creation of the world – in order to remind itself of their maker – but it should at the same time also bring to its attention the sayings of the Gospel. It should reflect upon the Son of God, who made Himself manifest to us and who made promises of reconciliation, and it should say: I invoke you, omnipotent, everlasting and living God, eternal Father of our Lord Jesus Christ, who made yourself manifest because of your boundless goodness, and called through your Son, our Lord Jesus Christ: Hear this! Maker and preserver of all things, with your equally eternal son, our Lord Jesus Christ and the Holy Spirit, have mercy on me because of your son Jesus Christ, whom you wished to be a victim for us. Sustain, help and renew me with your Holy Spirit, sustain and preserve your Church and the states that offer hospitality to the wretched churches.'

This form distinguishes the Christian prayer from the pagan, the Jewish and the Muhammadan prayer. It is necessary to understand this distinction, to hold it up as a model and to drive it home constantly – and, indeed, it cannot be explained without erudition and the comparison of opinions. Therefore God wants the Scriptures and the good arts to be always fostered in the Church, and He protects the schools in an astonishing way, so that learning may not be extinguished altogether. He wants us all to listen to the Church as to a teacher, as it is conveyed very neatly in the history of Samson: 'If you had not ploughed with my heifer, you would not have found out my riddle' [Judges 14:18].

We have learnt the Gospel from the people of Israel, as it was spread among the nations by the Apostles. God has always given a succession of teachers to the Church, and He has wanted continuous witness to his teaching. Therefore the rulers and states and we ourselves, who perform the task of teaching, declare that the preservation and spreading of learning is the highest of all human achievements, and each one strives in his own place, so that the schools may flourish and be honoured.

The ingratitude is most reprehensible by which we neglect and scorn God's great generosity towards us and His great gifts, when God in His boundless goodness and compassion made Himself manifest and imparted to us His concealed will from His heart, practically attested in these written records, in order to give us a share of the eternal good by that very voice and by these tokens. Let us give thanks to God for stirring our most illustrious prince's heart, so that he desired his churches to be taught with sagacity and led in accordance with the truth, and the study of the Scriptures to be restored.

By its example the most distinguished senate of this town, too, benevolently embraces and furthers the University; although the latter possesses many honours, it has nothing greater or more divine (if one is to judge truthfully) than the possession of this teaching. Indeed, only that city is to be considered upright in which the understanding of God and the knowledge of the other honourable arts are added to the political system.

However, in some way it also depends on us to make this possession a lasting one. The universities should be aristocracies, as the beehive is for the bees; let each one perform his duty correctly, let us teach what is useful, let us join our activities good-naturedly, let us help one another, and let us preserve general harmony by philosophical moderation. Let us think of ourselves as living in a Christian, or at least human, community, and let us not rejoice in the brutality of the Cyclopes, in which, according to Euripides [*Cyclops* 120], 'no one listens to anything from anybody' (*akousi ouden oudeis oudenos*). Do not let ambition fan competition among different ranks, or among the professors, but let private desires take second place to the common good. Let public peace be preferred to private passions.

When I consider and desire this, I am always reminded of Pliny's story about the two goats [*Natural History* VIII.76, 201f.]: when they met on a bridge so narrow that there was not enough room for one to pass next to the other, they made way for themselves in an extraordinary fashion. For one lay down on the bridge in such a way that the other could step on its body and walk across it. There are many cases in which, if no one yields to the other, great upheavals occur necessarily. We need to understand these examples for the state and rein in our impulses.

Some go wild because of works and honours, others because of party politics, when it would be much more righteous to restrain oneself and to heal the rifts by moderation of the mind, just as those she-goats yielded to each other. If we do so, God will support our schools and studies – for He demands faith in doing one's duty as well as care in safeguarding harmony, and He promises great prizes for each virtue.

You will remember the Gospel parable in which Christ praises the servant who applied his talent well. [Matthew 25:21–3] And the psalm about harmony says: 'For there the Lord commanded the blessing' [Psalms 133:3]. What example does Christ command us to imitate in washing the feet of His disciples? Not servitude, but a virtue dear to God, namely to bear private injuries, the avoidance of which would harm public order.

Let us impress this upon ourselves, and let us accustom ourselves to these true and philosophical duties with the diligence in which we can sense God, who will protect the school all the more because of our moderation.

Let us lay this before ourselves and before others, in order to impress on ourselves as well as others that the schools are necessary for the conservation of piety, religion, civil order and also for the administration of the state. The truth must be told in either case: if men can be moved, in order that they embrace it and live – lies are death and their father has always been a murderer – or, if they do not embrace it, in order that there be some evidence of their incorrigible impropriety.

What, I beseech you, is the future shape of kingdoms or states without erudition or teaching of the Scriptures? There is no need for argumentation; let us just cast a look at those places in which learning once had a home, where the schools even now retain these scholarly titles, but abuse them for promotions in rank and the achievement of honours. We can see how much turpitude is apparent there all the time. They accordingly begin to be held in contempt by their own members and by those outside them, and gradually they crumble and fall in ruins. Their ignorance and uncouthness increase, though, so that in some places they lean towards destructive evils, calling down upon themselves grievous ruin. For those who rise against the truth and against Christ can in no way prevail, but, as one says, they rush with horns against bronze. Their bad example should move and admonish us to grant safety to schools both in the state and in the Church of Christ.

There are many proud-hearted people who, once they have advanced to honours and have found a place in the light within the state, quickly forget from where they have risen. It is certain, though, that no other esteem or fame can carry men higher than those of doctrine. But what perversity possesses some, so that they despise the rank of scholars as being humble and are unjust towards them as towards an enemy, or at least they neglect them as though they were strangers? And what about some others, rich and well-to-do men, who were once slaves to superstition; what do they do now that the truth of religion has been revealed to them? They repay their benefactors as snakes would, and, having acquired freedom, they abuse it for the indulgence of their desires.

There are still some schools left in Germany; these assemblies of priests, already wavering before, are ready to fall under their bulk. The monks have almost sunk into oblivion through their obtuseness and ignorance and through ridiculous superstitions. The schools themselves in some places are barely supporting themselves, elsewhere they lie deserted. I dread to say, because the prognostic is so sad, what will ensue when even these are destroyed.

Therefore let all of us, of all ranks and positions, harmonise our minds and our wills, let us join together our work and studies, and support each other by mutual duties. For just as otherwise no community can flourish and endure for long, so the civil administration and that of schools cannot be torn apart and divided without danger to the state. Let the princes and cities defend, cherish and protect the scholars, and lift them up, or rather exalt them, by their generosity. Let the scholars honour, increase, adorn and celebrate the princes and cities. Let them provide for the courts, the senate and the palace, and for the foremost churches ministers who are good, useful and distinguished in doctrine and piety.

God will approve of this joining together, and He will favour and promote our efforts, studies and work therein, guiding it all towards the praise of His holy name and towards the increase of the Church of Jesus Christ. I pray with all my heart through the Son as mediator that He may preserve the remains of His Church at a time when the world is in such commotion, and that He may protect pious studies in this university and elsewhere. Amen. I have spoken.

3 On the distinction between the Gospel and philosophy[1]

CR XII, 689–91

When Paul says: 'See to it that no one makes a prey of you by philosophy' [Colossians 2:8], he does not reject philosophy but its abuse – just as, when someone says: 'Take care not to be ensnared by wine', he does not disparage wine but its abuse.

Paul is speaking of the kind of abuse that is most harmful in the Church, namely when Scripture is received as though it taught nothing other than a knowledge of human reason. For it is easy for cunning men to transform the Gospel, by skilful explanation, into philosophy, that is, the teaching of human reason. Thus Julian the Apostate[2] charged the Christians with ignorance, because they had brought forth absurd beliefs, having misunderstood the figures of speech of Scripture.

Philosophy contains the art of rhetoric, physiology and precepts on civic morals. This teaching is a good creation of God, and the principal among all natural gifts. And it is a thing that is necessary in this corporal and civic life, such as food, drink, or such as public laws, etc.

Moral philosophy is the very law of God on civic morals.

The most absurd men of all are those who imagine that philosophy and the Gospel differ in such a way that either teaching is a law on morals, but that the Gospel adds a few laws on external works, such as that one must not take revenge, and other similar ones.

On the contrary, if anyone takes away from the Gospel any law on civic life that conflicts with philosophy or the laws of the emperors, he should immediately be despised.

Just as the hands of Jacob resemble the hands of Esau, so the Gospel certainly teaches nothing else regarding civic life than what philosophy and the laws themselves teach.

Pomponius Atticus[3] and the Apostle Paul differ, because they disagree about God. The one doubts whether God cares about human affairs, and

---

[1] This is a record of a disputation rather than a full oration, and thus lists the main points that were argued. It belongs to a series of disputations on Colossians 2.8 delivered by Melanchthon in 1527, when he dramatically changed the meaning of this passage; see further S. Kusukawa, *The Transformation of Natural Philosophy: the Case of Philip Melanchthon* (Cambridge, 1995), pp. 65–9. For Melanchthon's interpretation of the passage; see also Melanchthon, *Paul's Letter to the Colossians*, trans. D. C. Parker (Sheffield), 1989, pp. 46–56.

[2] Julian the Apostate (*d.* 363), a nephew of Constantine, carried out a strict anti-Christian policy. He wrote the *Adversus Christianos*, which can be reconstructed from its refutation by Cyril of Alexandria.

[3] Titus Pomponius Atticus (109–32 BC) was a close friend of Cicero. See his *Letters to Atticus*.

lives without God, the other declares that God truly punishes; similarly, that He forgives for the sake of Christ, and that He has regard for and hears us. They do not disagree in what regards civic morals.

Joseph, David, Isaiah and Daniel are statesmen just like Fabius, Scipio and Themistocles.[4] They do not differ in the civic form of their life, but they differ in their faith in God.

The Gospel is not a philosophy or a law, but it is the forgiveness of sins and the promise of reconciliation and eternal life for the sake of Christ, and human reason by itself cannot apprehend any of these things.

Since, therefore, the Gospel teaches about God's will towards us, but philosophy teaches about matters subject to reason and does not assert anything about the will of God, it is sufficiently clear that the Gospel is not philosophy.

And however much reason judges about the will of God, certainly on its own it neither concludes nor asserts that God wants to forgive us without us giving anything in return, for the sake of Christ.

The Gospel approves of laws on good morals, and commands us to obey them.

Just as the Christian makes pious use of the law of God, so he can make pious use of philosophy, too. And since he knows that philosophy is the law of God, he should all the more respect the teaching of the philosophers and the true opinions of good writers.

That philosophy is the law of God can also be understood from the fact that it is the knowledge of natural causes and effects, and since these are things arranged by God, it follows that philosophy is the law of God, which is the teaching of that divine order.

Just as astronomy is the knowledge of the heavenly motions, which are arranged by God, so moral philosophy is the knowledge of the works, that is, of the causes and effects that God has arranged in the mind of man.

Thus we call philosophy not all the beliefs of everyone, but only that teaching which has demonstrations.

There is only one truth, as the philosophers say, therefore only one philosophy is true, that is, the one that strays least from demonstrations.

Stoic philosophy does not judge correctly on freedom from emotion

---

[4] Quintus Fabius Maximus (*c.* 275–203 BC), renowned Roman general and consul of the Second Punic War. Publius Cornelius Scipio Aemilianus (*c.* 185–129 BC) achieved military success against Carthage and Numantia on behalf of Rome. He is known also as an orator and patron of letters. Cf. Cicero, *The Dream of Scipio*. Themistocles (*c.* 524–*c.* 459 BC), Athenian statesman and commander who achieved military success in the second Persian War.

(*apatheia*) and philosophises in a ridiculous way about things to be promoted (*proëgmenois*) and things in the second rank (*apoproëgmenois*), and
those are most absurd who have said that no kind of philosophy is more
similar to the Gospel than the teaching of the Stoics.

Augustine, too, is being absurd when he says that he has found the
doctrine of the Christians in the Platonists, except for that one part: 'The
Word became flesh' [John 1:14].

Augustine would have spoken correctly if he had said that he had found
those laws on morals in the philosophers which are read in the Christian
writers. For philosophers are completely ignorant of the Gospel, not knowing that, because of Christ, reconciliation is achieved through faith. For the
rest they share the laws on civic morals with the Christians.

And Christ did not appear for the purpose of bringing out new laws on
morals, since reason knew laws before that time. And it is a matter for
magistrates to bring out laws, and there is no need of a new revelation for
establishing them; for this is a matter for the judgement of reason.

And the Epicurean philosophy does not judge correctly about the purpose
of moral goods, and Valla[5] is being absurd when he prefers Epicurus alone
to all the philosophers.

Aristotle's philosophy searches for demonstrations most assiduously,
and therefore it surpasses all sects by far. And it judges correctly about the
purpose of moral goods and the nature of virtue, at least if it is understood
as being about civic life and civic virtues.

Nevertheless, philosophy is not contained within such narrow confines
that one need assume that it is all included in the books written by Aristotle
that have come down to us, but its elements are in Aristotle. Mathematicians,
physicians and lawyers build on these as if on foundations.

Thus far we have spoken about the distinction between the Gospel and
philosophy. It is another matter, however, to examine the distinction
between divine law and philosophy. These agree with each other just as the
Decalogue and the law of nature agree, because philosophy – to the extent
that it has demonstrations – is the law of nature itself. But the Decalogue
gives clearer precepts regarding the motions of the heart towards God.

---

[5] Lorenzo Valla (1407–57) wrote the *De Voluptate* (later revised as *De Vero Bono*) which examined
Stoic, Epicurean and Christian ideas of goodness. The Wittenberg University Library held two
copies of this work: see S. Kusukawa, *A Wittenberg University Library Catalogue of 1536* (Cambridge,
1995), nos. 950d and 979a.

The arts course

4 On the study of languages (1533)

CR XI, 231–9

Oration of Veit Dietrich, of Nuremberg, on the study of languages, held at the graduation of Masters, 1533[1]

To begin with, I thank you, most learned men, for coming together here both in our honour and in order to adorn the study of the most important arts. As I assume that your duty is concerned with the honour of education, I hope that you have put yourself in such a frame of mind as to confer on us the kindness of not listening to us unwillingly. For we do not come on to the podium to announce anything that is worthy of your wisdom and authority – a task which should not be demanded from the witlessness of our youth. This whole talk is held for the benefit of these young men; you have joined us as spectators, so that the young will understand that these first studies are approved of by you. Although your kindness in all aspects is known and evident to us, it is nevertheless also our duty to ask you respectfully to listen to us with good will. Therefore I beseech you to consider my youthful oration favourably, and to lend me your authority in the cause which I have taken up to plead, a cause which I hope will be most agreeable to you.

I have determined to speak about the study of languages, as they call them. Although for the most part it is usually philosophy that is spoken about here, nevertheless this topic of languages is not so far removed from philosophy, if one considers it properly. Indeed, that part of philosophy that is most agreeable appears to me to depend chiefly on the knowledge of languages. In fact, I have not chosen this subject out of a desire for novelty, nor did I propose that, at my age, I could deal satisfactorily with a new subject. However, public necessity urges not only me but also all good men to rouse and stir up the young, as much as we all can, to the study of languages. In truth it would have been most appropriate to summon not a tongue-tied man but an eloquent one for pleading the case of languages, a man who could praise them for their dignity, and illustrate the great usefulness which results from the knowledge of them. Although I realised that this could not be done by me, I nevertheless judged that I should not neglect the public cause, especially on this topic, on which the university

---

[1] Veit Dietrich (1506–49) was Dean of the arts faculty at Wittenberg and presided over the promotion of Masters on 6 February 1533.

magistrate has commanded me to speak. I hoped that there would be as much authority in this oration as you attribute to the entire assembly of most learned men, who consigned this duty to me and wished to state their opinion to you through my oration, of whatever quality the latter may be. Since they excel in teaching, judgement and experience, and furthermore wish with the greatest faith for a plan for your studies and for the entire state, it is most proper for you to prepare yourself willingly and studiously for their admonitions.

But now I come to the subject; since not enough can be said about it because of lack of time, I shall adduce briefly the special usefulness that incites us all to the study of languages – I am talking about Latin, Greek and Hebrew.

Since different people have different purposes in their studies, and not all follow the same kind of learning, it is necessary to speak about the different professions, as they call them, in turn. First, I do not think that there is a need for a long debate about theology, for it is clear that the sources of theology are contained in Hebrew and Greek writings. The languages cannot be translated in such a way that there is no need for the sources if we want to pass judgement on obscure passages, as one has to do in many very serious controversies. So many times the Scriptures themselves recommend to us the ministry of the word, and they admonish us never to see the will of God unless in these writings. It is therefore easy to understand how necessary it is to grasp perfectly the nature of discourse, which nobody can achieve without a knowledge of languages or without the practice of eloquence.

Therefore each one must aspire to a perfect knowledge of sacred discourse, both for his own salvation and for the common good of the Church. First we experience in private how the mind is strengthened in a wonderful way as, among such variety of opinions, we are led, as it were, to the present case, when we look at the genuine words of the Scriptures. Furthermore, teachers are hardly capable of proclaiming with a clear conscience in public regarding great and difficult controversies, if they do not understand the form of speech in the evidence from which the whole matter needs to be judged. Many heresies are the result of ignorance of languages and of the forms of speech; this can be demonstrated easily in the history of ecclesiastic strife. Although that is not the only important point, in the interpretation of the Holy Scriptures the first thing is to understand the form of speech; having understood that, one can come to a conclusion on many things, most

of which are disputed even now. Therefore there is no doubt that knowledge
of languages is necessary for theology.

Do not let uneducated men deter you from that skill, who not only condemn the study of languages, but hate all the good arts bitterly, so that they
alone will appear to have knowledge. If the case needs to be resolved by
witnesses, oppose them with examples as well as the opinions of Jerome,
Augustine and many others, who believed that knowledge of languages is
necessary for explaining the Holy Scriptures. God Himself judges this to
be so, who, by giving us the gift of languages with the Gospel, proves that
the knowledge of languages is necessary.[2] Truly, if anyone thinks that there
is no use for it in the Church, he has an insolent opinion of the divine gift.
If that evidence does not move the adversaries at all, then they should at
least heed the canonical writings, whose authority is sacrosanct to them.
There are decrees about languages, and also regulations composed in the
synods, which enjoin the most famous universities to teach languages. Why
would the synod decree this with great authority if this kind of study were
not useful?

I have heard that sixty years ago Gregorius Tiphernas[3] arrived in Paris
and demanded a stipend from the senate of the university for him to agree
to teach Greek there. However, it seemed impolite to some that he had
dared to solicit a stipend, when the university senate had neither invited
him nor notified him that they were going to use his services, nor even had
a lector for Greek. Until then, in France as well as here, Greek was totally
unknown. Therefore, when he was asked what sort of despotism this was,
to more or less order the university senate to pay a stipend, the man, who
was prepared for this, cited the regulation regarding the study of languages,
in which the University of Paris was specifically mentioned. The senate
did not take offence at this liberty, but praised the man's sense and zeal; the
stipend was decreed by general consensus. The Parisian senate were not
going to do this, though, if they had not approved of the papal regulations, or
if they had considered that kind of study useless for the Church.

However, I desist from discussing this matter at greater length, given
that Erasmus demonstrates in his well-grounded volumes that the
knowledge of languages is necessary for the interpretation of the Holy

---

[2] I supply the passage in italics from *Declamationum D. P. Melanthonis*, ed. J. Richard (3 vols., Strasburg,
1558), vol. 1, p. 309: 'Quid quod ita Deus ipse indicat, qui cum Evangelio linguarum *donum largiens,
testatur, Ecclesiae linguarum* cognitionem necessariam esse.'

[3] Gregorius Tiphernas (1413–1464) taught at the University of Paris between 1456 and 1459: see G.
Mancini, 'Gregorio Tifernate', *Archivio Storico Italiano* 8 (1923), 89f.

Scriptures.[4] Remember that on this subject Doctor Martin Luther not only encourages you, but also severely reproves our laziness and idleness. If you defer to his judgement as much as his outstanding teaching and experience demand, you will certainly study foreign languages more eagerly and you will put much more work into the study of eloquence. However, given that theology is now held in dislike, the young everywhere cast from them the study of languages and eloquence, together with the Holy Scriptures, and embrace the arts that are universally more saleable and more gainful.

I do not disparage these arts, though, for the state needs a great variety of arts, and it is well said that 'a state is not made up from doctors and doctors, but from doctors and farmers'.[5] Those people need to be rebuked, though, who either lead everyone away from the Holy Scriptures or, having devoted themselves to other arts, do not think that any part of studying should be invested in the Holy Scriptures, and, as I can see, ridicule all of us who do not entirely abstain from the Holy Scriptures, and even consider us mad.

But let us not say anything here of those who are either irreverent against God or cruel towards the Church, and who, if it were up to them, would efface all religion. I shall address myself to others who are more moderate.

First I would like to consider, good young men, that the teaching of religion concerns everyone. Just as it is said that men are not born for themselves only but for their country, I could say even more truthfully that all good men have to consider themselves born chiefly for the Church. Thus, even if some commendable considerations call us to other arts (and I do not disparage them), nevertheless Christian teaching must not be neglected. Some part of our time and effort needs to be allocated to it for the purpose of strengthening our own minds as well as for preparing ourselves for the common good of the Church. Ambrose was active in the law-court and in judgements, but in the meantime he nevertheless read the Holy Scriptures and united the Greek theologians with the Latin ones.

Furthermore, the knowledge of languages is not only beneficial to theologians, it is also of surpassing usefulness in the other arts; I want this to be understood this way, and I ask you to pay attention, so that no one thinks that I detract from the dignity of the other professions. So I declare that those who will be undertaking the study of medicine or law should be

---

[4] For Erasmus' promotion of the study of languages for the study of the Bible, see his *Annotationes in Novum Testamentum*.

[5] See note 3 to oration 2, p. 10.

educated in advance in some noble teaching that contains philosophy and a knowledge of the ancient world. The practice of public speaking also has to be added. By these subjects the minds will be shaped towards both pleasantness and humanity and sharpened as well as instructed, so that they are able to grasp and manage the other arts in a more productive way.

If anyone believes that it is possible to have a perfect knowledge of philosophy without Greek, I certainly hold him to be fortunate in his belief. However, it is even said that there are many among those who interpret Aristotle and who have learnt Greek who are also inept. When they cannot explain the extremely weighty things transmitted by the authors, they come up with some new kind of teaching, full of strange dreams, that is of no use for life or for public business. Furthermore, they damage philosophy who circumscribe it by such narrow boundaries that they attribute nothing to it except those well-known precepts from Aristotle that are taught in the schools. Without speaking of mathematics, I for one am convinced that the knowledge of antiquity, of poems and histories, is assuredly an important part of philosophy, for it contains the teaching of humanity, as it displays precepts and examples for all duties.

Nothing can happen in private life or in the state of which there is not a likeness in the most wisely written histories. By my judgement it is most profitable for those intending to undertake great things to look at these likenesses as in a mirror, and to see decisions and the outcome of good and bad decisions. Furthermore, there is even much in secular as well as ecclesiastical affairs that can neither be understood nor judged without a knowledge of antiquity. How many times does one have to speak about the vicissitudes of nations? How often, in the Church, does one have to inquire into ancient disputes about the greatest things? These cannot be known in any way without Greek and Latin. And some matters concerning the Church are written in Greek only. Also, as far as the variety and quantity of topics and examples are concerned, the Greek poets as well as the historians are far superior to the Latin ones. For the Romans only strove to honour their domestic affairs with elegance,[6] whereas the Greeks included the histories of all peoples and all realms, and they described them in such a way that they philosophised more truly in the explanation of their affairs and decisions than those who teach the bare precepts in the schools. Indeed, the Greeks lead philosophy out of the shadow into the sun and the dust, that is, they show its usefulness for life and for business.

[6] Reading *ornate* for *ornare*.

Although this teaching would be desirable simply because it is pleasant, there are still other good reasons to learn Greek. For what pleasure could be more worthy of the minds of those present than the one gained from the knowledge of the greatest things? And since these pleasures pertain in some way to manners, I believe that they lead the mind to humanity and pleasantness by their delight.

However, I am not only discussing pleasure, but I am speaking of profit and necessity, for without the noble teaching contained mainly in Greek writings no one is sufficiently suitable for managing the other arts or for performing great things. That is not all. Even though any kind of teaching is advantageous for rousing one to virtue and for forming the mind, I do not hesitate to declare that the kind of teaching of which I am talking is most conducive to this.

Certainly, it cannot be denied that this teaching is needed for managing the other arts. Medicine is to a large extent Greek, and cannot be grasped without philosophy. And those who dedicate themselves to the law do not only strive to acquire the rhetoric of the law-court in order to apply it to their occupation, but they also seek a teaching that will be of use to the state and, as they themselves say, a philosophy that is not feigned. In order to protect themselves with dignity they will surely also need some other kind of teaching, that is, the knowledge of religion and of antiquity, eloquence and those writings which, because they contain the sources of laws, are no less often employed for deliberations on public duties than the laws themselves.

There are, however, some young men who, because of their idleness, flee the toil of learning and rush straight into the highest professions, with whose titles they disguise their sloth. They disparage our studies, so that they may appear to spurn these arts. They become, so to speak, denuded Solons, without grammar, without dialectics, knowledge of religion or philosophy, and finally without any humanity. Indeed I marvel with what cheek they dare look at the law books, whose authors were obviously learned in the arts that we are discussing. How much do they derive from the Greek and Latin histories? With how much reverence do they defer to Homer, how often do they quote his words like an oracle? In one place they cite from the words of Demosthenes, in another they copy the sayings of Plato *verbatim*. And some more recent lawyers dispute the authority of philosophers and poets in law-cases, because they describe in a very wise way the institutions of the ancients, the morals and weighty considerations of noble duties and finally all the power of the natural law. Now, what impudence is this, to hold in contempt the writings which the law-makers themselves consider most noble?

Accordingly, I urge modest and good minds, when they consider the greatness of the profession to which they aspire, to follow the example of their authors and think that some of their effort needs to be bestowed upon these our arts and writings. I do not wish to fight with those who spurn not only our judgement but also the example of their authors. Different things are good for different people, as is well said: 'Anacharsis errs against propriety among the Athenians, the Athenians do so among the Scythians.'[7] These people are not touched by the sweetness of the arts that we admire, nor do their judgements lure us away from the study of the best things.

When you busy yourself with your studies, young men, reflect that you also have to apply perseverance and endurance, for no virtue can be practised or retained without endurance. Therefore, do not allow the study of these our arts and languages to be cast out of you by the unreasonable judgements of the crowd and of the uneducated. 'Endure and preserve yourselves for happiness' [Virgil, *Aeneid* 1.207] – why should I not use that most brave man's words, according to the poet, particularly as I am using them for a much greater cause? For he sought a dwelling-place for himself and his comrades. Your studies relate to the entire Church and to all posterity, and what greater cause can there be than what concerns the preservation of the Church?

I have often heard that Capnio, when he had been sent to Rome to the pope because of a certain business, went to the lecture-hall of Argyropoulos, who at the time was teaching Greek in Rome with great success.[8] Capnio greeted Argyropoulos respectfully and, in the assembly of very learned men, explained to him that he, Capnio, was a German passionate about the study of Greek, and that he congratulated himself upon the good luck of having found an opportunity to hear him – for at the time there was no one who lectured more learnedly on philosophy and Greek – and he entreated him to give him permission to listen to him. Argyropoulos was delighted with Capnio's speech and, having kindly promised him his service, he asked him whether he had studied Greek before. Capnio said that he had heard the basics of the language in Basle in Germany. By chance Argyropoulos

---

[7] This must be a reference to a passage in *Letters of Anacharsis*, see note 10, oration 7, p. 65.

[8] Melanchthon's great-uncle, Johann Reuchlin (1454/5–1522) was also known under the Latin name of Capnio. He must have met Johannes Argyropoulos (1415–87) in the spring of 1482, when he accompanied Count Eberhard the Bearded of Württemberg on a journey to Florence and Rome.

was explaining Thucydides, and he showed it to Capnio and told him
to read and then to translate as well. When Capnio both pronounced it
beautifully (I have heard that he was extremely devoted to the study of
correct pronunciation) and rendered the sentence in Latin satisfactorily,
the Greek, astonished, turned to the audience and exclaimed: 'Here you
see that by our exile Greece had flown across the Alps.' Although he spoke
the truth, because the Greeks in exile kindled these studies among the
Latin nations, you must nevertheless consider that this happened by divine
providence, so that, when the Turks had invaded Greece and the Greek
nation had been destroyed, the language most necessary to the Church
would not be destroyed also.[9] And so it was spread among these nations by
the special favour of God. It cannot be denied that it has brought more light
to the other arts as well as to the Holy Scriptures. It assists the study of
eloquence in a wonderful way, for the Latin writers could not be understood without the Greek authors. It opened a door for German philosophy,
and not only to Aristotle and the Greek doctors, but also to the excellent
mathematical authors. How much we owe to those who translated Euclid
and Ptolemy into Latin! We can see that later Johannes Regiomontanus,[10]
a fellow-citizen of mine, was greatly assisted by the Greek language in
elaborating these works and in illustrating all the arts of that kind. And now,
too, in Germany, some who excel in the knowledge of the Greek language
join their efforts to honour the authors of that kind. Once the sources had
been made available, good men began to love the Holy Scriptures more and
to consider them more complete.

If the arts that I have recounted were to be consigned to oblivion and
annihilated, it would be sadder than if the sun were taken from the world.
Without the knowledge of foreign languages, though, it is not possible to
retain their assets. One can judge easily from this that the knowledge of
languages is not a trivial or commonplace gift from God. What impiety,
what a crime, to spurn such a gift, the usefulness of which is so obvious,
and to reject it again and expel it after it has been brought to these nations
by divine providence! The laws punish sacrilege horribly in public, but it
is a greater sacrilege to strip the Church of the knowledge of languages than
of golden or silver ornaments. For these heavenly gifts bring light to the
Gospel, and they are more truly ornaments of the Church than any golden

[9] Constantinople fell on 28 May 1453.
[10] Johannes Regiomontanus (1436–76), astronomer and mathematician, who set up a printing shop
and observatory in Nuremberg. See further oration no. 29, pp. 236–55.

object. And there is no doubt that God has added the gift of languages to the Gospel for the purpose that they call us and that they lead to an explanation of the Holy Scriptures. Therefore consider those contemptuous of languages sacrilegious, who once rushed at the altars and into the temples with great rage and threatened the devastation and ruin of religion and of the noble arts, and do not doubt that they will have to pay God their penalty. If we, however, strive to be pleasing to God and loyal towards the Church, let us recognise the favour of God and protect and conserve it for the use of the Church. If someone is deterred from these studies by the fact that the prizes do not appear to be adequate to the toil, then he does not have sufficient religious feeling for God. For if God promises prodigious recompense for piety in every case, His trustworthiness is not to be doubted. Elsewhere He promises vast crops of fruits of the earth, if the people generously joined together for the use of the temple. Therefore the recompense will not be lacking for us, if we join our efforts for the use of the Church; and it is piety to have regard for the Church in expectation of that promise. I have spoken.

5 Preface to Homer (1538?)

CR XI, 397–413

Preface to the Homer of Veit Winsheim[1]

Since I am about to enter upon the interpretation of the Homeric poem in a few days, it has seemed right that I commend, as I can, that lecture and these studies to the young by an oration in this place. I believe I can do so quite rightly, given that the matter is most worthy of commendation, and also much needed in these present times and amidst such corrupt judgements of men. I consider in my mind these admirable gifts of God, namely the study of literature and of the humanities – and apart from the Gospel of Christ this world holds nothing more splendid nor more divine – and I also consider, on the other hand, by what blindness the minds of men are enveloped in unnatural and Cimmerian[2] darkness; they spurn these true and greatest gifts, and with great effort they pursue means for their wishes and desires that are not only inferior but also ruinous and destructive to themselves. When I weigh these things in my heart, I am violently moved, for it comes to my mind by what dense darkness and, so to speak, black night the hearts of men are surrounded. I am not further astonished, if men are blind in things that are divine and beyond human understanding, when I see them thus treading under foot these their own and personal goods for which they are intended by divine providence, and which they could have comprehended and cherished.

We disdain, and make the butt of our jokes, the study of classics, by which that part of us that alone deserves the name 'man', that is made in the image of God and for the possession of true and everlasting happiness, was meant to be refined and roused. Instead of these, we pursue with mad and blind effort I know not what illusions held out by Satan, and worthless shadows, and hitherto have not had the reverence to look at that sun. That unceasing enemy of humankind leads our minds away from admiration and love for what is true and good by whatever kind of deceit he can, and he blinds our eyes by false appearances and obscures them to such an extent that we see and cherish anything rather than that which we should have seen and cherished most.

---

[1] Veit Winsheim (1501–78), as the Dean of the arts faculty at Wittenberg, presided over the promotion of Bachelors of Arts in February 1538.

[2] The phrase 'Cimmerian darkness', alluding to the Cimmerii (a mythical people said to live in perpetual darkness), indicates deep obscurity or darkness of the mind; Erasmus, *Adages*, II.vi.34.

What happens to the Muses and the study of them now is the same as Strabo[3] [XIV.2.21] reports as having once happened in Iassus to a singer accompanying himself on the cithara. When he was singing learnedly and sweetly in the theatre there and the Iassians were listening to him, as soon as a bell rang (which was the sign of the sale of fish on offer), immediately all left the singer behind and scattered to buy fish, with the exception of one somewhat deaf man who alone remained, not having heard the sound of the bell. The singer thereupon turned to him and said: 'I am immensely grateful to you – because of the enthusiasm for music as well as because of the honour to me – for not dashing out immediately at the ringing of the bell, like all the others, in order to buy fish.' The man said: ' What do you say? Has the bell rung yet then?' When the singer confirmed this, he said: 'Good luck to you', rose and forthwith he, too, ran out to buy fish. The singer was abandoned alone, and in a city of that size he did not find anyone who cared more for music than for rotten fish.

In such a way these studies and writings are neglected in our times. Each one rushes towards the mean and gainful arts, they are slaves to their detestable desires and to their stomachs, and they know no god besides these. Only very few take care to refine and honour their minds, the better and more divine part of them. Just as in a noisy and drunken banquet men talk nonsense, laugh, bawl and make loud noise while some famous musician is playing, and they neither pay attention nor receive in their ears and hearts the sweetness of the music, nor enjoy it thoroughly, so our times, as if intoxicated and frantic with their desires, neither listen to the voices of the Muses nor pay attention to them. Those who by their authority and efforts should have eminently fostered and honoured these studies, the majority being barbarians and without education, greatly desire rather to see them oppressed and annihilated. When Herod, the king of the Jewish people, was raised to royal honours from humble and obscure origins, he ordered all books containing genealogies to be burnt and destroyed so that, the distinction between nobility and obscurity being removed, the obscurity of his own origins would be less disreputable. In just the same way uneducated men hate literature and want it destroyed, hoping that thereby they can hide their own ignorance better.

So it happens that literature is attacked by some and abandoned by others; blind desire carries away each one in a different way, and we admire

---

[3] Strabo (c. 64 BC–AD 19), a Stoic who wrote the *Geographica* describing the geography, history and customs of the chief countries in the Roman world.

anything rather than the true good, and we do not even recognise it. So Satan holds human minds shackled by his fetters, and he leads them astray to whatever place he wants, and indeed now the disgrace of ignorance is considered the least of ills; if we were not insane and enslaved in our minds, we would not consider anything sadder or more worth fleeing. In the mean time some pursue honours, others the basest pleasures and the majority riches and money. They value these possessions alone at an enormous price, selling their life and soul at a profit, as one says. The wretched people measure happiness by these things, not considering how often that unhappy happiness is not merely interrupted by a slight change, but truly and absolutely turned upside down. Many have learnt this lesson from experience, the teacher of the foolish.

But what shall I say? We can see that it happens generally that the best things are held in utmost contempt and, on the other hand, that the worst things are made great. Therefore, if the same happens to literature and the teaching of classics, this must not appear to us as something new or excessively astonishing, nor is it fitting for us to be alienated from loving and cherishing these studies by the exceedingly bad judgement and error of the crowds. The matter itself and indignation move me to say this beforehand, as I am about to speak of Homer and of these our studies. For who would not be moved, seeing such extraordinary contempt for the best things? In your kindness, bear with me in this complaint that my distress and the indignity of the matter have wrung out of me.

But to get down to our actual topic, I have, as I said, decided to expound – with the help of the gods – Homer's poem; I chose to speak briefly about it first on this occasion. I do so also in order to be able to commend it to the young by this oration, and to honour it with worthy praise, although it can never be honoured as it deserves, and Homer's splendour surpasses any oration. But just as great deities are sometimes worshipped with sacrifices of coarse grain and salt, so we bestow upon the praise of such a great writer what little we can in our insignificance. We shall not be talking here about the birth, country and life of Homer, for this has been expounded with sufficient accuracy and at length by others; we shall discuss, briefly and as well as the short time will allow, the poem itself and the usefulness that scholars can derive from it. For those who read Homer in such a way that they derive nothing but pleasure from it, and aphorisms collected like little flowers, act like someone who tends a very fertile field only for the sake of their mind, so that he may occasionally crown himself with flowers growing there, neglecting care for the produce that he could reap in great abundance. Someone said, correctly, I believe, that such a man is not a sufficiently judicious steward. Even though one can obtain such pleasure from reading Homer as from hardly any other author – and it is entirely so arranged by nature that the highest true pleasure is matched with the highest usefulness – this must nevertheless not be the foremost object of attention. There is another one that is greater and preferable, beyond question; just as the heads of families are usually circumspect in what concerns their family, so immediately in the beginning we should devise a method in our minds if we are to attach any value to the task of reading this or that author. If we do this in studying Homer, then immediately the endless multitude of benefits becomes clear to us, as a throng of good things (*myrmēkia agathōn*), which we can demand from that text abundantly and to our fill, as they say. If anyone were to include and enumerate them all in a single oration, it would be as Virgil said [*Georgics* 2.105–8]: 'We who would have knowledge of this world would likewise fain to learn how many grains of sand on the Lybian plain are stirred by the Westwind, or when the East falls in unwonted fury on the ships, would know how many billows of the Ionian Sea roll shoreward.'[4] To speak the truth, although I have not so completely forgotten who I am as to dare claim that I could perceive and know all those prodigious and countless riches of the Homeric poem, of which no doubt only the smallest part is known, nevertheless I feel that it is clearly happening to me that, as one says, the abundance is making me needy. For when I contemplate this work, manifold things, appearing from every side like divine miracles, leave me stupefied and anxious, so that it is difficult to judge where I should begin and where I should stop. For I fear that I should fare like those who, having deliberated greatly and at length, have to choose from an enormous heap of precious things certain treasures (*keimēlia*) and sometimes err through excessive care and doubt, and, leaving the best behind, set apart the less precious. In the same way I, too, fear that, passing by the better things which others perhaps admire more, I may choose the inferior ones; but whether this is noticed I do not regard it as being of great moment. For it does not escape me that the keenness of people's minds is usually blunted by the splendour of the Homeric song, just as the eyes' keenness and faculty are overpowered by the rays of the sun. We shall therefore assemble a few examples out of an infinite variety – a task like

[4] As translated by H. Rushton Fairclough in Virgil, *Eclogues, Georgics, Aeneid I-VI* (Cambridge, MA and London, 1967), pp. 123–5.

enclosing the sea in narrow water-pipes – and enumerate summarily and briefly those which have seemed to us the most admirable in that poem.

First I declare that no work has been brought forth by any human mind since the beginning of the world, in any language or nation – with the exception of the holy writings – in which there is such a wealth of teaching or of elegance and pleasantness. I am not unaware that this is a daring statement and one that excites ill will, but at the same time I do not doubt that nobly educated minds, who have tasted Homer only lightly and, as they say, with the foremost part of the lips,[5] will agree ardently with me on this. But now I shall not talk about that teaching which contains the nature of things, which transmits the positions of the celestial circles and the stars and their rising and setting, which shows the harmony of the temperature of the human body, the symmetry (*symmetrian*) of its members and their various conditions. I shall not speak about the hidden learning with which the Homeric poem is filled and crowded throughout, for the short time does not allow us to enumerate the individual examples; let us come to our better-known ones. What moral injunction will you give me for ordering one's life well and happily, that has ever been uttered by wise men, for which there is not some splendid and distinguished example in Homer? What duty is there in life or what matter is there altogether of which there is not a likeness portrayed in it? They are the most refined, the sweetest and at the same time the wisest thoughts about all things and matters that can be conceived by any human mind. For what is sweeter or more ethical (*ēthikon*) to think, what can one be admonished more seriously for, than that which Homer repeats in several passages of his poem to those who are angry for a not unreasonable cause – *ameinō d'aisima panta* – that is, nothing is better in all things than moderation, readiness to be appeased and forbearance? What is more just and human than the utterance of Diomedes in book nine of the *Iliad* to decree, as the first law in the assembly, freedom for those who speak and patience for those who listen? Do we not see how our century is afflicted more than anything else by the fact that the mighty cannot bear free speech, and not even any thought of freedom? What is more heroic than Hector saying: 'There is one perfect omen, to defend one's country' [*Iliad* XII.243] – that there is one most auspicious sign, and that is to fight bravely and to die nobly for one's country? If the princes of our times had this sentence before their eyes and inscribed in their hearts, we would not see the Turks attack Germany and the Christian

---

[5] To take a brief sample of something: see Erasmus, *Adages* I.ix.92.

world again and again with impunity, nor would we fear their arrival quite so much. What is more divine than when he writes that he who has not rendered thanks to his parents for his nursing dies a premature death, among the first. Likewise, he says: 'Ill deeds do not attain to virtue, and even a slow man catches up with a fast one' [*Odyssey* viii.329] – that evil deeds do not lead to success or have a good outcome, and that the wicked man, however fast he may be and however versed in deceit, is nevertheless caught, and even by one who is lame. There is no doubt that this kind of saying was first uttered by the holy fathers and transmitted to posterity. Then they were passed on from one to the other, one could say from hand to hand, and finally extended to the men by whom they were included in these written monuments, so that, put in an illustrious and perspicuous place, they could be kept in the memory of all posterity and beheld with admiration.

Homer's poem is full of such sentences that have almost the weight and authority of laws, and which had to be by right respected with extraordinary scrupulousness, like oracles or divine responses, and committed to memory and always kept before one's eyes. And it seems that what Cicero said of Euripides – that he believed his individual verses to be separate testimonies – can be said much more truly of Homer, since Euripides and the other poets gush forth from Homer like rivulets from a never-failing source.

In any kind of art some principles and common notions are passed on, to which those who occupy themselves with those arts turn their thoughts as by the Lesbian rule.[6] You will remember, young men, that Boethius in his dialectics calls common preconceptions (*prolēpseis*) of that kind maxims. I should say that the entire Homeric poem consists of such maxims, that is of common and most useful rules and precepts for morals, life and civil duties, for which there is widespread use in every life and in all its actions. He teaches many things, admonishes wisely on many, and instils in the young the most honourable and agreeable notions of modesty, respect and the other virtues. No one is a better teacher of the habits of pleasantness and humanity than he; he demonstrates and accomplishes a certain experience of life in the young, which is otherwise held in highest praise, but is attributed only to old age. The passage from the Latin poet is well known:

---

[6] The Lesbian rule alludes to a lead rule used in Lesbian architecture. The rule changed to fit the shape of the stone and hence did not remain a rule. The phrase 'by the Lesbian rule' is used when things are done the wrong way round: see Erasmus, *Adages*, I.v.93.

'... older age does not have only what we flee; experience comes with advanced years' [Ovid, *Metamorphoses*, VI.28f]. Indeed, reading Homer performs this divine service, namely to impress the prudence of the old upon the youthful mind, for they can obtain and draw from this poem, by a short-cut, as from a treasure or a spring those things which old people usually learn from long experience, and which numerous years, the variety of things and the experiences of human life teach them. For the teaching of how to live rightly and happily is not delivered less successfully there than in any writings of the philosophers, as Horace said truthfully of Homer [*Letters* I. 2. 4]: 'What could there be that is ugly, that is beautiful and that is useful, that he did not teach more clearly and better than Chrysippus or Crantor?' Indeed, he envelops the most serious and holy tenets in the sweetest and most pleasant poetic images, so that noble and inquiring (*syzētika*) minds are educated with, as Plutarch says, a sense of beauty.

Nor is ethics (*to ēthikon*), that is the grace and gentleness of manners, and the moderation and humanity of the mind, expressed in any writings as it is in Homer's poem. Therefore, if it is true that, as they say, studies are transformed into manners, there can be no anger, but rather, by contact with the most humane and delightful poet, minds also grow gentle and become more humane and peaceful. I believe that great men endowed with outstanding intellects have noticed this, and some call the Homeric poem the workshop of humanity, others the fountain of all pleasantness and beauty. Pliny calls Homer the most eminent father of higher teaching and of antiquity, while Plato calls him the best teacher for life [*Laches* 201b1]. In order to understand that these magnificent titles have been rightly attributed to Homer, and to understand his poem, let us display to ourselves the entire body of the work, so that we do not have to conjecture, as with a ruined statue, from the mutilated parts and limbs.

The Homeric poem has two themes; one is entitled *Iliad*, the other *Odyssey*. Plutarch judges that in the *Iliad* Homer celebrates physical strength, in the *Odyssey* the powers of the intellect [*Fortune of Alexander* 327f.]. In the *Iliad* he describes, according to tradition, the most noble and therefore the honourable and pious war which the Greeks waged against the barbarians in defence of conjugal virtue, in order to avenge adultery and the violation of hospitality. The *Odyssey* contains the wanderings of Ulysses by whose image the poet wanted to describe a wise and civil man cast about by varied storms of fortune, who knew how to sway and temper fortune by judgement.

I believe that there is only little for me to say here about that part [i.e. the *Odyssey*], as we have decided to expound it first. There is no doubt that in the *Iliad* the poet wanted to describe the arts of the military and of war, in the *Odyssey* those of peace; and so in the entire poem he meant to form, educate and prepare the kind of intellect that one day must rule the state by either kind of art. Accordingly, in the *Odyssey* he paints a picture of civil and peaceful life, but in the *Iliad* he sets out military examples; for by these arts states and kingdoms are acquired, held and ruled, and whoever will some day lead the state must be instructed in these arts. Homer's verse to that effect is well known, of which they say that Alexander the Great was so pleased by it that he always kept quoting it: 'Both a good king and a strong fighter' [*Iliad* III.179].

But let us see what Homer assigns to that man whom he conceives as a civil man, a prince in the state and endowed with such gifts of the intellect and such arts and virtues. First of all he assigns to him a great love for his country, and we know that after the love for God this is the highest degree of piety and justice. As Herodotus reports, Solon, when staying with Croesus, ascribes the highest degree of happiness to him who dies for his country, and the next degree to him who fulfils his duty towards his parents [*Histories*, I. 30f.]. In order that Ulysses be filled with this love for his country and that he be made more distinguished, the poet conceives many opportunities and various obstacles by which his return to his country is hindered, against all of which he struggles with counsel, reason and the powers of the mind, and all of which he surmounts in the end. And what is the country that he holds so dear? To be sure, a barren, narrow island, attached to the roughest rocks like a bird's nest, as Cicero says [*On the Orator* I.xliv.196]. He has such longing and love for it that he would not hesitate to prefer the smoke coming from there to immortality. And we can see that this fondness has been extraordinary in all great and distinguished men. Demosthenes writes [*Letters* II.20] that when he was in exile in Calauria, he used to climb every day to the top of the sanctuary where he had taken refuge, and, measuring the distance with his eyes, gazed in the direction of Athens with great longing and love; although his country had been ungrateful and wicked towards him, it was still dearer to him than his life or his soul.

The next degree of virtue, to return to our topic, is duty towards one's parents, spouse and children, and, for the prince, especially towards his citizens and subjects, which Homer attributes to Ulysses to the highest degree. How piously does he cherish and revere his parents! With what love does he embrace his son or his wife, from whom he would not suffer himself to be torn away, not even by familiarity with immortal goddesses! With what care and solicitude does he protect the life of his companions, even though they do not deserve it! How he keeps watch for them and does not decline any kind of trouble or toil when considering their safety!

Because the poet makes him a most wise and constant man, he contrives various opportunities in which these virtues can be seen, and he exposes him to various misfortunes and dangers in which his fortitude is shown and his ready power of judgement shines forth. For we know that adverse fortune is like a practice-field and a gymnasium, where strength of the mind and uncommon virtue are exercised and seen. It is also remarkable that he makes him most wise and most eloquent, and attributes to him speech flowing like rivers swollen with the snows of winter, and he opposes and compares two completely perfect ways of speaking in Menelaus and Ulysses. Moreover, he pretends that Ulysses is ruled and protected by Minerva, in order to show that great men are dear to God and that, supported by His help, they can accomplish great things.

Then he makes him fight with the Cyclops and with the suitors, that is with tyrants and with quarrelsome and vicious men occupying the bed and possessions of others, because for heroic and distinguished men there have always been struggles and contests with these two types of men. And, what needs to be observed in particular, Homer conceives him as being most patient and persevering in what he has determined. In order to keep his course and to achieve what he wants, he does not let himself be defeated or broken by any trouble or toil or by any abuse. When he already seems to have done with dangers and ills, even in his own house he endures much that is unbearable, he withstands being torn and needy, being made sport of, being beaten, having bones thrown at him by the suitors and being mocked by his household. He conceals everything for a time, waiting for the opportunity to regain his house, take possession of his things and take revenge. That virtue is unique in distinguished men – not only to achieve great and memorable things for the good of their country and of many men at risk of their life, but also to withstand and endure injustice, disgrace, abuse and disrepute, and persevere on their determined course, aiming for and following only what is honourable and beneficial. The phrase by Ennius about Fabius is well known: 'For he did not put reputation above safety.' It is clearly Ulysses' kind of wisdom, by which unfortunate and miserable facts are sustained and endured. I shall desist from talking about Ulysses, whom Philostratus [*Lives of the Sophists* 1.8.3] calls Homer's delight (*athyrma*), since I would run out of time more quickly than of things to say. For in Homer there are countless passages intended and devised as if by divine providence (and Horace has said not rashly that they are wonderful), and throughout they are all created with incredible elegance and pleasantness, diversified by various moods, chiefly the dispositions (*ēthesi*), however, and by many splendid and pleasant accidents – indeed arranged with such order and economy (*oikonomiai*) of things that I would consider anyone who is not charmed by reading Homer lacking in any sense of humanity: an animal, not a man.

There is in that work a perfect and absolute image of human wisdom, as much as can ever exist and be imagined altogether, and in every kind of teaching there is nothing sweeter, nothing more splendid and nothing in which greater splendour of eloquence shines forth. It was rightly said by Fabius [Quintilian, *Education of the Orator* x.i.46] that just as the courses of all streams and springs take their origin from the ocean, Homer had given a model and origin to all parts of eloquence. For he did not collect rainwater, as Pindar says, but he rushes forth in a living river, created by the gift of divine providence so that he might thereby test all his strength by eloquence.

Although after his age there flourished a considerable number of poets, he himself nevertheless always kept his, that is the highest and noblest, place, and he alone snatches away the palm of victory from all poets that any age has brought forth, and he leaves them all far behind. He achieved this, namely that it requires a great nature and a great mind to follow his virtues, not by emulation, which is impossible, but at least with the intellect. Manilius sings of him, splendidly as well as truthfully:

> Yet all posterity has for its verse drawn on the rich
> stream issuing from his lips and, daring to
> channel his river into slender rills, has
> become fertile by the wealth of One. [*Astronomica* II. 8–11][7]

And Theocritus says that if the birds of the Muses, that is the other poets, dared compete with Homer, they would toil in vain and it would be like the cry of the cuckoo compared to the sweet song of the nightingale. Philostratus, too, declares that Homer is not like the sculptor Euphranor,

---

[7] As translated by G. P. Goold in Manilius, *Astronomica* (Cambridge, MA, and London, 1977), p. 83.

who excelled among the others in his art by certain virtues, but is most distinguished in all of them, any of which would be highly praised in one person. He records an agreeable story about Homer which I thought was not inappropriate to relate briefly here.

He says that, as a youth, Achilles was stirred with astonishing enthusiasm and love for music and poetry, so that he entreated the Muses every day with prayers to be made into an outstanding musician with their help. When he would not stop pleading, finally the Muse Calliope appeared to him and warned him not to fight against destiny, for it pleased the gods otherwise, to make him not a singer but an outstanding warrior, who would perform such deeds that poets would take them as a subject for their writings. Indeed, after a hundred years there would be a bard by the name of Homer, who would celebrate his exploits and brave deeds in an immortal song. This is what Philostratus says of Homer. Without doubt he means that Homer was roused by divine power and sang his song inspired by divine virtue.

It can be seen in many passages that he sang as if from the innermost part of the temple or from the tripod of Apollo, higher and more divine than human understanding. This is shown by a few oracles scattered in his poem, which could not have been conceived by the human mind without the inspiration of a god – such as the one about the descendants of Aeneas and the everlasting existence of the future Roman empire, which is rendered by Virgil in the following verse: 'And the sons of your sons, and those who are born from them' [*Aeneid* 3.98]. Therefore Democritus says, not without reason, that Homer had been assigned a soul with the gift of divination [*Fragment* 21.1].

However, this is neither the place nor the time to pursue this argument. Let us therefore return to our subject and to what is more befitting our studies and manners. At the present occasion I have no leisure to consider these hidden topics of philosophy (*ta philosophoumena*) concerning the origins of things, the motion of the celestial bodies and stars, the elements, the earth and counter-earth,[8] the constitution of man, the soul and its parts, the seat of the faculties of the soul, the single faculties, the emotions (praiseworthy and corrupt ones), then reason and intellect, and sensation and appetite which are locked in constant struggle with the former, the more divine part of man and his dumb part. Even if, as I say, I am not at

---

[8] For the concept of counter-earth, see G. E. R. Lloyd, *Early Greek Science: Thales to Aristotle* (London, 1970), pp. 27–9.

liberty to consider these, the students should nevertheless know that the seeds and origins of all these things are in Homer. And there has been no better or more outstanding painter of our nobler and more divine part than Homer.

Therefore, in Silius [*Punica* XIII.778–97], Scipio lauds Homer's shade, that he has seen in the netherworld, with great but not false praise, and, in a passage of great skill, he wishes for such a poet for his own times. For the sake of the young men here it is not troublesome to quote the passage; this is what he says:

> And he saw, walking along the boundaries of Elysium,
> the figure of a youth, his hair bound by a purple fillet
> and flowing over his shining neck.
> 'Tell me, young maid', he said, 'who is he? For with a light beyond compare
> shines the man's venerable brow, and many souls
> follow him in admiration, surrounding him with joyous cries.
> That countenance, were it not in the Stygian shadows,
> I would easily believe to be a god.' 'You would not be wrong,' said
> the wise handmaid of Trivia, 'he is worthy of being held to be a god,
> and a great genius dwells in his mighty mind.
> He described the Earth, the sea and the stars,
> and he matched the Muses in song, Phoebus in honour.
> Before he ever saw it, all this region, he revealed in order to the world,
> and he raised fame of your Troy up to the stars.'
> Scipio gazed with joyful eyes at the ghost of Homer, and said:
> 'If Fate would suffer such a poet to sing the deeds of Rome
> for all the world to hear, how much greater impression the same
> deeds would make upon posterity, if Homer testified to them!
> How fortunate was Aeacid [Achilles], whose lot it was to be made known to all
> by such a voice. The hew was made greater by the poet's verse.'[9]

So much about Scipio's praise of Homer in Silius.

However, we meet with an objection, and indeed from that most distinguished and learned man, Plato, who, condemning Homer as for a capital crime, excludes him from his Republic, and thrusts him out and despatches him into exile. I can echo the words of Chrysostom on this accusation: it is difficult to judge between such great men, just as it is difficult to utter a verdict when two men, both good, both eminent and honourable, both

---

[9] Translation based on that of J. D. Duff in Silius Italicus, *Punica* (Cambridge, MA, and London, 1961), vol. 2, pp. 261–3.

friends, disagree in their judgements on some serious and weighty matter, so that one does not appear to condemn the judgement of one of them by one's speech. But let us see what moved Plato to expel Homer from the city created by him [*Republic* III.9.398a]. For one must not think that he is doing so rashly, especially when he himself called him the best and most divine of poets (*ariston kai theiotaton tōn poiētōn*).

So what has that innocent nightingale done to deserve being banished from the Platonic fields? It can be objected that he had related some ridiculous and absurd things about the immortal gods and about religion. I agree, a great and capital crime. But let Plato or another champion of his judgement tell me what else Homer could have related about the gods or about religion, as it was then in Greece, and whether Plato himself knew and recounted anything much better. Homer himself followed what was then customary regarding religion or the immortal gods, and in those times there was no other form of religion among these people than the one Homer describes. I shall not discuss here whether it was true or false. Certainly Homer agrees in this with Plato and some most distinguished men, that there is a God and that He cares for human affairs; therefore he assembles so many counsels of the gods, in order to show that human affairs do not arise fortuitously or by chance, but are arranged and ruled by the immortal gods. He makes God loving of humans (*philanthropon*), and therefore Jupiter is shown by him lamenting that he is affected by human vicissitudes, and that he grieves about the ills and miseries of mankind; he declares that the good are protected and showered with good things, the wicked punished by divine power. Minerva commends Ulysses in the first book of the *Odyssey*, first of all for his virtue and nobility, and then also because of his zeal for piety and religion, or the worship of the gods. If human nature strives by its own powers, what better or more sublime can it imagine about the will of God than that He loves, protects and helps the good, hates the impious and the wicked and afflicts them with punishment, and attends to and rules human affairs?

As for what allegorical themes other than these he has added, it can easily be understood that he pursued another objective, and that he alluded to the manners of men and to the nature of things, and that he concealed serious and ponderous tenets in these poetic images, as was the custom in those times. Since Plato, too, sometimes sports in that way with the immortal gods, in order to demonstrate something else, he who wants to be such a strict judge of others can be convicted of just the same crime. Furthermore, one can also retort what Chrysostom says, namely that Homer described 'some things according to belief, others according to truth' (*ta men kata doxan, tade kat' alētheian*) [*Orations*, LIII.4.6]. And that is sufficient for me to say about the first issue.

The second objection made is that he attributed tears to great and heroic men; I do not see why this should merit rebuke. On the contrary, it seems praiseworthy to me that he did not think idly of the stupid and imaginary Stoic freedom from passions (*apatheia*), but presented such images of affairs and men as they are in the nature of things and in life; he did not invent marvellous opinions remote from human common sense, but expressed in his song the things that are most usual in life and consistent with common sense. He intended to show how great men are faced with very serious and sad vicissitudes, and are overcome by great emotions of the soul – as the Roman poet says of his Aeneas: 'he feigns hope on his face and deep in his heart stifles anguish' [Virgil, *Aeneid* I.209].[10] And elsewhere: 'he rages with the mighty fire of anger' [*ibid.* IV.532]. For the poets described the heroes as they were, without doubt also exposed to human vicissitudes and moved by them. They set before us familiar images of emotions, actions and duties in life, and of men, and they did not follow the strange paradoxes (*atopōtata paradoxa*) which some of the philosophers greatly enjoy.

Furthermore, the third crime held against Homer by Plato, I believe, was that he invented the underworld, for he is thought to inspire in men the fear of death, when they imagine for themselves after this life the horrors of what he depicts in the underworld, and thus the reading of Homer's poem appears to sap the strength of the mind. We shall reply to this briefly that Homer intended to celebrate the tenet of the immortality of the soul, to which the more sagacious and noble men of all centuries have adhered. He wanted to show that there was some place and abode after this life, where the souls of the good and the wicked live, and where there is some honour for the good and the wicked are punished. Furthermore he followed the familiar opinion that men then had of the netherworld. He did not contrive anything new or unheard of, or alien to the common judgement of that age, as the philosophers did.

These are the capital crimes for which Homer is punished with exile by Plato, and is relegated from the Platonic city to I know not what lonely lands, to the Scythians, I believe, or the Garamantes. Nor is this done at random, for Chrysostom is witness [*Orations* XXXVI.9.7] that even those

---

[10] As translated by H. Rushton Fairclough in Virgil, *Eclogues, Georgics, Aeneid I–VI*, pp. 255, 435.

who were barbarians and unacquainted with Greek learning, softened by the sweetness of the Homeric song, began, for that one reason, to make themselves acquainted with Greek writing, so that they could learn that poem by heart, and it was even repeated among the Indians. So, to whatever people Plato banished Homer from his Greece, he made it immediately more cultivated and more human by acquaintance and contact with him, as by the arrival of a god.

To Plato's stance in this matter we can also oppose the unanimity of all the best and wisest men who have flourished in all the centuries since Homer through the praise of their intellect, teaching, virtue or wisdom. For there was no one among them who did not praise Homer's poem with a loud voice or did not cherish him and worship him like a god. Archelaus, the best and wisest king of the Spartans, never used to go to bed, nor go out when he had arisen from his bed, without first reading with attention, almost solemnly, something from Homer; whenever he had some time free from his duties, he immediately rushed to his Homer, saying that he went to his lover and darling.

Nor is it unknown how much Alexander of Macedon relished Homer's poem. Whether he dealt with serious things or jests, even when he armed himself for war, he used to repeat Homer's songs. When a casket from the spoils of Babylon, made of gold and gems, of enormous value, was brought to him and the others assigned it to various uses for the keeping of precious things, Alexander replied that there was nothing for which the box was more appropriate than for keeping the Homeric poem; for the most noble treasure a no less noble vessel in which to preserve it was proper.[11] We, however, young men, who do not possess golden vessels or ones adorned with jewels, let us nevertheless emulate Alexander the Great and store this valuable treasure in a no less noble casket, namely in our hearts, and adorn and enrich the more excellent and divine part of ourselves by it.

'What are you telling me about treasures and riches?' some may ask, and indeed we can see that Homer, in his lifetime, was destitute, and that so far none of his disciples has become rich. We know that this is true, and that it is all too true in these our times; but we have to remember that it is certain and evident proof of public misfortune that we see these studies despised. But these ignoble thoughts and most sordid words should not concern us. Those who spurn those far more excellent goods for the sake

---

[11] The casket for Homer was from the spoils after the battle of Gaugamela, not Babylon. For the casket, see Plutarch, *Fortunes of Alexander*, XXVI.1.

of sordid gain are not worth being initiated into these sacred rites of the Muses, or admitted to this sanctuary of humanity and virtue. Homer does not swell the purse with gold or silver, nor the stomach with fat, nor does he encircle the fingers with rings adorned with jewels; but he certainly fills the mind with treasure, which is the more excellent and immortal part of ourselves, and adorns and enriches it. It should not deter us that Homer was destitute and despised in his lifetime, and that those who cherish studies of this kind are destitute. It is a condition universal to all the best things that they are despised in this miserable life full of errors and blindness. In what way have those who proclaim the word of God, the preachers of eternal salvation, who announce liberation from death, from sin and from eternal torment in the underworld, always been received and treated by the ungrateful world, and how are they treated today? It must not appear greatly surprising or new to us that the good things are neglected and the lesser ones, by contrast, become great; this is not a new situation in the world, and it is already beginning to be almost customary from a depraved habit. Let us, on the other hand, consider it thus that Homer does not serve gain, but that he is better than that; for virtue and the Muses refuse to prostitute themselves and, as the saying goes, to sit in the place of the harlots [Ovid, *Letters from Pontus* II.iii.20]. Those who consider everything in relation to its usefulness for them, and who measure happiness by the possession of the goods of fortune, should remember that they are grasping fragile and most unstable goods that are often destructive for those who own them, and that by the movement of one moment their entire happiness and they themselves can be completely overturned. If these studies are prevented because of indigence and contempt then, by the same move, humanity, virtue and nobility are excluded, the disciples of the Muses, to whom Homer is father and tutor, and all that is truly good, holy and pious in the world is excluded. On to all this one can inscribe the epigram (*epigramma*) that someone set up on his dwellings: 'This is not a large house, what of it? Often virtue gifted with genius is hidden under a poor roof.' I have spoken.

6 On the usefulness of fables (1526?)

CR XI, 116–20

I do not doubt that the more modest someone is the more he will wonder, and justly, what has come to my mind that I, a boy barely out of swaddling-clothes, should decide to speak here in the assembly of most learned youths. Indeed, we have not to such an extent laid aside all sense of shame that we would dare mutter, so to speak, in this lecture-room, unless most honourable reasons forced us to do so. For since it is unseemly to step forward here unless one can defend one's position with honour, with eloquence as well as authority, I fear that I shall be ridiculous if I undertake such a thing at an age of which everyone knows what it can do and how much it knows. However, if you do not expect perfect erudition, reverence should deserve the first praise in youthful minds; if I did not realise how far removed from it this theatrical show is, I should clearly be stupid. But my teacher's authority overcomes these reasonings; in order to try my intellect, he imposed on me this duty of speaking, and if I had refused it, I would not have appeared sufficiently dutiful. For I believe that a well-behaved young man has to obey his teacher even in an unjust matter. And so I preferred to be seen as no matter what, rather than to detract from my teacher's authority. I hope that this dutifulness will free me easily from any false accusation, and will persuade you to take it in good part that I strive to do the will of my teacher with some risk to myself. In the meantime, he himself will know to what purpose he wanted to put me to the test. He enjoined me to speak in praise of fables, which is an argument of a somewhat childish aspect, and fitting for my age. On the other hand, if one observes this argument more closely, one can understand that even the eloquence of the most sagacious men is hardly a match for it. For what part of literature or of life does not borrow something from the fables? But let me deal with the matter according to the measure of my wits, provided that it is not tedious to listen to a childish oration. If hope does not fail me, I intend to make you understand that no other kind of literature has been found to be more useful than fables.

In order that this be plausible, let me first reveal why, in my view, they were composed by preceding generations. They saw that, by a universal condition, mortals were born not only with weak bodies, but also with weak minds, and I believe that nature established this law in this way in order to increase in the parents the concern for rearing and protecting their offspring. The mouth is first unprotected and toothless, and very late the tongue, hands and feet begin to perform their function. There is such weakness of all members in the delicate body that, if the infant did not cry one would almost not know that it is alive. With extraordinary benefit, nature has made a nourishment appropriate for that state of the body in the mother's breasts, because the mouth is not straight away strong enough for more solid foods. So the infant is nourished by its mother's milk until, its small strength having increased, it tolerates more solid food – and there are medical authors who believe that infants should be nourished with only milk for a full two-year period – then little by little more solid food is given, but for a while only food that is chewed in advance. Then it is put into the infant's mouth by the nurse's hand, until its own hand can perform this function. I do not mention with how much assiduity and care it is placed in the cradle in childhood, in order that a good condition may be provided for the limbs, and some comeliness for the features.

Unless I am mistaken, by that condition of the body nature represents the weakness of the mind, as if by some spectacle, and it reminds us by what care it wants us to train and educate the unformed minds of the children. For minds, too, have their infancy: we see how late they recognise even members of the family, they are without hope or fear, and they have no sense of absent things. Therefore wise men, having observed the power of nature more closely, discovered – not, I believe, mindlessly or without the will of the gods – that the mind also needs some kind of milk. I ask you, would it not be ridiculous, if someone carried a one-year-old infant around several cities and ordered him to observe and memorise their location and also the names of their hosts accurately, so that, having returned home, he could recount it to those of the same age? I judge that those are being equally absurd who set such things before children as their understanding cannot yet grasp. There is altogether nothing more beautiful and pleasant than the truth, but it is too far removed from the sight and the eyes of men for it to be beheld and known fortuitously. The minds of children need to be guided and attracted to it as if step by step by various enticements, so that they may then contemplate more closely the thing that is the most beautiful of all, but, alas, all too unclear and unknown to mortals. And just as those who want to be loved by children attract them with sugar and similar things, so the truth needs to be made agreeable with some allurements, and needs to be introduced into uncultivated minds.

Therefore, extremely sagacious men have devised some tales which first rouse by wonder the children's minds that are sleeping as if in lethargy. For what seems more unusual to us than that a wolf speak with a horse, a lion with a little fox or an oak with a gourd, all in the manner of men? Quietly we wonder to ourselves what emotions and what language the animals would have; and this wonder gives rise to a desire to know the matter better, and it is useful to learn for what reason the stories are invented. When the mind has been stimulated little by little, it raises itself up to the contemplation of human matters, and begins to recognise the distinction between virtues and vices. Thereafter both the words and the meanings of the arguments which we heard with wonder remain rooted more deeply, and, so to speak, leave spines behind in the mind by which we are inflamed with a concern to investigate these things which are taught to us by the novel device.

I believe that fables were first invented with that intention, because it appeared that the indolent minds of children could not be roused more quickly by any other way of speaking. Perhaps the authors of the fables also did this in order to make the children's minds gentler by pleasant arguments. For in that age – like in fresh apples – there is something harsh and wild, which changes into barbarity and beast-like cruelty unless it is set right by a more humane education. For we see that the most serious and wisest of men have used this kind of teaching, and I cannot say easily what a great public evil it is that it is now banished from the schools. The learned admire the sagaciousness of the poet Homer so greatly that they place him beyond the common condition of mortals and clearly think that his mind was roused by some divine power. Yet he wrote about the war between frogs and mice [*Batrachomyomachia*] for the children whom he taught everywhere in Greece, in order both to delight the delicate minds with a very beautiful fable and to teach how much better it is to ignore a wrong than to avenge it, how uncertain is the outcome of all quarrels or wars, and that it happens not infrequently that the stronger are defeated by the weaker, and that often all ill turns itself against the instigator. For when the mice – provoked by some wrong – preferred to avenge that wrong with arms rather than ignore it, and trusted too much in their strength against the unwarlike frogs, the gods gave the victory to those who were less warlike, and the instigators of the war received a just punishment for their obstinacy. I ask you what is as important as implanting in children's minds a hatred of war and strife, a zeal for tolerance and other similar human arts?

It seems that Hesiod was of such sagacity that those who believed that he was made a poet by receiving his pen from the Muses wanted his poem to be seen as divine. And yet, since he wanted it to be most clearly established for his fellow citizens that nothing is uglier or more monstrous than violence or wrongdoing, he painted the matter as if in a picture by composing the fable about the hawk and the nightingale [*Works and Days* 203ff.]. He, too, instructed the young Greeks, and one must not despise the writers who recorded the fables invented by Aesop.

I have said for what purpose I believe fables to have been invented, and it is possible to judge from this, as if from a source, their value and usefulness. For such wise men as the authors of the fables would never have been so delighted by these trifles had they not thought that they were most useful for educating the minds of children. What of the fact that fables were beneficial not only for children, but also for the most famous cities? When the Roman people disagreed with the Senate and had withdrawn to the Sacer Mons, and were not brought round by any fierce speech, Agrippa was sent, and he so charmed the entire multitude by a beautiful fable about the stomach and the other parts of the human body that they immediately resolved to return into favour with the Senate.[1]

When Macedon was to make a truce with Athens on the condition that those orators who had provoked the minds of the citizens against Macedon with continuous orations surrendered themselves, the eminent orator Demosthenes opposed the highly unjust condition of the state with a humorous fable, although the people, being distressed by the long war, did not shrink from the condition so much. For since he wanted to teach them that the orators were required to surrender so that the city, deprived of the protection of the orators, would be the easy victim of a royal tyranny, he set the intention of the Macedonians before the eyes of the multitude with admirable clarity and perspicuity with the following fiction. The wolves once made an agreement with the shepherds that from then on they would not attack the sheepfolds, if the dogs were surrendered to them. The agreement pleased the stupid shepherds, and the dogs were surrendered. Accordingly, as soon as the wolves saw that the guardians of the sheepfold were removed they began to attack the flock. Since this fable taught how important it was to protect the orators, it protected the state for as long as the decision to do so was valid. Assuredly these examples testify that there

---

[1] Mons Sacer is a mountain near Rome, whither the Roman populace withdrew in a tumult, which led to the formation of the Tribunes (magistrates of free plebeian birth charged with the protection of the people). Menenius Agrippa, a Roman general, appeased the populace of Rome by a fable of the belly and limbs: see Livy, *History of Rome*, II.32, cf. also Cicero, *On Duties*, III.v.22 and 1 Corinthians 12:12.

is some admirable power in fables; for it needs to have been a most powerful speech that wrenched the weapons from the hands of the implacably angered Roman citizens, and that led the grievously distressed Athenians, even though they all demanded peace with one voice, nevertheless to prefer war.

Someone may now invoke the staff of Mercury, by which the ancients pretended that souls were called from the underworld, or the cithern of Orpheus, by which they say that woods and rocks were attracted, but it seems to me that the music is no less to be admired by which the power of an excited multitude is calmed than that which softens beasts and rocks. I do not know if those who invented those things about Mercury and Orpheus wanted to express that uncouth mortals and wild animals are tamed by some special kind of speaking. If this is true, it is according to reason that this is achieved by the fable, a kind of speech by which the minds of the inexperienced are charmed. Surely those who founded the laws for their peoples left to following generations many things closely resembling fables. For what is that scene by Lycurgus? Did he not present a fable when he taught with the example of the two whelps that nature and innate strength are overcome by training and habit? I do not wish to enumerate here foreign laws and practices, since there are so many fables in the Holy Scriptures that it is sufficiently clear that the heavenly God Himself considered this kind of speech most powerful for bending the minds of men. I ask you, what greater praise can fall to fables than that the heavenly God also approves of them?

I believe that you have long since been wearied by these childish trifles, and I think that it is my function not to belabour you any longer, although the topic pleases me so much that I believe that it cannot be sufficiently praised by any oration. For what kind of speech is there in which the utmost grace is joined to the utmost usefulness in the same manner? For Horace said most truly that he who mingled the useful and the pleasant carried off all the applause [*Art of Poetry* 343]. For what speech expresses morals, studies and the intellects of men more accurately than fables? And this is done with such charm that the minds of men cannot be enchanted more quickly by any lyrics than they are grasped by the fables. Therefore I encourage those of my age to devote themselves wholeheartedly to the study of fables, if my oration has any merit. There are some who wear away their wits in investigating I do not know what obscure authors, and learn with great toil to be foolish. But the fables rouse, cheer and educate the minds of children most successfully. Since, furthermore, they exist in

Latin, they nourish the speech as if with some mild juice. Indeed, if you seek either precepts for shaping morals or an example of speaking correctly, no explanations would perform either more successfully than fables. I have spoken.

7. Praise of eloquence (1523)

StA III, 44–62 & CR XI, 50–66

Philip Melanchthon's oration on the topic that the arts of speaking are necessary for every kind of studies (or, praise of eloquence)

Just as Hesiod grieves that the mortals ignore how much comfort the mallow and asphodel can bring to human affairs [*Works and Days* 41], as if they were worthless herbs, we, too, are mourning – not for the first time – that the young ignore how much importance the arts of speaking have in preparing a perfect education. These do not promise as a pretence anything of that kind which the masses applaud, and furthermore, in their usefulness they easily surpass all human affairs. For there is nothing anywhere, in the entire totality of things, which yields greater comfort for mortals than that kind of art. But, since the young ignore their value, it happens that to most they seem mean and are judged least worthy of devoting one's energies to. It is excellent to be called a philosopher, wonderful to listen to a lawyer and these days nothing is more worthy of applause to the masses than a theological title; but the arts of speaking are not paid any regard, like those of the Megarites.[1]

For this reason, it seems appropriate to demonstrate on this occasion which facts should most commend their study to us. Here I wish for the word-power of Pericles, while I exert myself to call back to the right path the foolish young, who partly spurn elegant philology out of error – because they consider it unnecessary for achieving the other disciplines – and partly flee it out of sloth. For the nature of literature and equally other good things is such that they do not fall to anyone without the greatest toil. For it is known that what is beautiful is also difficult.

Although nothing, however hard, will deter from the study of these arts the person who is aware of how little trouble will bring such great gain, and who has kept in view the greatness of the advantages; if you do not know these, you cannot even realize how unsuccessfully you will be dealing with the other disciplines. Therefore hear with open minds which reasons have brought me here, and why I judge elegant literature clearly necessary for human affairs.

---

[1] The Megarites were considered in antiquity to be exceptionally idle and worthless people and thus had no claims to respect at all: see Erasmus, *Adages*, II.i.79.

First, no one is so foolish as not to see that we need a fixed method of speaking, by which we can clearly explain the thoughts of our minds, whatever matter we need to discuss, in public or in private. Perhaps it would be ridiculous to discuss here how indispensable speech is for man. For those who despise scholarship do not quite want to appear to be depriving man of speech, but they spurn the cultivation of discourse. Therefore I shall indicate in a few words how important it is to have a method of speaking. Those who wish to weigh up the matter correctly should understand that it does not make such a difference whether you are simply mute or employ no art for speaking. For it is not feasible that you can express what you think as it should be understood unless you acquire and strengthen the ability to speak by art.

Wise men have learnt from usage that nothing is more difficult than to speak clearly and perspicuously about any topic. For, first, unless you support the power and weight of the words by your speech, what listener will understand your discourse? For since words are tried by use like coins, one must use those which one has received, which are free of obscurity because eloquent men have passed them on to following generations as if from hand to hand. In a past century, when each forged his own words, and foreign words mingled with Latin ones, in this manner a language became melted together which could not even be understood by the men of that age.

There is too much lacking for posterity to understand. For who would understand Scotus[2] or another writer of the same kind in that age? Furthermore, the most practised could scarcely vouch that they would not somewhere violate the structure or the diction of the language; if these were corrupted, the speech would necessarily become more obscure. And how much do even the educated utter improperly? How often do they render their speech obscure by incongruous and silly metaphors? For who can bear Apuleius and his monkeys? But Apuleius speaks rightly when, portraying the ass, he wanted to bray rather than speak.

Finally, if you know the words and diction well enough, it is nevertheless very difficult to distribute them each in their place, to suppress some and render others conspicuous, to contract some briefly, and extend others more generously, to dissemble and conceal some, and expose others to view, so that they stand out and become conspicuous like lights among shadows.

---

[2] Johannes Duns Scotus (*c*.1265–1308), a Franciscan philosopher, became a great scholastic authority and was dubbed the 'subtle doctor' for the subtle distinctions he drew in his commentaries.

For eloquence is something altogether greater than a noisy mass of words. But yet, I see the young fall into error; since they know neither the power nor the nature of eloquence, they do not consider it worth the effort of acquiring it with some zeal and struggle. They believe that it is praised by us little teachers in a vulgar manner, in the way in which the drug-sellers praise their ointments. Nor are they convinced by the authority of the best and most sagacious men, who, with one voice, summon the young with a universal trumpet-call. How miserable is the condition of men when the better a thing is, the further it recedes from our sight and the less it is recognised. And I do not doubt that if the merit of eloquence could be seen by the eyes, it would rouse wonderful love for it, as it is said. But since the young live by chance and not by reason, they slide, with inconsiderate impulse, towards those things which are most praised among the masses.

Therefore, if someone is not an ignorant judge of things, he should first ponder in his mind that there is nothing that is of such wide-ranging usefulness as the advantage of speech. The whole community of men, the method of organising life in public and in private, procuring everything by which we preserve life, and also all communication, are held together by speech.

Then he should persuade himself that no one will be able to speak suitably and clearly about anything unless he has shaped his speech by some art, by imitation of the best, and with great care, by that language which we use in public. Once he has noticed this, he will no doubt esteem nothing better and nothing more preferable than to learn the arts of speaking. Be it that others have to be helped by advice, or that they have to be taught, or be it that some dogma is to be defended or that one needs to speak about fair and good laws and equality, you will not achieve any more than mute people do on a stage, unless you bring to it a speech worked out with art, which places obscure things in the light, so to speak.

I know that there are those who separate elegance from the method of speaking correctly, and believe that it does not matter – as long as they declare the intent – what kind of speech they use. If they looked at the matter more closely, they would judge that by no means is an assumed[3] and superfluous pretence needed by the teachers of eloquence. The very purity and fundamental aspect of speech is elegance; if you do not preserve it, you will speak in a way that is impure and not beautiful, as well as

[3] Reading *ascitum* for *asciticium*.

inappropriate, obscure and foolish. In shaping bodies there is elegance only when all the members agree among themselves in the right proportion, and, if you make anything otherwise, it becomes monstrous. In just the same way, if you spoil the genuine form of a speech by a new arrangement you make it simply monstrous and silly. In a letter in which he defends the barbaric writers of philosophy, Pico – joking, I believe – separates elegance from the method of speaking correctly, in an improbable (*adoxoi*) argument, and reckons that things can be explained in any kind of speech.[4] Indeed, I am not at all angry with him, who no more defends barbarism than Favorinus praised fever. I am astonished that there are those whom such trifling subtleties convince in earnest that it does not matter how we speak. Does the painter imitate the body correctly if he guides his brush without any method, and if his hand is moved at random and the lines are not drawn with art? In the same way you will not put the sentiment of your mind in front of the others' eyes unless you use appropriate and distinct words, a fitting arrangement of words and the right order of sentences. For, just as we represent bodies by colours, we represent the sentiment of our mind by speech. Therefore it is necessary for one who speaks to conceive a certain image through art, which marks out the faces – so to speak – of the sentences against each other.

It is a scourge, when someone shows a roundabout path to one who does not know the way; and how often do those who lack the care for speaking correctly not lead the reader away from the path? How often are they not deceived by the misuse of one word? Repeatedly in philosophy and in the Holy Scriptures solecisms are inflicted upon our translators. For who has ever understood Paul's sentence to the Corinthians, where those crickets,[5] the despisers of elegance, have translated: 'in front of many persons'?[6] [2 Corinthians 1:11]. What storm carries away Augustine, so that he does not keep to the argument in explaining what is in John:

---

[4] Giovanni Pico della Mirandola (1463–94) wrote a defence of the scholastics after Ermolao Barbaro (1454–93) had criticised them for their lack of eloquence. Another defence of eloquence 'on behalf of Barbaro' was printed and circulated under Melanchthon's name, but it is now shown to be the work of a student, Franz Burchard: see Erika Rummel, '*Epistola Hermolai nova ac subditicia:* a Declamation Falsely Ascribed to Philip Melanchthon', *Archiv für Reformationsgeschichte* 83 (1992), 302–5.

[5] 'Grylli' or crickets are figures painted in absurd costumes: see Pliny, *Natural History*, XXXV.xxxvii.114.

[6] The exact meaning of the phrase in the Vulgate, 'ex multis facierum personis', was frequently disputed. Melanchthon understood it to mean 'by the means of many persons' who give thanks to God for various different reasons: see Melanchthon, *Commentary on Corinthians*, CR XV, cols. 1206f.

'that I said unto you from the beginning' (*tēn archēn, ho kai lalō hymin*)? [John 8:25].[7]

There are countless examples of that kind, where barbarisms deceived even the fairly educated. Indeed, you will not satisfy the reader by just any kind of speech, but the ability has to be acquired by care and zeal, by which you can put the sentiment of your mind clearly before the gaze of others, and state suitably everything that the matter requires, for that is to speak elegantly.

Therefore, let us rather administer hellebore[8] to those who disdain the beauty of speech, who are strangers to human common sense to such an extent that they do not even understand what it means to speak. It was necessity that brought forth elegance, because everything that is barbarous is undetermined, and because what is illustrated by oratorical embellishments is understood more clearly. [Marcus] Fabius [Quintilianus] wrote that rhetorical figures are employed for that purpose, and he thinks that it is never correct to divide true appearance from usefulness [*Education of the Orator*, VIII.3.11]. In the sacred writings – to leave out the secular ones – what, I ask you, do you lack in rhetorical figures? I believe that the prophets would not have used them if they had judged that they contributed nothing to the matter.

You can see for what reason I commend the study of eloquence to you – because we can neither explain what we ourselves want, nor understand the surviving writings that have been excellently written by our ancestors, unless we have thoroughly studied a fixed rule for speaking. For my part, I do not see how there could be others who wish neither to explain what they think, nor to understand what is excellently said. Therefore, even if eloquence has neither dignity nor grace, it is nevertheless important, in order that we do not, as they say, use fire, air or water in several places. For how would human affairs endure, if eloquence deserted the defence of the sacred and secular laws, if speech that can be understood were not employed in public and private counsels, or if exploits could not be transmitted to later generations by any writings? What remnant of humanity

---

[7] The interpretation of the word 'principium' (*tēn archēn*) had been problematic in this passage: medieval tradition took it to be nominative, which was known to Augustine as impossible: see Augustine, *The Literal Meaning of Genesis*, 1.10 and *The Gospel of St John*, 38.11. Erasmus followed Chrysostom in taking it as adverbial, but Melanchthon followed Nonnos in translating it as 'plainly': see Timothy J. Wengert, *Philip Melanchthon's Annotationes in Johannem in Relation to its Predecessors and Contemporaries* (Geneva, 1987), p. 129.

[8] From antiquity, hellebore was considered a strong purgative effective for treating mental disorders: see Erasmus, *Adages*, I.viii.51.

would remain in such a state? Furthermore, how little different from that was the earlier age, when hardly anybody still understood the language of the sacred books, and the sacred laws were daily fixed and re-fixed by the judgement of stupid sophists?

The exploits of those times lie buried in eternal darkness, for there was no one who could bring them to the light of literature. All subjects were rendered so obscure by the style of speaking that not even the very teachers who taught them had sufficient knowledge. They fought among themselves about the philosopher's figures of speech, as if blindfolded[9] by darkness, and none of them were understood clearly even by their followers. That man said rightly: 'Anacharsis speaks incorrectly among the Athenians, the Athenians among the Scythians. (*Anacharsin par' Athēnaiois soloikisin, Athēnaious de para Skythais.*)'[10] They spoke incorrectly in their own home-country, and they mixed in their individual dialect with astonishing liberty. The laws were a pleasure to them, not otherwise than to Heraclitus, but they spread darkness over the rest of the mortals.

Since it is already very clear how much the contempt of eloquence has brought about for us, why do we not abominate barbarism like a most harmful plague? Why do we not hiss it out of the schools by general consent? Why do we begrudge ourselves eloquence for so long, when the sun sees nothing better and nothing greater in all the lands?

So far we have been teaching that necessity compels us to pursue and preserve a fixed method of speaking; if anyone is little moved by these things, the gods would give donkey's ears to him more justly than to Midas. To this let us add the not despicable reward of the study of eloquence, because minds are roused and educated by the use of the arts by which eloquence is comprised, so that they discern more sagaciously all human affairs, and the shadow does not follow the body more closely than eloquence accompanies sagacity. As yet I speak of human matters, later I shall speak about sacred matters. Our ancestors saw that those two – the knowledge of speaking well and the mind's judgement – are connected by nature. Therefore they also said that the speech of one who is not foolish is the displayed thought of the mind. And the poet Homer attributed eloquence and sagacity to the same persons. Leaving aside the others, to Ulysses, whose speech he compares to the snows of winter [*Iliad* III.222], he attributed both

---

[9] *Andabata* are those who enter a battle with their eyes closed or blindfolded: see Erasmus, *Adages*, I.iv.33.

[10] *Letters of Anacharsis*, I. *To the Athenians.* Aldus Manutius published an edition of this in 1499.

in one little verse, when he said: 'In you both the form of your words and your intelligence are excellent.' (*Soi d'eni men morphē epeōn, eni de phrenes esthlai* [*Odyssey* XI.367].) And I do not restrain myself from recounting what was also expressed in Latin by some erudite man: 'You have a strong mind, and together with it the charm of fluent words.' Oh, what a divine sentence that is much more worthy of being carefully implanted in the hearts of the young than several Delphic decrees! For what else did the excellent old man [Homer] see than that sagacity and eloquence are linked together to such an extent that they cannot be torn asunder for any reason? If only all young men considered that little verse set before them, whither they may direct all their studies and considerations, as if at a target, and think that they have to direct all work, care, industry, thought and also intellect towards acquiring these arts. Without doubt Homer mentioned them for the reason that he wanted them to appear – as they are – the most beautiful and the most useful of all human matters.

What do you believe was on the mind of the ancient Romans that they called the arts of speaking humanity? They judged that, indisputably, by the study of these disciplines not only was the tongue refined, but also the wildness and barbarity of people's minds was amended. For, just as by training many strip off their rustic nature, the intellect is rendered mild and tamed.

There are two reasons for which the mind's judgement is sharpened by the study of speaking. The first is that those who bestow care on these arts need to compare themselves to the examples of such writers as have achieved the highest sagacity by habit of doing and dealing with the greatest things. By contact with them it happens that the readers acquire something of their judgement, just as those who walk about in the sun become tanned. It is customary to set before young minds an example of speaking and thinking in the right way, from which they should learn the power of words, the structure of speech and the figures of arrangement. For imitation assists the method of speaking as well as the other arts. For it is not likely that so much beauty and grace could have been applied to the art of painting by Apelles, if those who first painted paintings of one colour (*monochrōmata*) and then also oblique images (*katagrapha*) had not much earlier demonstrated the method of shaping the strokes. In the same way a fixed method and form (*kai idea*) of speaking and judging is to be taken in from the best writers, which you can follow, whatever matter you need to discuss.

Therefore, those who have in their hands the work of eloquent writers should reflect on what it is most seemly to admire, praise and imitate in any one of them. The first whom the young are encouraged to get to know are the poets and the historians. Even those who summon them only for pleasure, like women cithara-players at banquets, do not greatly harm the appraisal of those most excellent men. For they wanted[11] to be useful, and excellent things are a great delight to worthy minds [Cf. Horace, *Art of Poetry* 333]. So one needs to seek to acquire the form of speech from them, and one also needs to observe how they usually judged on general things.

I often laugh about the crowd of Greek grammarians who relate Homer's entire song to physiology, and whom it pleases wonderfully when, by a new metamorphosis, as charming jokers they turn Jupiter into ether and Juno into air – things that Homer would not ever have dreamt of, not even in a fever. How much more satisfactory would it have been to show the things that he wanted readers to admire in particular, that is, his propriety and clarity in arranging the management (*oikonomia*) of the song, when he musters various counsels and various happenings in admirable order, when he adapts suitable opportunities to new events; how great is his solicitude to preserve decorum; how great also is the abundance and variety of words and figures of speech in those places, where he wants to engage the reader? You see how the description of the mutiny in the second book of the *Iliad* is not in the least feeble or spiritless [*Iliad* II.101ff.]. Good God, how perspicaciously and how weightily does he treat the opportunity for the agitation, and the anger of the crowd, and the mutinous speeches of some, which, as they say, poured cold water on the crowd! And the character of Thersites, the evidence of his character, and his appearance! Also the very weighty speeches of the two who calmed the minds of the crowd; of those, that of Ulysses is the more violent, and that of Nestor the gentler speech. You would not easily find a more complete original of speaking correctly, all of whose elegance and virtues should be studied especially closely by those who would attempt to imitate it and express it in writing. For beware of thinking that Homer is simply called orator by M[arcus] Cicero fortuitously [*Brutus* 10.40], and that Fabius [Quintilian, *Education of the Orator* x.1.46f.] wrote without consideration that this poet excelled in all rhetorical virtues. What play has presented human affairs better than Homer's song, so that it is impossible that we be not touched again and again by admiration of the subject-matter when we contemplate his style? Furthermore, there

[11] Reading *voluerunt* for *voluere*.

are examples of manners to be seen: the affection between the princes and the people; various counsels of exploits. If Arcesilaus had not thought that the mind was educated by these things, he would never have called Homer his lover. It seems to me that, among all that human intellect has achieved, there is no more sagacious work than Homer's. Nor would I hesitate to declare that, as Horace reckoned [*Letters* I.2.3f.], Homer teaches better than Chrysippus or Crantor what is right and what is useful. I ask you, in what manner could the kings' rashness be indicated more agreeably than when he invents that Agamemnon, moved by a dream, leads the entire Greek army into danger [*Iliad* II.1ff.]? For it is well known that princes sometimes throw everything into confusion for trifling reasons. What is on Achilles's shield [*Iliad* XVIII.428ff.]? Did he not represent beautifully the elements of things and the brightest stars, and furthermore also their position and paths, from where later the philosophers, too, learnt the method of measuring the heavens [*Iliad* XVIII.485f.]? For he says that Arcton never sets, and that Orion lies in a region opposite to it; by that sentence he comprises a good part of astronomy. What shall be said of this, that in the same place he compares with each other the good of peace with the calamities of war, when he depicts two cities, one flourishing in peace, and the other devastated by war; how could he better have shown how hateful – as I believe – war is most destructive for all that is excellent? In the peaceful city, a wedding is taking place, judgements are carried out, law-cases are discussed, and the orators are admired. In the other, children are slaughtered, the laws are silent, the forum mute, and finally the destruction of all civil things is to be pitied. What, tell me, could have been more sagaciously thought out than that fiction?

It has not seemed right to touch upon too many passages in Homer here. I have only indicated those passages in order that I give confidence to the studious young that not only the mouth and the tongue, but also the heart, are shaped by the knowledge of the good writers. I believe that this was formerly the Greeks' purpose, for which they wanted Homer to be most intimately known to their men. For Solon and Peisistratus established by law that his song be arranged in order. For in that golden age the princes considered it their responsibility to warrant that some useful work be not lost. Nowadays there is nothing royal that is not also without refinement (*amouson*).[12] It was established soon afterwards that the Homeric poem be sung in public in the theatres by rhapsodes,

[12] Erasmus, *Adages*, II.vi.18.

68

or *Homeristai*,[13] so that the ears of the young might be constantly filled with sound by the divine song and that the rule of speaking and judging correctly might be always at hand.

Among the Romans, Virgil competed most successfully with Homer, and clearly, unless I am mistaken, equal praise is due to both, whether you look at the diction or at the weightiness of the sentences. What do the tragedians present, if not – with many examples – the habits and fates of tyrants? And what is comedy, if not a mirror of private life? Fabius [Quintilianus] indicated how poetry could serve students in everything [*Education of the Orator* x.1.27]. I see that it furnishes an abundance of figures to our speech, and that the mind is educated as well as delighted by their variety. Demosthenes believed that judgement was shaped and the faculty of speech increased by history, when he familiarised himself with Thucydides to such an extent that he copied his works eight times. Cicero loved Xenophon, too [*On Divination* I.xxiv.52]. And since universal history is some kind of state (*politeia*), it represents various forms of establishing a state. For, not to mention anything else here, what is more admirable than the comparison of states (*tōn politeiōn*) in Herodotus, where some Persian satraps approve of democracy (*demarchian*), others of oligarchy (*oligarchian*) and others of monarchy (*monarchian*) [Herodotus III.8off.]? In that passage you see that that most serious writer painted all diseases and vices of cities as if in a picture. In truth, no one is so ignorant as not to notice that the histories are written with the intention that examples of all human duties be seen as if put in an elevated place. If these do not lead to educating and rousing the minds of mortals, why would it have been that Scipio felt that he had risen to virtue by contemplating the images of famous men?

When orators administer states, and when, engaged in trials, they discourse so much about fair and good laws, it is well known that they teach many useful things. For what topic of moral philosophy is there that Demosthenes or Cicero did not touch upon? No one has painted (*ezōgraphese*) the best state (*politeian*) as they did in their plots, when they attack violent and rebellious citizens with their pen as if with a sword, and when they defend the states against the hostile power by their advice. What could be devised about peace that is more popular and true than what Cicero said in the oration in which he advises against the agrarian law? [*On Duties* II.22.78.] What is more civil than the praise of the laws which was transcribed by the lawyer Aristogeiton (*kat' Aristogeitonos*) into

---

13 Rhapsodes are bards who made a living by reciting the poems of Homer.

his commentaries from the oration of Demosthenes? But where would it lead to weave a more extensive praise (*enkōmion*) of writers here? Rather, make the attempt yourselves: what each one preserves from the classics, with what clarity and grace he explains everything, and how sagaciously he assembles everything that pertains to his purpose. For unless you apply yourself to the imitation of them, you have to despair utterly of attaining the ability to speak and judge in the right way.

It remains for us to judge also the other reason – why we declared that the power of judgement is sharpened by the study of eloquence. This is the case because care for speaking well in itself makes the mind more vigorous, so that it perceives more correctly what is most fitting or profitable in whatever matter. For, just as we see that the vigour of the body is strengthened by exercise, so it cannot happen but that the minds of those grow dull who are not roused by any intellectual toil. No one doubts that the perusal of good writers is very profitable. In truth, unless you add to this the habit of writing and speaking you will be able neither to understand with sufficient incisiveness their opinion, nor to conceive in your mind the fixed rule for judging and deliberating. Therefore, in order to obtain the ability to speak and judge, nothing is as indispensable as the exercise of the pen. For what else did Afranius[14] intend, when he claimed that Wisdom was the child of Habit, than that the mind is awakened and educated by the study of speaking and deliberating? Anaxagoras left a maxim worthy of the memory of posterity in the sentence that the hand is the cause of wisdom (*Tēn cheira sophias aitian einai*) [*Testimonies*, fr. 102.1], because he saw that all the arts are obtained by habit, and that the mind grows totally barren with leisure.

For just as we learn the mechanical arts by experience, and no one is so deranged as to be assured that he will be an Apelles as soon as he has a paint-brush in his hands, so the mind needs to be inured by much habit to direct itself more sharply towards everything. In the same way M[arcus] Cicero had such a high opinion of the pen that he wrote that it was the best and most excellent author and teacher [*On the Orator* I.xxxiii.150], and he used to translate some things from Greek into Latin for leisure, prepare others anew, and declaim some of them. By this industry he both preserved the power and vigour of his intellect, and enriched his fluency. For so he says about himself in the *Brutus* – lest I appear to invent something at random. We,

---

[14] Lucius Afranius (*c*.150–120 BC) received qualified praise in Quintilian, *The Education of an Orator*, x.i.100. Afranius' fragments were included in the *Fragmenta poetarum* (Paris, 1564).

too, did not desist from increasing with any kind of exercise, and mainly with the pen, that which was ours, however little it was. Demosthenes hid himself in a cave for some time in order to ponder an oration, and they say that he used to work by night most tenaciously, sacrificing his enjoyment, and the author Plutarch used up the night with constant lanterns, until he reached his fiftieth year. These most sagacious men taught by their habit what could not be said clearly and appropriately by vulgar skills. And how few among our young men have decided to write a little verse in this whole decade? Many believe that it is a short road to obtaining erudition, if they hear and read as much as possible. In the same way, others run hither and thither every day, and crawl through all the schools, and listen to teachers here and there, admiring those whom they do not understand, listen to the lessons, write refutations of the commentaries in inch-high letters, and illuminate them in vermilion. Those commentators are in repute who protract the time as much as possible by dictating, and no-one would acquire a teacher who deviated by as much as a finger's breadth from that usage. Then again, others never set foot outside their houses, bind themselves to books as to some drudgery, turn pages and turn them again, and consider themselves happy when they have passed through a large number of pages every day. Do they not both appear wretched, if with so much toil and such damage to their health they only learn how to act foolishly?

For if first the mind is not roused by the pen, it becomes dull by itself, and then, if these people overwhelm it with immoderate listening or reading, they blunt the sharpness of the intellect, if such there is. Lack of judgement also comes about if they hear and read just the worst things eagerly, and do not range through many things. If anyone asked them, as if appealing to a judge of one's own city, what they are aiming for with this method of learning, and what purpose or what goal they have set before their mind, he would realise that – like those deprived of sense – they do not know. For they do not heed the opinions or the language of the writers, since they lack the attention to imitate. They busy only their eyes and ears, but in the meantime the mind sleeps the sleep of Epimenides,[15] and, since they do not strive to imitate any fixed model, it comes about that their method of speaking and of judging becomes perverted.

Demosthenes congratulates himself when he is about to speak among the Athenians [*Olynthian Orations* I.I.], because they perceive by themselves what is excellent. And we commend the exercise of the pen to those

---

15 Epimenides was a Cretan poet said to have slept for fifty-seven years.

who have never experienced the matter, and do not even see as if through a lattice[16] the advantages which that exercise brings. All the more I fear that our oration will have little credibility, since we value the pen so highly. Truly, if anyone is not utterly unsuited to the Muses, let him ponder in his mind what was the method of teaching of the ancients, by which all disciplines were not only rendered illustrious, but also increased. Few authors, but only the best, were proposed in schools, whom the young were to imitate. There is a rule for agriculture that the land should not be larger than one can cultivate properly, for Virgil says: 'Large fields are to be praised, but small ones cultivated' [*Georgics* II.412f.]. In the same way the ancients, when they saw that many authors could not be taught thoroughly or imitated, and that the young minds were confounded rather than educated by the throng of writers, they admitted fewer authors, with whom the students should familiarise themselves as much as possible. Likewise, they declaimed assiduously, some wrote verse, and others free style; and since they competed in their zeal to speak well, their attention and care sharpened their judgement. While there was no more pleasing sight than this instruction, there was also nothing more useful that could be done in private or in public. For from these schools came forth most renowned men in past centuries – Greeks and Romans, and also many Christians. If our contemporaries strove to imitate them, good God, how much more would human affairs flourish, and how much more successfully would the Holy Scriptures be dealt with? Furthermore, since the ancients put so much effort into exercising the pen, since neither erudition nor a certain eloquence can be obtained without this study, and since what is written sagaciously by others cannot be understood unless we rouse our intellect by the use of the pen, please allow me to ask you that you sometimes put your powers to the test by the pen. I request something that is not very difficult, and is profitable, for there is no greater addition to your studies from any other thing.

You should master both verse and free speech; for I see that those who do not attain poetry speak somewhat more tediously, and merely crawl on the ground, and have neither weightiness of words nor any strength of figures of speech. Since it is moreover by far the easiest thing to detect rough and uneven compositions in verse, it happens that those who make poems judge correctly about the rhythms of free speech. And I do not know

---

[16] Seeing through a lattice is a saying derived from the practice of shopkeepers of erecting screens in front of articles which they did not want handled. The phrase means a distant inspection in outline rather than a close and detailed examination of things: see Erasmus, *Adages*, III.i.49.

whether it applies to all writing, when people begin to despise poetry. For it comes about that the ornaments and splendour of words are not held in regard, people write with less care, everything is read more negligently, and the zeal for inquiring into things flags.

Therefore, in Roman times too the contempt for poetry led to unbelievable ignorance of all things, as well as lack of eloquence. And thus in our times, if our men began to make verses, poetry would return to favour with the better writings. I do not see how one could preserve whatever elegance has blossomed anew in this century unless the young reflect upon poems by exercising their pen. M[arcus] Cicero, too, thought that fluency was nourished by writing verse, and it is well known that for that reason he often wrote poems, and was very fond of poetry. Posterity can see several of his epigrams, and today there survive some passages from famous poets, most clearly expounded by him in Latin verse. The orator Pliny [the Younger], by his published poems, testifies that his power of speech was assisted by that study. Therefore, those who wish to employ their time well in studying should imitate the example of the ancients and, as Quintilian says, by the trustworthy pen achieve fluency and sharpen their judgement [*Institutes of Oratory* x.7.7]. For those are greatly deceived who hope to advance themselves in writing without that practice. The sea is more likely to bear grapes than that he achieve erudition or the ability to speak, who – just like one who is rendered unconscious by mandrake[17] – never grows warm, in order to awaken his intellect by writing.

I have expounded the reasons which attract me to the study of the arts of speaking, without doubt because both a fixed method of speaking needs to be observed, and some power of judgement is conveyed to the student by the habit of these arts. If anyone thinks that this has nothing to do with him, he is without doubt very far removed from any feeling of humanity. Good men, on the other hand, will rush to these studies, with sails and oars, as they say [Cicero, *Tusculan Disputations* iii.11.25], as soon as they have contemplated the strength of the advantages which we gain from speech, and have realised both that a fixed method of speaking is needed and that by these arts the mind is rendered more cultivated.

In truth there are not too few, in particular in these times, who hinder the course of good men; these deny that the knowledge of the arts of speaking contributes to the study of theological writings, and this error – spread

---

[17] From antiquity, mandrake was known to induce sleep and was thus used to cure insomnia: see Erasmus, *Adages*, iv.v.64.

widely as if by some contagion – has seized many who spurn the humanities in order not to appear to be theologising improperly. I certainly wish that they practised theology seriously, and offered those things which are suitable for the Christian mind. I see that nowadays the name of theology is only a pretext for sloth, and that furthermore it resembles nothing less than what they declare.

For while it irks them to study eloquence and fret themselves by expounding most difficult writers and exercising the pen (for no knowledge of any writings is achieved without zealous study), occasionally when they return home well drunk they may read some trifling speech. Then, when they have plucked from it what suits their taste, they declaim it here and there at banquets – for there they are especially clever. And since the crowd applauds, in truth, presently they appear only to themselves[18] as perfect theologians, since vulgar men discuss the weightiest matters with a filthy mouth and without any religion. And when Paul prohibits hawking the word of God (*kapēleuein logon theou*) [2 *Corinthians* 2:17], no one trades in the word of God more impudently than those who – since they cannot prove themselves either by good morals or by good education – would purchase the favour of the crowds by an impious treatment of the Holy Scriptures. What is the penalty? You can see them spurn our writings, in which all good and worthy things, piety, public morals, and indeed Christ, are related. If we had a well-established state, we would not chastise them by our speech, but the magistrate would do so by force. For what torture would those not deserve, who, even if they do not transgress otherwise, divert the young from writings by their example?

Unless these writings are studied, we shall have a posterity that is in no way more sane than past centuries, when the ignorance of writings had overthrown all human and divine matters. Indeed, therefore we think of it in that way, that in time past, when God was sorely angered against the Church, writings were snatched away, and ignorance of holy things followed. For when God wanted to speak in our words, those who were inexperienced in the arts of speaking judged foolishly on the divine word. Furthermore, what blindness possessed men's minds in those times? How few knew Christ? Indeed, the literature that contained sacred matters had already fallen into disuse. The Parisians fashioned clauses which for a time the world worshipped as though they were divine laws; there was nothing pious, except for what they dreamt up. And, since they had no writings

[18] Omitting *non*.

from which to learn how to be wise, the charming men devised that foolish sophistry, and began to argue about fabricated compositions of words, so that they would even speechify about what the difference was between 'The Pope I saw' and 'I saw the Pope'. A Parisian clause still exists today: '"I runs" (*Ego currit*) is said badly in Latin; whoever disagrees is a heretic.' Does it not seem that the neglected writings have sufficiently avenged the affront? For who would believe that the authors of such nonsense had a brain?

In truth that misfortune is to be attributed to a large extent to the ignorance of writings; for the holy things were not accessible, as though cut off by thickets and foliage, whence the method for educating the mind properly would be available, and the skilful writers, too, who would teach about human matters, were neglected. How much more bearable would it have been for the Church to be struck by a plague or by a scarcity of produce than by such madness? I am wholly convinced that it is an example of certain divine wrath, if ever literature is snatched away from the world. For the pious, too, are often touched by other punishments, but public impiety accompanies ignorance of literature. In recent times, indeed, when the excellent Father had begun again to turn His attention to the wretched, and was going to give back to us the Gospel, because of His generosity He also restored writings, by which the study of the Gospel would be assisted. The gift of tongues bestowed upon the Apostles must not be seen as more extraordinary than the fact that from such foulness these writings were recovered from a darkness greater than that of the infernal regions[19] and brought back to light.

It is not unknown that the knowledge of writings is a help to some good men in renewing theology. First, therefore, it would be ingratitude to spurn the heavenly gift; furthermore, since the holy things were renewed by the help of the writings, we would be impious if we had no knowledge of the things without which theology could not continue. And to say in a few words what I judge that the knowledge of languages can contribute to the study of the Holy Scriptures, I am not so mistaken that I declare that sacred matters can be penetrated by the industry of human minds. There are things in sacred matters which no one would ever behold, were it not that God shows them to us, nor does Christ become known to us, unless

---

[19] The reference to infernal regions (*Tartareis*) is possibly a pun on the name of Petrus Tartaretus, a Scotist at the Sorbonne active around 1480 to 1490. His scholastic textbooks were originally taught at Wittenberg: see Kusukawa, *The Transformation of Natural Philosophy*, pp. 15–18.

the Holy Spirit teach us. For Christ Himself says that he is magnified (*doxasthenai*) by the Holy Spirit. Certainly, because of prophecy, the power of words must be known, in which divine mysteries are hidden as if in a shrine. For what is it, to pronounce words you do not understand in the way of magic? Is that not like telling a story to a deaf man?[20] But no one could judge correctly about speech unless he had thoroughly studied the method of speaking correctly. For what is easier than to be deceived by some word or figure of speech? Recently, when one of our masters explained what is related of Melchizedek in Genesis [14:18] – *rex Salem panem ac vinum obtulit* – he did not realise that Salem is the name of a place, and discoursed much about the strength and nature of the seasoning, for the similarity of the words tricked the good man.[21] For those who do not train their intellect by the arts of speaking read everything negligently.

These word-forms have tricked even the educated, for no amount of practice in speaking and writing makes one sufficiently prudent. The other day, some learned man asked me what Paul means when he says in the letter to Timothy: 'She shall be saved in the childbearing, if they continue in faith' [1 *Timothy* 2:15] – for the Greeks express the verb in the plural. Since I had no good answer, I consulted the commentaries. And behold Chrysostom, how nicely he talks nonsense, when he relates the verb 'they continue' (*meinōsi*) to the offspring. It is easy to judge that this does not fit Paul's purpose. The old man does not see that there is a grammatical compound, as he expresses the neutral with a verb in the plural. The daily usage of writers will supply similar examples.

Finally, for what other reason did the sophists devise a new kind of theology, having banished the Holy Scriptures, than because they did not understand their language and method of arguing? If anyone is not deterred from barbarity by their example, he must be punished not by speech, but by cudgelling to death.[22] For if the young continue to despise good writings, it will no doubt happen that – while the best things are neglected – again all holy and good things go to ruin. For whoever thinks that these bad theologians are barbarians in their words only, and not also in their minds, is mistaken. Again, if at some time Church dogma needs to be defended, what, I ask you, can one offer who cannot express what he

---

[20] Cf. Terence, *Heauton Timorumenos* II.1.10.
[21] The correct meaning of the passage is: 'Melchizedek king of Salem brought forth bread and wine'. The Latin for salt is *sal*, the accusative of which is *salem*, and thus could be confused with the town Salem, in which case Melchizedek the king would have 'brought forth salt, bread and wine'.
[22] Cudgelling to death was a military punishment for desertion: see Cicero, *Philippic*, III.vi.14.

thinks? Or should he bring to it some miscellaneous or Stoic oration, in which he disputes the placing of points between words? If the listener expected from him a clear treatment of the holy dogma, he would, just like the gaping raven,[23] go away vexed with troublesome distinctions which are continued for a long time to no purpose. In like manner, those who are involved in the study of piety should fulfil the duty, both towards Christ and towards the public necessity of the Church, to learn how to speak correctly. Paul also calls for this, when, in the letter to the Corinthians, he commends the study of languages [1 Corinthians 14:5 and 39]. His authority should be deservedly strong among you, in whose mouth he is so often.

I have indicated in a few words what the knowledge of speaking correctly contributes to the study of secular or sacred writings. Now it is your task to be reconciled with more elegant writings, and to embrace them avidly. I see many hasten prematurely towards the more serious disciplines, as they call them; some the hope for gain drags away towards studying law or medicine, others direct their course towards theology, before building up some strength in the study of the arts of speaking. If they undertook these things in their order, good God, how much more successfully would they deal with the matter? Now they delay themselves by their ill-advised shortcut.

There was among us a fool, who carried wood into the master's kitchen in a foolish way. He used to pull away logs from the bottom of the pile, which could not be moved without great exertion. Asked why he did this, he answered that he would complete the most difficult work first, and that those on top would be easier to move, and he did not see how much it would profit to take the individual ones in order. Those seem to me most similar to him, who disdain these arts and hasten forth towards lofty things. For both the toil of learning is increased and everything is treated in a more unsuitable way if they are not refined by the first principles. Immortal God, how unfortunate that it was granted to our ancestors to bring these things about. There is no form of the arts that in past centuries was not basely defiled by those who – since they did not apply themselves to elegant writings – rushed into the best and weightiest disciplines like swine into roses. Theology was utterly overwhelmed by stupid and ungodly questions. Those who taught philosophy did not even understand the name of the art sufficiently. It was not enough for fair and good laws that some rational men mingled with those who were ignorant of elegant writings, because the discipline itself is derived right from the humanities, and the

---

[23] Legacy-hunters are called gaping ravens in Horace, *Satires*, II.v.56.

writings of the ancient lawyers are full of antique and true erudition. Now I do not reproach only the filthiness of speech of the teachers of the arts, but the imprudence, a vice from which those whose intellect is not refined by the arts of speaking cannot free themselves.

Therefore I do not cease from encouraging you to the study of eloquence and of these arts, without which it is impossible not to treat other disciplines in an unsuitable way, because it is proper for you and public necessity requests it. For where barbarity mars the weightier disciplines, men's morals are usually also imperilled. For it is much truer that morals are achieved by knowledge than, as Plato wrote, from the songs of the musicians. I have spoken.

8 Preface to Cicero's *On Duties* (1534)[1]

CR XI, 257–61

It appears to me that the Greeks have laid down, with unique judgement, in the definition of art that it must have some usefulness for life. For all arts are tools for either preserving private life or for ruling the state. There is no need for expounding the individual arts here, or for showing the use for which they were invented and transmitted with great care from the elders to posterity. Rather it is necessary to exhort those who enter upon these studies of literature to consider at the beginning what the goal of these arts is, what benefit is to be derived from them, so that those who know may recognise the power and dignity of the arts more clearly, and choose more carefully the one that is most profitable to learn. They never achieve the perfect teaching whose minds do not look out for the certain goal of their studies, and they wander at random and without order or reason from one discipline to the other. 'An art is the compound of concepts practised for some useful purpose in life' (*Technē esti systēma enkatalēpseōn engegymnas-menōn pros ti telos euchreston tōn eni tōi biōi*) [Galen, *Medical Definitions* XIX.350]; it is proved from the definition of art itself that the goal or benefit in all arts has to be envisaged from the beginning. This was also the reason why Quintilian searched for the purpose of rhetoric with such great care in chapter eighteen of book two.[2]

Every teaching contains knowledge either of things or of words, and since words are the signs of things, the knowledge of words comes first; and although the arts of grammar, dialectic and rhetoric are necessary for obtaining that knowledge, nevertheless the arts are ineffectual without examples. Therefore we must read good authors from whom we may learn the diction of a language, and from the imitation of whom we may obtain for ourselves the kind of speech which can be applied to the explanation of serious subjects, and which can shed light on obscure matters, such as when people need to be taught about great things, as happens frequently. Now everyone knows that Cicero is the best master of speech. Indeed, this book has great qualities, it contains many commonplaces and there is a great variety of figures of speech in them, as well as accounts which contribute greatly to eloquence. Antony says in Cicero that the part of a speech

---

[1] In 1534, Melanchthon taught the *On Duties*. K. Hartfelder, *Philip Melanchthon als Praeceptor Germaniae* (Berlin, 1889), p. 560.

[2] Marcus Fabius Quintilianus (*c.* 35–*c.*95), author of the *Education of the Orator* (*Institutio Oratoria*), a highly influential text on rhetoric.

which is most difficult to achieve is a clear narrative. Therefore it is very profitable to have outstanding examples of narration, which we set out for ourselves to consider with attention, so that in speaking we may achieve something similar to them.

First, therefore, at the beginning of this work the reader will think that perusal will be useful for promoting his skill with words. And so, while contemplating the entire sequence and diction of speech, he may pick out, like flowers, remarkable figures of speech, pleasant narrations and particularly memorable sentences, for we must constantly strive to convey something from there to our own use, so that our speech becomes enriched by it. For these works are not to be glanced at in passing, as we behold admirably painted pictures set before us to look at, only for the sake of enjoyment, and obtain nothing from them for ourselves, but we should contemplate them like the most pleasant gardens, in which here and there we gather the most delightful fruit and flowers.

There should be a further consideration of the knowledge of things, of which we can introduce scientific knowledge, knowledge of which we can adduce here. It is profitable to hold and grasp in one's mind some order of the arts, and to see their purposes and uses. Some discuss the nature of things, others involve religion, others the method of ruling the state and of judging disputes in the law-court, others involve the precepts for civic morals, which are necessary in all walks of life. Therefore, when we read anything, we need to ponder to which order of arts it belongs: whether it will be useful for the administration of the state or for private life; and this consideration not only stimulates studying, but it also contributes very much to understanding and grasping the arts better. For it is easier to grasp those whose territories, so to speak, lie wide open, and of which we discern the boundaries.

This book of Cicero concerns moral philosophy, for it contains the definitions of virtues, and, besides the definitions, many precepts for civic morals, and most of this in oratorical mode, in the style of a popular oration, so that men endowed with common sense can understand them and imitate them in the habit of everyday life; for dry disputations, such as are found in Aristotle, contain some teaching that is not ignoble, but somewhat obscure and almost deliberately distant from the intellect and judgement of the inexperienced. Cicero's definitions can more easily be understood and adapted to everyday use in life. Moreover it is generally acknowledged that everyone needs some teaching on morals and a description of virtues, so that we understand in our manners and in judging about human business what is proper and what is not, what is done rightly and what is ill done. Accordingly, it is necessary to have forms and images of virtues, which we follow in all decisions and in our judgements on all matters. This teaching is strictly speaking to be called humanity, and it shows the way to live properly and as a citizen; those who do not know it are not very different from beasts.

Although it may on other occasions be more appropriate to show what the distinction is between that teaching and that of the Gospel, I have nevertheless thought that listeners need to be warned to banish the error which already occupied their minds, namely that the writings of the pagans are unworthy of being read by Christian people, and that Christians should give a wide berth to philosophy. Let me therefore expound my opinion on this matter. Philosophy does not provide confirmation of the will of God, nor does it instruct on the fear of God and the trust in Him; that pertains properly to the Gospel. However, apart from these things, precepts for civic life are necessary, which teach how men may live peacefully with each other. These are propounded in philosophy, and their causes are put in relation and perceived by excellent men. And one must not think that Christ came into this world to teach these precepts; He expounded something else, about the will of God and trust in God, which human reason could not understand. However, God also favours civic duties and requires them from all ages, and by that discipline He wants men to be restrained, in no other way than by the laws and institutions of the magistrates, which have great affinity with those precepts, for all laws and all justice has sprung from them as if from springs. For this reason this teaching is very useful, because, by demonstrating the causes of the laws and of public justice, it helps much with the understanding of all discussions of civic matters. Since Christians should cherish and support this civil society, this teaching of civic morals and duties has to be known by them. It is not piety to live like the Cyclopes, without justice, without laws, without teaching, or without any of the other things helpful for life that are contained in literature. Therefore those who disparage philosophy not only wage war against human nature, but they also severely injure the glory of the Gospel, which commands that men be restrained by civic discipline; and nature decorates with the highest prizes the honourable institutions that contain the civil society of men. Therefore philosophers and other writers teaching honourable precepts for life are not to be spurned, but they are to be read diligently, so that they may sharpen one's judgement on public affairs and on morals. Wise men occupied with the state can admonish much that they know by habit, which makes us more prudent in performing great things.

I have expounded what these books contribute to the richness of words as well as to the knowledge of things, for they nourish the power of speech and confirm one's judgement on morals, and both of these are highly necessary in life. But there is another use to these books, pertaining to eloquence; it is pre-eminent, or it seems so to me. All learned men enjoin us to furnish ourselves with commonplaces, from which we may take a speech on honourable things whenever there is the need. For all business in life is judged from commonplaces on virtues and vices, and because of that one has to refer to them [i.e. commonplaces] in a speech, whatever the topic. First of all it is useful to have passages that one knows perfectly, because the subject itself, when perfectly grasped, produces the discourse. It is even more useful, though, to have at the ready topics discussed and embellished by Cicero, so that we can borrow words or embellishments from there, or at least imitate them. For what does Cicero do if not collect commonplaces, that is, definitions of the virtues? All civic business of which one has to speak has to look to them. If you write a letter in which you thank a friend who has done you a favour, how many embellishments will Cicero supply in the passage that contains the precepts on gratitude! There are many similes there, and many arguments which we can accommodate to our use. If, in a decision, there is conflict between utility and honour, as it often happens, how much can be gained from the third book! What can one say on such a controversy that is more weighty than the story of Cyrsilus, whom the Athenians stoned for giving useful but dishonourable advice, and the Athenian women stoned his wife.[3] So strong did the Athenians want the power of honour to be that they thought to censure him who had judged utility to be preferable to honour with a new punishment. When such embellishments are ably transferred into our speech, they not only produce gracefulness, but also authority. I spoke above of words and sentences to be excerpted, but it will be even more useful to know entire passages in sequence, and to keep hold of their figures of speech, which we can either imitate or take over when there is need for them. Since all matters in life are related to these passages, it is necessary

---

[3] Cyrsilus was stoned to death by his fellow Athenians for advising them to receive the army of Xerxes and submit to the power of Persia. Demosthenes, *On the Crown*, XVIII.203, mentions that his wife was also stoned. Cf. Cicero, *On Duties*, III.xi.48.

to have them stocked and ready in great number; he who lacks these treasures will not be able to judge any matter correctly or expound it clearly. I have spoken.

9 Dedicatory letter to the *Questions on Dialectics*

CR VI, 653-58

Greetings from Philip Melanchthon to Johannes Camerarius, son of the most illustrious D. Joachim Camerarius[1]

'Slight is the field of toil, but not slight the glory',[2] to use Virgil's words [*Georgics*, IV.6], in having studied dialectic properly, and in being so accustomed to the boundaries of the art that you can follow the threads that are as though appointed by the art, in the explanation of things that are worth knowing, in order that the explanation be true, appropriate, simple, clear, certain and powerful; furthermore, in order that you be able to judge and refute those straying from the boundaries, and recall them, so to speak, to the path and within the limits.

If some clever men, without erudition and this basic knowledge, see by a natural light the sources of arguments and connections of parts of discourse in many debates, and can do many things similar to those done by the masters, the art is not to be neglected for that reason. For such a swift intelligence is not common to all, and there are far more mediocre intellects which, unless trained by the art, would remain in perpetual darkness. Furthermore, even though keenness of intellect, directness and skill are great goods, there are nevertheless two of the highest effects of the art which not even clever men can achieve without knowledge or erudition. The first is to see the causes of certitude, that is, why the beliefs we embrace are fixed, and why what we construct needs to be consistent. The other is to refute deceits by showing the faulty places and the causes of the deceits, and to distinguish the parts of arguments by the naming of the arts, as if by unfailing marks, so that the adversary feels himself held in check by these bonds – like the captive Proteus – and is finally led to the precepts of certainty, called criteria (*kritēria*), where he recognises that he is overcome and condemned by the divine voice. For these precepts – experience, principles and understanding of consequences – are indeed the divine voice; and to this we add the doctrine passed on to the Church by divine providence, which we will discuss in due course.

---

[1] Johannes Camerarius was the son of Melanchthon's close friend, Joachim Camerarius. Melanchthon often dedicated books and textbooks to the family of his friends (e.g. dedication to Anna Camerarius in the German translation of the *Loci Communes*, CR, VIII, cols. 33f.). See also the dedications to orations 11, 17 and 19.

[2] Translated by H. Rushton Fairclough, *Eclogues, Georgics, Aeneid I-VI* (Cambridge, MA, and London, 1967), p. 197.

In the same way, the ingenious painter who is experienced by practice may often paint the shadows correctly but nevertheless, without a knowledge of optics, he does not see the causes, nor can he point out his errors to one who is going astray. Therefore, even though there is great power in natural disposition, there are nevertheless some tasks peculiar to masters which the uneducated cannot perform. Often it also happens to the clever that – either through their confidence or by flattering their own intellect – they ramble too long in discussions, play their tricks and defend and strengthen false ideas, as did the Academics, Arcesilaus, Pyrrho[3] and others who indulged themselves too much; nor are examples lacking in other ages. Therefore there is no doubt that the art is necessary which instructs and assists mediocre intellects, rules and forces within limits those that are outstanding and accustoms one to seeking and loving certain truth. But why do I discuss whether there is need for the art? If I had some authority, it would be much more appropriate for me to rebuke those who scorn knowledge than to refute them by debating. For contempt of the arts indicates not excellence of intellect, but barbarous savagery. For certainly, just as unrestrained natures hate the bonds of law in morals, many flee the precepts of the arts as though they were a prison. And just as in life they want licence to be granted to all their desires, so also in religion, philosophy and the forum they love boundless liberty, which is ruinous both to themselves and to the Church of God in defending and rejecting ideas. Even though such wanton natures are not moved by our admonition, those whose intellects are more moderate must not be abandoned.[4] I urge and entreat them, for the sake of the glory of God and the welfare of the Church, not to neglect dialectic, nor to applaud the foolish speeches of those who disparage it and loudly claim that it is useless for the Church.

But it is plausible that before our times dialectic came to be scorned and hated, because what was taught was not the art itself but some vague shadow of the art, and indeed inextricable labyrinths were displayed which not even the teachers understood. So far were they removed from being able to assist those engaged in other arts that they were corrupting them,

---

[3] Arcesilaus (*c.* 315–240 BC) was the founder of the Middle Academy and introduced the teachings of Pyrrho of Elis (365–275 BC), who claimed that it was impossible to achieve certainty in knowledge and that one should therefore suspend judgement and strive to achieve mental quietude. Before the publication of Sextus Empiricus' *Outlines of Pyrrhonism* in 1562, the major source of classical scepticism was Cicero's works: see Charles B. Schmitt, *Cicero Scepticus: A Study of the Influence of the 'Academica' in the Renaissance* (The Hague, 1972).

[4] Supplying the passage in italics from the 1555 (Wittenberg, J. Crato) edition, Aiii^v: *tamen alii quorum ingenia . . . non deserendi* est.

rather. I, on the other hand, profess the true uncorrupted and original dialectic, which we have received from Aristotle as well as from some of his reliable commentators, Alexander of Aphrodisias and Boethius.[5] I declare that it is very useful, not only in the forum and in trials, but also in the Church.

And, to speak of the Church now, the facts show that in the books passed on by God through divine providence the most far-reaching knowledge is displayed regarding law, sin, the Gospel and other similar topics. If anyone said regarding these matters that there is nothing to be defined or distinguished, that there is no need to demonstrate the distinction between human judgements and the decisions brought forth from the hidden bosom of the eternal Father which are beyond and outside the grasp of the human mind, nor that a way and an order need be employed in explanation, it would be true, as one says, that he has strayed beyond the stars.[6] Certainly there is a need for dialectic, not only so that the doctrine receive some light, but also so that it be the chain of concord. For in order that the voice of those who teach be one and unanimous, it is necessary to keep the substance of knowledge enclosed within the confines of the arts, held together by specific language and order. For when these restraints of the arts are broken and knowledge is spread in an unsuitable language, without order, definitions or distinctions, disagreement necessarily follows, since each receives and repeats the rules differently. It is therefore necessary to maintain dialectic in the Church, but let it be erudite, respectful, serious and loving of truth, and let it not be garrulous, quarrelsome or deceitful. And let us not be deterred from the study of dialectic for the reason that some have written that with the weapons of dialectic the truth has been overthrown by the authors of warped tenets – for this is not a rebuke of the art, but of evil minds and distorted instruction. As in other studies, the student's disposition should be upright and loving of truth, and he should study the art cautiously, and employ it modestly and seriously for the examination and elucidation of the truth. Sophistry should not be practised, and fallacious arguments and tricks should not be enjoyed, in the way in which many distorted natures – like Autolycus, Sisyphus, Eurybatus[7] and other impostors

---

[5] Alexander of Aphrodisias' (second century AD) commentary on the *Topics* was first published in Greek in 1513, and that on the *Prior Analytics* and *Sophistical Refutations* in 1520; and Boethius' (455–525) commentary on the *Topics* was first published separately in 1528.

[6] 'Toto coelo errare', is to be entirely astray (by the sky): see Erasmus, *Adages*, 1.i.49.

[7] In Greek myth, Autolycus, son of Hermes, was a master of trickery and thieving; Sisyphus in Greek myth had a reputation as the most cunning of men; Eurybatus came to be known as Agamemnon's herald who kidnapped Achilles' favourite mistress, Briseis: Ovid, *Heroides*, III.9f. Cf. Homer, *Iliad*, I.v.32.

– delight in games of fallacious arguments and subterfuge. It is sufficiently clear that there have been, and are, many dealers in tenets, if I may say so, similar to these, who by no means are or were dialecticians, but rather sophists or impostors, and the corrupters not only of other teachings, but also of dialectic.

Just as the knowledge of numbers is both a great gift from God and very necessary for the life of men, so we know that the true way of teaching and reasoning is God's gift and is necessary in expounding the heavenly doctrine and in the examination of the truth in other things. Thus, when Paul commands that the heavenly word be divided correctly in teaching – or *orthotomein*,[8] as he says – he demands that care definitely be employed in distinguishing the various parts of doctrine, such as the law, the Gospel, philosophy, civic government and many other things. And it appears that the word *orthotomein* is taken from the ceremony of sacrifices. For it was not allowed to tear the meat of the victims in a random way, but certain parts were to be burnt for God, such as the fat, the loins and the tail; some belonged to the priests, such as the breast and the shoulders. It was therefore an art to divide the limbs, because God willed these very practices to be admonitions of greater things. He bestowed the breasts and the shoulders upon the priests, not only because these parts, having more meat on them and being more muscular, supply more food, but also because the breast signifies wisdom and the shoulders signify carriers of burdens. It is necessary for the priests to excel in erudition and wisdom, and particularly to sustain the great burden of governing. The tail was burnt for God to signify that all actions are to be related to that end, that is, to worshipping God. But I omit an overly long explanation of that ceremony. For I only brought these things to mind in order to remind the young of the Pauline word *orthotomein*, which is taken from the language of sacrifices. Just as the victims were to be cut up in a fixed way, so the heavenly notions are to be divided by a fixed method. Since the way of this matter is taught properly in dialectic only, this art could be considered the knife for this division. Everywhere there are ready examples which show how widely the use of the art lies open and how necessary it is.

But now I shall briefly admonish readers about one matter, namely the invocation of God. In order that it be done properly, not only the learned but also others, those unacquainted with letters, need to be assisted by dialectic. For the more learned need to instruct the people regarding what

---

[8] In 1545, Melanchthon composed an oration on the term *orthotomein*: see CR XI, cols. 684–9.

things one needs to think in prayer, what God is, what God we address and how He is to be distinguished from imaginary deities. Also, in every serious invocation, a difficult struggle is kindled, since we contend whether and why in fact we are accepted, and our lamentation and prayers are granted. Our transgressions reproach us, and anxious and perplexed minds flee God. In this confusion and flight they must not be abandoned. For that reason the reproach must be opposed with the voice of the Gospel which confirms that, although defiled, we are nevertheless in fact accepted on account of the Son of God, without doing anything in return. This is the learned argument on which the learned and uneducated likewise need to reflect. For that to happen, the people, too, are to be instructed, so that they do not stray from God in this reasoning. I have often spoken and written about the benefits of dialectic elsewhere, and I wanted to call them to mind here so that there would be a testimony of my judgement – that I encourage worthy minds, so that they may love and study dialectic as well as the other true parts of philosophy; but they should also add the doctrine of God that is passed on in the prophetic and apostolic writings. I shall mention also the books on dialectic of which I particularly approve. Even though many disparage Aristotle's books, and say that they are like the scattered planks of a wrecked ship, I declare that – if I have any judgement – they teach dialectic properly and can be understood by those who are refined by liberal teaching. It appears that the books are distorted in places by the ignorance of those copying them, since no codex is without blunder, but nevertheless the substance of the work is unimpaired. Although I strongly urge those who are talented to study Aristotle himself, and in Greek, it is nevertheless beneficial to bring the first principles to the reading, so that he can be understood more easily. I judge that these can be learnt properly either from the book by Johannes Caesarius or from the *Erotemata* of Jodocus Willichius.[9] I, too, have included in this publication almost the entire art, and I believe that this method of teaching the art would be useful for the studies of the young. And I have introduced some technical (*technologika*) matters which show the sources of the tenets; but nevertheless I yield the judgement on the book itself and on the entire intention of this little discourse to the learned who will judge frankly.

---

[9] Johannes Caesarius' (*c.* 1468–1550) *Dialectica* was first printed in 1520, with more than thirty reprints; Jodocus Willichius' (1501–52) *Erotemata dialectices* was first printed in 1540. See Wilhelm Risse, *Bibliographia logica. Verzeichnis der Druckschriften zur Logik mit Angabe ihrer Fundorte*, I. *1472–1800* (Hildesheim, 1965).

But to you, dearest son, I dedicate this work so that you may have this ever so slight monument to the friendship that I have with that excellent and most learned man, your father, and also an expression of my benevolence towards you. You will learn dialectic either from this book or from others, according to the judgement of your father, which is most weighty. Know me to be one who encourages you and your most delightful brothers, as well as other talented youths, to the study not only of this art, but also of the other parts of philosophy. I have also dedicated it to you all the more willingly, not only to enjoin you and your brothers – since you have in your family the most beautiful examples of all the virtues, namely the wisdom, justice, seriousness and moderation in every duty of your grandfather, uncle and father, and indeed also your father's erudition – to contemplate with attention these ornaments of your family, and to rouse yourself to virtue by contemplating them. But I have done so also in order to enjoin other worthy minds to imitate the studies and excellent morals of your father. I pray to the eternal God, Father of our Lord Jesus Christ, Maker of humankind and of His Church, and fount of true wisdom and knowledge, that He may always gather for Himself the eternal Church among us, and encourage the beneficial study of doctrine, so that the Church can in no way lack erudition. May He also keep your most worthy parents unharmed, and also you and your most delightful brothers and sisters. Wittenberg, first of September, 1547.

10 Preface to arithmetic (1536)

CR XI, 284-92

Preface to arithmetic read by Georg Joachim Rheticus[1]

I believe that in the beginning I need to expound to you the reason why I begin to teach publicly, so that no one thinks that I have come forth in this hall inconsiderately by my own decision. For I am rather shy by nature, and I cherish most those arts that love hiding-places and do not earn applause among the crowds; furthermore, I see not only what abundance of knowledge [i.e. of things to be known] there is, but also how much dexterity and fertility of intellect is needed, especially for treating of these subtle arts, and I am indeed conscious of my stupidity. Therefore I did not strive to be here, and for a long time I objected to our teachers who encouraged me to teach in public the precepts of the arts with which I have busied myself in an unremarkable way, in particular at this time, when the other lectures in mathematics have ceased by the death of that most learned man, Johannes Volmar.[2] However, they entreated me to take into account, in this matter, not only my friendship for them but also the benefit for the young, as it is greatly profitable that these elements be assiduously inculcated and practised in the schools. Thus the teachers' authority prevailed, as well as their excellent disposition towards education. I saw that they did not confer this duty upon me out of private favour but in order to be mindful of the young, and to attract them, as far as possible, to the arts that are the true beginning of philosophy.

Therefore, while I did not want my effort to be lacking for the use of the state and of the young, they nevertheless urged me to promise that I would take the risk. I entreat you, therefore, to consider that because of this duty I have come forth in public not out of arrogance, but out of great trust. Moreover, I shall repent my willingness less if I recognise that your attendance and diligence respond to the excellent disposition of the teachers, who imposed this rôle on me for the sake of your benefit. It will therefore

---

[1] Georg Joachim Rheticus (1514–74) was promoted to MA at the University of Wittenberg on 27 April 1536. He is best known for having persuaded Nicholas Copernicus to publish the *De revolutionibus*: see K. H. Burmeister, *Georg Joachim Rhetikus, 1514–1574, Eine Bio-Bibliographie*, 3 vols. (Wiesbaden, 1967–8).

[2] Johannes Volmar (*d.* 1536) was a lecturer in mathematics at the University of Wittenberg from 1518 to 1536. His notes on astrology and astronomy survive at the University Library of Jena: see J. C. Mylius, *Memorabilia bibliothecae academicae Jenesis* (Jena, 1746), pp. 348, 405f.

be a sign of your sagacity and humanity to take my effort in good part. For I hope to satisfy you as far as teaching the precepts themselves is concerned, but I ask your forgiveness if you find something lacking in my speech or my delivery. I admit that I am hampered by embarrassment and fear, and that by nature I am not suited to theatrical performance. However, it is a characteristic of an effeminate and peevish mind to shrink from these arts because of these inconveniences, and thrust away the study of them, even if a teacher is expert in his own discipline. Indeed, even if I do not assume anything for myself, I shall nevertheless teach these precepts with faith and diligence in the hope that they will be grasped and understood.

I have expounded the reason why I have come forth in public, which, I hope, will free me from the suspicion of arrogance with the good and the learned. Now I shall speak of my opinion, or rather of that of our teachers. They enjoined me to teach the elements of arithmetic and geometry and, since the nature of these arts demands it, I shall begin from arithmetic. Would that I were so effective, both in authority and in eloquence, as to rouse and inflame the young to the study of these arts. For what could be more desirable for the teacher than to have listeners who are kindled and aflame with the desire to learn? But since our teachers daily encourage the students to learn these arts, and their benefit is evident, I hope that most of those who are endowed with superior minds are sufficiently inspired to cherish these studies.

The Greeks tell the story of Pallas [Athena] who, when Mercury had given her the flute he had recently invented, walked to a stream and began to play it. Although she was charmed by the sound, she nevertheless threw away the flute immediately when she saw in her reflection in the water that her face was ridiculously deformed by the blown-up cheeks. The Satyrs who had approached, attracted by the novelty of the sound, immediately took up what she had thrown away, and thus the flute, spurned by Pallas, began to be the favourite of the Satyrs. In the same way let ignoble minds rejoice in other rustic arts, or rather divulge some fragments of the arts, either for the sake of gain or in order to win over public opinion. But it is characteristic of the honourable mind not to love anything more ardently than truth, and, inspired by this desire, to seek a genuine science of universal nature, of religions, of the movements and effects of the heavens, of the causes of change, not only of animated bodies but also of cities and realms, of the origins of noble duties and of other such things. If we are held by admiration and love for this perfect science, then we also need to value those elements of numbers and measures that provide access to the other parts of philosophy, although even on their own they are of great nobility and benefit.

For you see how great is the use of arithmetic in economy, and Aristotle writes in the *Republic*[3] that there are some Thracians who cannot count beyond four. I ask you whether you think that the management – I am not even saying of a large market or of mines of metals, but of some medium-sized household – can be entrusted to such men? Would we think that such men can unravel and settle an even slightly intricate computation? By no means. But when it comes to long and obscure computations, all those who are deprived of the assistance of this art are similar to those Thracians. This art is necessary not only on the market and for metals for coining money, but in many other public and private computations. Those who busy themselves for the state must know the calculation of finances. In the courts of justice there often occur problems which require learned calculations. Therefore it is not sufficient to know the numbers through the kindness of nature, but the art has to be added without which certainly no difficult calculations can be settled. Therefore in Plato [*Laws* 819ff.] Socrates makes it one of the laws that the citizens be compelled to learn arithmetic. But what is the use of speaking at length about a known fact? For there is no one who does not see that in every life the greatest use is made of arithmetic – unless he is more stupid than those Thracians who cannot count beyond four. And these everyday benefits should attract equally all the young to the study and the practice of this art, for many eventualities can arise in which arithmetic can be of great use to the individual. Therefore the Romans, too, took great care so that their children grasp arithmetic as well, together with the first steps in reading and writing. You will remember that verse of Horace [*Art of Poetry*, 325–8]: 'Roman boys learn, in long computations, to divide the *as*[4] into a hundred parts. "Let the son of Albinius answer: If one ounce is taken from five-twelfths, what remains?"' The benefit of geometry, too, is manifold, not only in building and in measuring vessels, but also to a statesman for cosmography, for understanding the distance between places. But I forsake these everyday benefits.

Those who busy themselves with studies and strive for complete knowledge should see clearly that there is no access to the science of celestial things except through arithmetic and geometry. Arithmetic is so important

---

[3] In fact, Aristotle's *Problems*, 911a2.   [4] An *as* is a copper coin of small value, a penny.

in the science of celestial things that almost everything in that science is accessible to even a mediocre arithmetician; he can certainly attain to a large part of that science without any trouble. See by what little toil you can obtain a great reward for your work! Nothing is easier than to teach these notions, as they call them, of the art of counting. If one knows them even imperfectly, one can immediately grasp almost all of astronomy without any difficulty.

In the *Phaedrus* [246c] Plato invents two kinds of soul, one of which he says is winged, the other has lost its wings. Then he says that those that have wings fly up to heaven and delight in meeting and conversing with God, and in the most beautiful sight of the heavenly ways, and he says that they contemplate the causes of all changes in inferior nature, in the air, in animated bodies, in the studies and manners of men and in the various vicissitudes of realms and cities. And, flying throughout all of heaven, these souls are charmed by the beauty of divine things and by the sweetness of the knowledge and of the virtue of that admirable order, and they wish to enjoy this one pleasure forever. They do not burden their souls with obscene pleasure, which perturbs the harmony of virtue in the souls and casts darkness in their way, so that they cannot behold the heavenly things.

The souls whose wings have fallen off wander about on the ground and desire impure pleasures from earthly things, and they do not behold that most beautiful light of heavenly things. Even if Plato thinks of the wings as heroic impulses of the minds, it is nevertheless not these impulses alone that lift up the minds, but the arts are also needed by which these impulses are raised up. Consequently, the wings of the human mind are arithmetic and geometry. If someone endowed with an intellect that is not mean attached these to himself, he would easily enter heaven and would wander freely in the heavenly company, and enjoy that light and wisdom.

Therefore those who are endowed with a mind that is not unnatural, and who desire to behold the things that are best and most admirable and worthy of knowledge, should attach those wings, that is, arithmetic and geometry, to themselves. Carried up to heaven by their help, you will be able to traverse with your eyes the entire nature of things, discern the intervals and boundaries of the greatest bodies, see the fateful meetings of the stars, and then understand the causes of the greatest things that happen in the life of man. I believe that noble minds can be attracted by such great benefit, and roused to learn and love those arts. For I know that you are certainly convinced that the science of celestial things has great dignity and usefulness, and that, as is proper, your ears and your souls shrink from the absurdities of Epicurus, who derides astronomy and thinks idly that the sun is vapour, which in the morning is kindled by its movement, and then either burns up or is extinguished in water. In the same way he also says that the stars are little clouds set alight by their fall. It is unworthy of a man to declare these monstrosities as the truth, much more so for a philosopher. There has not been a people so barbarous as not to feel that the stars are true and enduring works of God, and that they are carried by firm laws, because of some great purpose. Therefore it is an insult against God to invent this confusion of things, that the sun is a vapour set alight by its fall and carried by its fall, as Lucretius says: 'whither their food calls each and invites them as they go, grazing their fiery bodies all over the sky'.[5] The authority of the most learned men who refuted these absurdities with very serious arguments must have greater value for us, as well as the divine oracles in the Holy Scriptures, from which it is impiety to dissent. These prove clearly that the sun, the moon and the other stars are true and enduring works of God, and the Holy Scriptures add for what purpose the heavenly lights are made: Let them be signs and set apart the seasons and the years [Genesis 1:14]. Although this description is rather short, it nevertheless contains great things and approves the study of astronomy. For, leaving out the rest, if the sun is made in such a way that it brings about and rules the year, the observation of the course of the sun is necessary; for without the observation of its movement there is no distinction between the seasons and the years. It is therefore evident that it is considered good by God and that the observation of the movements of the heaven is enjoined. For, apart from bringing great benefit to universal life, this most beautiful order of movements also reminds us that nature does not exist by chance, but is created and governed by an eternal mind. Hence it strongly confirms in the mind worthy beliefs about God and providence. Consequently, among the philosophers only the Epicureans were ungodly (*atheoi*), because they did not want to behold these illustrious proofs of God, that is, the most firm laws of movements and this wonderful harmony. It is therefore proper for good minds to love this most worthy science, and, as far as possible, to put some effort into the examination of these great things. And those who are even moderately trained in arithmetic will easily understand many things.

---

[5] Lucretius, *On the Nature of Things*, v. 524f., though Melanchthon's text is slightly different from the modern text.

I shall therefore return to arithmetic, for that is what I specifically intended to talk about. After having recalled to mind all its benefits, which are, however, hardly indistinct, I have reckoned that something needs to be added briefly on its easiness. I know that the young are deterred from these arts by their reputation for difficulty. But as far as the beginnings of arithmetic are concerned, which are taught in schools and are employed for everyday use, they err greatly if they think that they are very difficult. The art originates from the very nature of the human mind and has very sure demonstrations. Therefore the beginnings can be neither unintelligible nor difficult; on the contrary, the first precepts are so clear that even boys can acquire them, because the whole thing originates from nature. Then the precepts of multiplications and divisions require a little more diligence, but the causes can be grasped quickly by the industrious. This art, like all the others, requires practice and habit. For it is very true what Anaxagoras says, that the hand is the cause of wisdom [*Testimonies*, fr. 102.1], meaning that without practice and experience the arts cannot be correctly understood. Therefore, wherever there is some difficulty, remember that there is no art that does not have some difficulty. And you are indeed mistaken if you believe that the practice of composition is easier than these beginnings of arithmetic; the schools are not made and established for the purpose of granting leisure to the idle for enjoying foolish pleasures, but they require studies, attention and sharp contest of minds. Nor do I deny that many things are sought out and observed by arithmeticians which elude the grasp of the inexperienced, for all the arts grow by practice. But I am talking about the beginnings that are usually taught to you and are employed for use. Therefore let the young thrust away the idea of difficulty, and approach the learning of this art with an open mind and some hope; if they do so, the sweetness of the things will engage them, and they will feel the difficulty diminish by the very connection of the things. I have expounded what benefits are to be sought from arithmetic, and I have also spoken about its efficacy. What remains are other benefits, but more obscure ones, of which I shall not say much. It is most true that, once one knows arithmetic, the other arts can be understood more easily. For arithmetic is among the first arts, which teaches us to distinguish and divide between one and many; it shows the order of things, and teaches us that confused things need to be unravelled and distinguished. These are the beginnings of reasoning in men. Therefore the understanding of numbers is foremost, and I believe that Pythagoras noticed that when he defined the mind as a number, for this means that the mind is capable of reasoning, it discerns things and perceives order. These are the main characteristics of the mind and its foremost functions. Therefore he rightly defined the mind as a number, that is, as something that counts. This is the reason why the ancient Greeks, too, taught arithmetic second after grammar, then in the third place they ranked dialectics and in the fourth geometry. For they saw that dialectics takes its beginning from arithmetic, and the practice of multiplication and division prepares the intellect for syllogisms in an excellent way. In the same way the power of demonstration can be better understood once one knows arithmetic, because it has extraordinarily distinct demonstrations.

Besides, there are many passages in the [ancient] authors which cannot be understood without this art. The Pythagoreans used arithmetical terms figuratively and transferred them to physics and to moral philosophy. For this is how Pythagoras defined God: God is that by which the greatest number exceeds the next number. Thus he meant to say that God is one, and indeed the highest nature, for he understands the unit of 10 as the highest number, and the one next to it is the unit of 9. The projection beyond 9 is unity; thus they wrapped all of philosophy in numbers.[6]

Even if it is better to teach the arts in the proper sense and not to wrap them all in figures and riddles, nevertheless other philosophers, too, who clearly intended to teach philosophy, employ examples from arithmetic which it is unseemly not to understand. When Plato is saying that the state changes because of heavenly causes which effect certain vicissitudes of affairs in cities and realms, he says: just as nature resides in tones, when the four thirds are joined to five, that is when a quarter (*dia tessarōn*) is added to a fifth (*dia pente*), that means when the harmony of all (*dia pasōn*) is complete. In just that way, when the period of realms has passed away, states fall and change. He adds the reason that, just as when plane squares are added up to form solids until nature can go no further, many dissimilar numbers are brought forth, so ignoble citizens who, descended from more outstanding ones, have nevertheless become masters of the state, little by little overturn the state until the overthrow. Not even these designations can be understood without arithmetic.

But these benefits are less weighty, and the ones that I mentioned above are great, namely that this art is needed in many other affairs in life and,

---

[6] According to Aristotle (*Metaphysics* I.v.3), the Pythagoreans considered the number 10 to be perfect, comprising the whole nature of numbers and tried to explain the universe with their number mysticism. For further details, see G. E. R. Lloyd, *Early Greek Science: Thales to Aristotle* (London, 1970), pp. 24–35.

without it, there is no access to that most excellent part of philosophy dealing with heavenly matters. That is the great and weighty reason which must kindle superior natures to this art, because those who seek complete knowledge worthy of great men must strive with all the powers of the intellect[7] to add to the other general disciplines the part dealing with the movements and effects of the heavens. We shall rightly call happy the man who has comprehended all of philosophy in his mind, and understands the hidden causes of most changes in nature and in the lives of men, the sources of virtue and of honourable duties – as Virgil, too, said most wisely: 'Happy is he who could know the causes of things' [Virgil, *Georgics* II.490]. I have spoken.

[7] Reading *ingenii viribus* for *ingeniis viribus*.

11 Preface to Johannes Vogelin's *Book on the Elements of Geometry* (1536)

CR III, 107–14

Greetings from Philip Melanchthon to Johannes Reiffensteyn[1]

I decided that no more fitting ornament can be added to the beginning of this book which provides access to geometry than the sign which Plato is said to have painted on the gates of his school, namely: 'Let no one enter who is not trained in geometry (*ageōmetrētos oudeis eisitō*).'[2] The interpretation of that saying has engaged the conjectures of many people. Some judge that Plato kept away from his school – as if they were defiled and impious – those inexperienced in geometry, the elements of which used to be taught then straight away from an early age to all those who were given a liberal education. Others transfer it to morals and believe that it meant, for students of philosophy, that they should preserve in all duties a certain moderateness and impartiality by analogy with geometry, just as in the *Gorgias*, when Plato rebukes the unjust opinion of Callicles, he says that the latter neglects geometry. Even though it is sufficiently clear from Plato's writings that he liked to apply geometrical examples to morals, nevertheless it cannot be doubted that, at the same time, by doing so he points out something about the order of subjects, and that he felt that those who were to undertake philosophy should be prepared in geometry. There are many most weighty reasons for his aphorism. For that art is not to be relegated to the mechanics who measure buildings, vessels or other trifling bodies, even though that practice also contains liberal teaching, and brings great benefits to life. But, for many other reasons, the philosopher needs geometry, for the beginnings of natural philosophy take their origin from there. And everywhere in all parts of natural philosophy many demonstrations are taken from that art: first those which show that the world is finite, that there are not several worlds and that no body is infinite. For these are the true beginnings of natural philosophy. Furthermore, since geometrical demonstrations are most distinct, no one without a knowledge of that art understands what is the power of demonstrations; without it no one will be

---

[1] Johannes Reiffensteyn was the son of Melanchthon's friend, Gulielmus Reiffensteyn, to whom he had earlier dedicated the *De Dialectica Libri Quatuor*. Later Melanchthon also dedicated the *Elementorum Rhetorices Libri II* to both Johannes and his brother Albertus (CR II, cols. 542–44). Johannes Vogelin (*d.* 1549) was a professor of mathematics at Vienna and then at Heilbronn.

[2] This phrase is discussed by Erasmus in *Adages*, III.iii.60.

a master of method. Therefore Plato, too, said that geometry needs to be studied for the reason that the knowledge of it leads to understanding the other arts more easily and correctly. But its most obvious benefit lies in measuring the size of the earth, of the heavenly bodies and of distances. And that is the greatest success of geometry, that it did not cleave to trifling and lower machines, but took flight to the heavens, and raised human minds, having cast off the earth, back to that heavenly abode, and showed us the wonderful construction and regulation of the world. Furthermore, it led exiled minds to their homeland and to acquaintance with the heavens, and even to the recognition of God. For that very teaching, in which the construction and the ruling of the world are beheld, has great power in strengthening worthy beliefs about God in the hearts of men.

Since, therefore, the origins of that most outstanding part of philosophy, on heavenly motions, are mainly in geometry, there is a sufficiently weighty reason why Plato admonished those who were about to undertake philosophy to add the study of geometry. I believe that this is what Plato meant by the inscription which I have repeated here, in order that Plato's authority might add some weight to our oration, since I wish to encourage the young to aspire to that art which has to be used as a guide towards many parts of philosophy. For every time the students take this book into their hands and read its Platonic inscription, they will think that they are being admonished by the voice of Plato, and indeed with the prayers and judgements of all the learned, so that they may aspire to that art because of the greatest benefits. Nor assuredly is there any doubt that the computation of measures in itself delights dispositions that are not warped, just as by nature we are captured by the comparison of numbers or the harmony of sounds. However, the greatness of this benefit must rouse and inflame noble and lofty minds to these studies, because this art opens the path to that most outstanding philosophy of heavenly things; how much dignity it has, and in what various ways it is useful for the life of men, is not in the least unclear, especially to those who are not utterly averse to studies of the true and old philosophy.

I know that these exhortations are of no avail when faced with those endowed with base minds, who do not discern the dignity of the outstanding disciplines, or pursue some more saleable arts for the purpose of gain. Plato certainly excludes them most strictly, since they are untrained in geometry (*ageometrētoi*), on two accounts. For they have monstrous minds, as well as reprehensibly throwing into disorder the geometrical proportion since they do not concede the arts their dignity. However, upright minds, even mediocre ones, can be stimulated by the admiration of the arts, if they are encouraged, and also if there happens to be a master who teaches them skilfully. Therefore I hope that I can provoke some to study, and I urge you, my Johannes, and those like you, that you consider first that those like yourself who aspire to true praise need to strive with all the powers of intellect and mind in order to obtain for themselves a firm and perfect knowledge which is of use to the state. For that purpose the entire circle of the arts is needed, tied and joined together, so that in the individual arts many things are to be adopted from others nearby. Indeed the two disciplines,[3] of numbers and of measures, have great usefulness in natural philosophy, while they also have also brought forth the entire teaching of heavenly things.

They say that when Aristippus had lost all his possessions in a shipwreck, and he himself had nevertheless safely reached the shore of Rhodes with a few others, he caught sight of some geometrical figures on some scaffoldings when walking along the shore. Although the sea had cast them off their journey and stranded them in an unknown place, when he had seen the geometrical figures he nevertheless bade his companions be of good cheer, saying that he had seen traces of men. And he congratulated himself and the others that they had not been stranded on a barbaric shore, and asserted that humanity towards strangers and the shipwrecked would not be lacking in these men among whom the studies of these arts were cherished. If only these traces of men which Aristippus saw there on the shore were even more numerous in the schools. For these arts have been lying abandoned and neglected for many centuries already. For the previous age lured away the young from true philosophy to the most absurd sophistries; now, after they have been driven out of the schools, one would need to take pains that pure and genuine philosophy be taught, which leads to achieving firm knowledge. For this our age shows us plainly how much the state needs excellent knowledge, because everywhere many – be it from lack of judgement, or because they cannot explain anything clearly – have spread or defend absurd and miscellaneous beliefs, from which great struggles and great discord in the Church have emerged. There will be no end to these ills unless the young are called back to the true and erudite system of studying. Those who lead the Church and the state would truly need to apply themselves to that task. But the same concern is also a matter for

[3] Reading *scientiae* for *scientia*.

our office, that is, for those who teach or study in the schools. For our office also pertains to the state. We are put in our position by divine providence in order to preserve and spread a knowledge useful for humankind. God demands this diligence from teachers and students in equal measure. Therefore the young should consider that they have a duty towards God to strive for firm and complete knowledge which will be of use to the Church and the state. As we bring our minds to the churches, we need to bring them to the school, that is, in order that we come to know divine things there and disclose them to others. If anyone comes to the school only in order to take away from there some particular discipline that he could direct to gain and idle show, he should know that he defiles the most holy temple of knowledge. In the same way, if the young understand their duty, if they know in what spirit they need to busy themselves with their studies, we shall easily obtain from those whose minds are not monstrous that they understand all the arts correctly and in order, and that they attempt to acquire not the empty shadow of erudition, but true knowledge.

Some are deterred by the difficulty of the subject. But these deliver the verdict before they examine, which is most unjust; before tasting the first principles, they reject and condemn the entire study. Certainly the beginnings can be understood without great trouble, and they are useful in life and in many arts. They would at all events need to know these first before they delivered a verdict on the difficulty. Furthermore the order, which is most convenient, particularly in geometry, alleviates the toil and adds much light. Finally, demonstrations are taught everywhere; although in the most advanced part of the art, as if in the pediment, they are far removed from our eyes and our sight, like cities which we see from afar, nevertheless in the other parts, being more exposed to the eyes, they contain much less difficulty. It is the utmost sloth to reject the study before you have made the attempt. And it is unjust weakness of the mind not to want to undertake any toil in studying, since it is a certain warfare to be engaged in education, and the state entrusts us with the care and preservation of the highest things which cannot be protected without the keenest striving of the minds.

Therefore both the dignity of the arts themselves and the public good should rouse us; and let us remember that to these studies of virtue we need also to add fortitude, which does not allow the mind to languish in sluggishness, and which makes its way by force, so to speak, through all difficulties. Noble and heroic natures which are urged to these highest arts about heavenly things by some divine inspiration and enthusiasm (*enthousiasmōi*) grasp these arts easily, just as those who have a natural talent for poetry quickly grasp the measures of syllables and feet. Nevertheless, as in other arts, even mediocre minds will achieve much through zeal and diligence. And if some do not dedicate themselves completely to this study, they have need, nevertheless, of a knowledge of the first principles of geometry, in order to shape their judgements and understand many topics which are common in Aristotle and in other famous authors.

Aristotle depicts justice most beautifully, in the fifth book of the *Ethics*, by these geometrical figures, and he distinguishes its forms by comparing them to arithmetical and geometrical proportions. And in that passage the precepts are taught that are necessary for those who desire to judge learnedly about the causes of the laws. A comparison taken from arithmetic and geometry sheds most light on those. However, since the commentators whose books have come down to us did not understand that comparison they not only obscured, but utterly falsified, Aristotle's entire opinion, just as if someone had sprinkled and covered with dirt and mud an outstanding painting by Apelles. Furthermore, it is not only shameful for the commentator, but also irksome for other readers to get stuck in such a passage as if in mud[4] and to be defrauded of the author's opinion. For Aristotle most sagaciously establishes two forms of justice, one of which orders the ranking of persons in choosing magistrates in positions of authority, in a city and in families. The other rules not only contracts, but any exchange of things, such as merchandise, damage, harm and penalties. Then surely, when it is explained why in exchanges the arithmetical proportion is needed, but in the other kind of justice – in choosing magistrates – geometry is applicable, the causes of justice become very clear. Aristotle took this comparison from Plato, who states with the greatest elegance and dignity that equality must be achieved in the cities, because equality creates mutual love: as one says: 'Same is dear to same (*ison isōi philon*)'.[5] However, he says that arithmetical equality is troublesome in positions of authority and in choosing magistrates, while geometrical equality is beneficial for cities. For it is geometrical equality when degrees are established and selection is employed, so that the highest commands are bestowed upon the best and most sagacious citizens in proportion, and the individual citizens understand which part of the public duty they support, and stay in their rank and

---

[4] People are said to be 'stuck in the mud' when they are involved in troublesome business from which they cannot extricate themselves: see Erasmus, *Adages*, I.ii.lxxxi.

[5] Cf. Erasmus, *Adages*, IV.vi.67.

do not upset the proportion. Plato proclaims this arrangement by saying that this geometry is divine, and that the cities then become happy indeed when God imparts to them a small part of that geometry. Then he adds that whatever is good proceeds from that geometry – just as if in the Church the highest authority belonged to the best and most learned, and individuals understood and performed their duty by their rank, and each one, as one says, adorned his own Sparta, and the inexperienced yielded to the opinions of the learned. What could be happier for the Church than if it were established by that geometrical proportion which prevents both tyranny and the wantonness of the people? For in a tyranny there are no degrees, but all the good are oppressed to an equal degree. In a democracy arithmetical equality rules, in consequence of which all the lowest men reach the highest commands without selection, and the condition is achieved which Achilles disparages most sharply in Homer, when he says that he does not want to be in a country in which there is no distinction between good and bad citizens: 'The bad and the good would be held in equal honour' (*en d'iēi timēi ēmen kakos, ēdē kai esthlos*) [*Iliad* IX.319]. What could be more desirable for all those who are good than if the geometrical proportion – which prevents both tyranny and the wantonness of the people – governed the Church Synod? Indeed, it is not without reason that the most learned men have been delighted by geometrical analogies. For they appear before us like paintings. Therefore, since they are understood, they greatly illuminate discussions, and inform us of many things that are worthy of admiration.

Therefore that reason, too, should attract the young to getting to know the first principles: they see that great men loved these figures, and that their writings cannot be understood without having tasted these arts. For although there are much greater benefits, of which I have spoken a little while ago, for noble minds it nevertheless also adds an incentive if they love the ideas of great authors as if they were the most precious gems, and desire to grasp their power completely. These examples show that it is not absurd to apply the maxim which Plato wrote on the entrance to the school – 'Let no one enter who is not trained in geometry' (*ageōmetrētos oudeis eisito*) – to morals. He excludes from discipleship those who upset the geometrical proportion, who neither understand nor preserve the degrees of honourable duties, and who rush, without law and inconsistently, wherever their impulse carries them. For that saying of Aeschylus is most true, that each man is suited to a different kind of city (*allon allēi pros polei tetagmenon*) [Plato, *Republic* VIII, 550c]. Therefore, just as these wild and barbarous minds are not suited for the philosophical city because they neither admire the arts nor can they be taught, so, on the other hand, those who are endowed with moderate minds are suited for the philosophical city, because they can be encouraged to cherish these best studies. Such men Plato invites, and at the same time he shows which disposition is capable of philosophy, what morals are appropriate for these studies, what minds can be roused to the love of philosophy and what kind of teaching is needed at the beginning.

Therefore, when the students read that Platonic inscription – *ageōmetrētos oudeis eisitō* – they should remember that they must take upon themselves geometrical equality in morals, and join the study of geometry to the other arts. Either is a great distinction and has to be striven after for many reasons.

But you, my Johannes, have been given by the favour of God a mind that is both moderate by nature and – as one can see from your drawings – talented for geometry, and clearly suited to the philosophical city. I hope that, roused by your father's and our encouragement, you are aflame with the desire to know that most beautiful teaching about the motions and effects of the heavens. The step towards this needs to be made through geometry. You will believe that you are also doing something pleasing to God by bestowing care upon these studies. For it is said most pleasantly by Plato that God always practises geometry (*theon aei geōmetrein*) [Plutarch, *Moralia* VIII.ii.718c-720c], that is, as I interpret it, He governs everything, and rules by a most firm law the heavenly courses and all of nature. Therefore without doubt He approves of the studies of those who by, observing the paths of these courses, so to speak, acknowledge and worship Him as the Ruler. Jakob Milich joined together, by a useful decision, the books on arithmetic and geometry most suited for schools, written by outstanding masters in the university which for some centuries was the main abode of these arts. For in Vienna the philosophy of celestial phenomena was almost reborn, promoted by Peuerbach,[6] and now they maintain its possession, as if by inheritance, with great success, and there it is made illustrious by other men as well as by Johannes Vogelin, the author of this book on the elements of geometry, which he describes with the brevity and arrangement which he hoped would be most useful to the students. May Christ guide your studies and those of the rest of the young to the good of the state. In the month of August, in the year 1536.

---

[6] See below, note 3 to oration 12, p. 107.

12 Preface to *On the Sphere* (1531)

CR II, 530–7

Philip Melanchthon sends greetings to Simon Grynaeus, a most learned man and an old friend[1]

Since it is beneficial in all arts to teach some brief elements at the beginning in order to prepare students for deeper knowledge, the greatest gratitude is due to the most excellent and learned men who wrote introductory works for us of those most beautiful disciplines, that is, of astronomy and cosmography. They deserve praise not only because of the merit of the arts themselves, but even more because of the difficulty of the matter. For it was a matter of great labour and sagacity to choose from such a wide and varied multitude of things those which would be most beneficial for the introduction and the beginning. For that reason I have always loved the wonderful book by Johannes de Sacrobosco[2] which appears to me to have grasped very aptly the first principles of this discipline, and I judge that I have seen in the universities most learned men who preferred this book to others of the same kind with great unanimity, and wanted it to be available in all schools, and to be in everyone's hands. 'The book that is to live needs to have genius', says Martial [*Epigrams* 6.60.10]. But such genius does not fall to the lot of works which do not have the commendation of usefulness. In order for the book to have favourable genius for so many centuries in all schools, among such a variety of opinions, it must be filled with the best things. For we see very few writings bear their age well, in particular in the schools, where they usually judge most capriciously. But this book has been read with the greatest approval of the learned, for many centuries already. Therefore let us, too, take care to transmit to coming generations this book which we have received into our hands from our ancestors, and let us preserve it as a public work for everyone's studies, so that it shows to the young in the schools the approach to the most beautiful arts, whose elements it

---

[1] Simon Grynaeus' (1494–1541) life-long friendship with Melanchthon went back to their school days at Pforzheim. Grynaeus held chairs of Greek at the University of Heidelberg and then at the University of Basle. This preface to Grynaeus was often censored in Catholic countries: see I. Pantin, 'La Lettre de Melanchthon à S. Grynaeus: les Avatars d'une Apologie de l'Astrologie', in *Divination et Controverse Religieuse en France au XVIe Siècle*, ed. R. Aulotte (Paris, 1987), pp. 85–101.

[2] Johannes de Sacrobosco (John of Holywood; *d.* 1256) was educated at the universities of Oxford and of Paris. At Paris, he became a professor of mathematics, renowned for his proficiency in astronomy. He composed the *De Sphaera* based on the works of Ptolemy and his Arabic commentators. It became the standard university textbook of astronomy.

teaches. For if we reckon that the knowledge of these arts is useful in life, these monuments, which open the path to them, must be preserved by us with great effort.

Who is so hard-hearted and so without feeling that he does not sometimes, looking up at the sky and beholding the most beautiful stars in it, marvel at these varied alternations which are produced by their motions, or desire to know the traces, so to speak, of their motions, that is, the fixed computation shown by divine providence? For such varied things, which are placed so far away, would not have been investigated or perceived by human sight had God not roused and advanced the studies of some outstanding men. Since therefore nature leads men to these arts, one has to consider as utterly lacking a human mind those who are in no way affected by the sweetness of these things and of knowledge. Plato very plainly says that men were given eyes for the sake of astronomy [*Timaeus* 47a; *Republic* VII, 530d]. He meant to say that there is nothing more beautiful among all the bodies than the heavenly lights, and that men are particularly drawn to enjoy that beauty. But it seems to me indeed that the eyes themselves have the greatest affinity with the stars. Just as the sun shines in the world, so in man, too – whom some call a 'small universe' (*mikron kosmon*) because of several similarities – his own lights or stars are created. Therefore those who disdain these related lights do not contemplate the work of nature, and for that reason they deserve to have their eyes plucked out, since they do not want to use them for the purpose for which they are chiefly made – especially since that knowledge puts us in mind of God and of our immortality. For it is not possible for the human mind not to conclude that there is a mind that rules and governs everything, if it contemplated these established courses and laws of the great circuits and stars. For no such thing can exist or continue by chance or by another power without a mind.

For this reason – if astronomy corroborates the belief about God in the minds of men – we have to consider that Plato said not only learnedly, but also piously that eyes are given to us because of astronomy. For they are certainly given to us chiefly for the reason that they may be our guides for searching for some knowledge of God. Furthermore, only those among the philosophers who spurned astronomy were professedly ungodly (*atheoi*); having done away with providence, they also removed the immortality of our souls. If they had reached this knowledge, they would have perceived the manifest traces of God in nature, and, having noticed them, they would have been forced to acknowledge that the universe is made and governed by a mind. But if someone also requires authority from the Holy Scriptures, which commend these studies, he has a most weighty testimony in *Genesis*, where it is written: 'They will be for signs, seasons and years' [*Genesis* 1:14]. How would the sun bring about the years for us if not by observing its orbit, and by marking off spaces and distances of its course and the seasons? Therefore that heavenly voice admonishes us to observe the motions of the heavenly bodies. Why should I recount the public benefits? What would the life of men be like if we did not have a defined relation of the seasons, or if we did not have the number of the years in history or in public business? Not to know anything about the sequence of the past, and not being able to establish an order of seasons in our present business would be more than barbarity; indeed, the life of beasts. In such ignorance neither religion of any kind nor public order could be preserved.

Therefore, since nature stirs us up and divine oracles admonish us (although the meaning of nature, too, is a divine inspiration and almost the voice of God), and the greatness of the benefits attracts one to this discipline, the studious young must cherish it diligently. In this matter it befits them to be moved also by the praises for our country, because this discipline has recently blossomed again after it had been neglected without honour for some centuries, re-established by two excellent men, Peuerbach and Regiomontanus,[3] of whom the one was from Nuremberg, the other from nearby Franconia. The facts prove that these two heroes were roused with extraordinary force by divine providence to make these arts illustrious. For when did these studies attain such light after they were extinguished in Egypt? For even though the Arabs seized with great energy the property relinquished by the Greeks, so much so that they propagated these arts to the West and as far as Spain, nevertheless their writings show that this inquisitive people did not take pains in observing the motions as much as in divinations. They were so desirous of the latter that – not satisfied with Ptolemy's astrology, which can be considered a part of natural philosophy – they also devised casting of lots and many other kinds of predictions for which no cause can be assigned (*anaitiologēta*) [*Tetrabiblos* 111].

But these men brought all their zeal to the chief part of knowledge; they rescued the most obscure demonstrations of Ptolemy and brought them to light, and, in order that the art be transmitted to coming generations, they

---

[3] Georg Peuerbach (1423–61) was born in Peuerbach, Austria, not Nuremberg, and does not have an obvious connection with Nuremberg; Johannes Regiomontanus (1436–76), Peuerbach's student, was born in Königsberg in Franconia. See oration 29 on Regiomontanus' life, p. 237.

provided us with more than one kind of commentary.[4] The ancients praise the dove of Archytas and various works by Archimedes, but that brief book, the *Theorica* of Peuerbach, is far more admirable.[5] It contains the whole of the very long work by Ptolemy, and sets before our eyes the position of the orbits. What should I say of the remaining works, the entire *Epitome* and the tables, in which they demonstrate the use of the rules, in order to complete the art.

Therefore, to that extent our men are successful in this discipline. For these authors sowed the seeds of that discipline throughout Germany, just as it is written that Triptolemus distributed the seeds of the fruits of the earth.[6] Therefore it would be a most vile thing for us to dismiss such noble possession of the best things.

However, there are some Epicurean theologians who mock this entire branch of learning. Not only do they take away credibility from the prophecies, but they also disparage knowledge of motion; let us leave them to play the fool with Epicurus. For they are in a condition such that they would need medical doctors rather than geometers. It is an obvious kind of madness to spurn the knowledge of the motions, which contains the most erudite and fixed computations – not to mention in particular the part concerned with divination, although neither Pico[7] nor anybody else can persuade me that the stars have no effect on the elements and on the bodies of animated beings and, besides, no import in this lower nature. For experience shows that the conjunctions of fiery stars indeed brings these bodies and droughts, and again that the meeting of humid stars increases the moisture. Furthermore, stars mixed in various ways, and variously[8]

---

[4] As a papal legate, Cardinal Johannes Bessarion (1403–73) went to Vienna in order to secure German participation in the campaign against the Turks. There, he commissioned a new translation of Ptolemy's *Almagest* and a more accessible digest of Ptolemaic astronomy from Peuerbach. Peuerbach, who knew no Greek, began the digest, entitled the *Epitome*, based on Gerard of Cremona's translation (from the Arabic), but died before its completion. His student Regiomontanus accompanied Bessarion to Rome in the autumn of 1461 to complete the *Epitome*, which was first printed in 1496. See N. M. Swerdlow, 'The Recovery of the Exact Sciences of Antiquity: Mathematics, Astronomy, Geography', in *Rome Reborn: the Vatican Library and Renaissance Culture*, ed. A. Grafton (Washington, New Haven, London and Vatican City, 1993), pp. 125–67.

[5] Archytas of Tarentum (*fl. c.* 400 BC), was a renowned mathematician and Pythagorean. He is said to have invented mathematical instruments, including wooden pigeons which could fly. Peuerbach composed the *Novae Theoricae Planetarum*, a new version of the medieval astronomical textbook, *Theorica Planetarum*, usually attributed to Gerard of Cremona.

[6] Unable to make him immortal, the goddess Ceres taught Triptolemus agriculture and commanded him to scatter seeds from her chariot: see Ovid, *Metamorphoses*, V.645–7.

[7] Giovanni Pico della Mirandola (1463–94) wrote against astrology in the *Disputationes adversus astrologiam divinatricem*, first published in 1496.

[8] Reading *varieque* for *variaeque*.

arranged qualities have different effects, like completely dissimilar and differently arranged things in remedies. Therefore I judge that Aristotle spoke rightly when he said that this lower world is governed by the higher one, and that the higher things are the cause of motion in the lower ones. He adds a very wisely considered reason: since the beginning of motion comes from the heavens, it follows that the motion of the heavens is also the cause of motion in everything else.

For these are his words, which we add so that the young may remember them like an oracle: 'This is necessarily continuous with the motions from above, so that all its power is governed from there, whence is the origin of motion; it needs to be considered the first cause for everything'[9] [*Meteorology* I.ii.339a22]. Just as in our bodies life, or the first motion that resides in the heart, stimulates motion in the other members, so, since without doubt the motion of the heavens is the first, it rouses the other bodies to effect each their own motions. Assuredly no one who is correctly versed in philosophy will think differently in any way. For the doctors, too, who tend to search for the causes of things in matter more than in the heavens, nevertheless relate many things to the constitutions of the stars. The book ascribed to Hippocrates, *Airs, Waters, Places*, demonstrates that.

And these things do not disagree with Christian doctrine which, although it teaches us that all things are governed by divine providence, nevertheless does not remove the natural actions and import of things. Thus it appears to be the case in nourishing the body: although God bestows life and motion on them, He nevertheless commands us to pamper and support them with food, drink and other things made for protecting life. And it is prudence worthy of a Christian to distinguish which are the actions of God together with nature and which those of God alone and placed above nature. To speak of man in particular, it often appears to me when I think about it that three kinds of action befall men. What springs from man's nature, by emotion and by reason, is very well known. The inclinations, which follow the mixtures of qualities, belong to this. For we see endless differences between minds, which certainly bring forth dissimilar actions, so that the poet spoke the truth when he said: 'Each one follows the seeds of his own nature.'[10]

---

[9] This passage was originally in Greek: *Esti d'ex anankēs suneches pōs houtos tais anothen phorais, hōste pasan autou tēn dunamin kubernasthai ekeithen, hothen gar hē tēs kinēseōs archē, pasin ekeinēn aitian nomisteon prōtēn*, which is very close to the corresponding passage in Aristotle, *Meterology*, I.ii.

[10] This is a paraphrase of Horace, *Art of Poetry*, 108–11, found verbatim in Fioravanti Octavianus Mirandula, *Illustrium poetarum flores* (Strasbourg: W. Rihel, 1538), CCXVIIʳ, a copy of which was in the Wittenberg University Libraray: S. Kusukawa, *A Wittenberg University Library Catalogue*, no. 907.

For what is so established among doctors as that the habits and passions (*ta ēthē kai ta pathē*) imitate the disposition of bodies? And the reality itself tells us that no habits (*ēthē*) can exist in a bilious man, but that immoderate impulses are roused in him, like storms, great and violent passions (*pathē*), which reason can only rule or curb with the greatest difficulty. If anyone contemplated the character of different regions and the minds of various peoples, what other cause for this difference could he show than the nature of the heavens? From this one can judge easily that in the mixing of the temperaments of bodies and minds the nature of light also concurs, among other things. And I do not judge[11] that education, habit, custom, laws and advice contribute nothing to ruling these inclinations, but I put these, too, under that category of action that springs from nature.

The second category is that of actions which exist in man by divine providence, above nature. For it is proper for the Christian mind to understand and feel that men are protected and governed by divine providence. But although God governs in such a way that He also leaves to nature its parts in some way, He nevertheless corrects many things in nature, and for many things He allows different outcomes than those that nature intended. For neither was Moses saved by the favour of the stars when he escaped by a road opened through the sea, nor was Peter freed by the favour of the constellations when he was led from prison by the angel, nor was Paul made pious from being an enemy of the Gospel by the power of the stars. No one fails to understand that God is to be considered exclusively responsible for such works. Therefore, just as we receive the powers of nature to such a degree that they do not take away the rule of Christ, so we concede to the star its powers to such a degree that it detracts nothing from the glory of Christ; since everything is subject to Him, rightfully, it should also be considered that the powers of the stars have to obey Him. Worthy minds must cheer and strengthen themselves by this belief against the sad signs which not rarely perturb the minds to an astonishing extent amidst such weakness of human nature. Just as otherwise we must prefer the word of God to our conjectures, so the mind[12] has to be strengthened against these signs by the word of God and the divine promises. The well-known saying taken from Jeremiah teaches this: 'Be not dismayed at the signs of heaven; for the heathen are dismayed at them' [Jeremiah 10:2]. For the prophet does not deny that they are signs, but since he names them signs, he means that they

---

[11] Reading *iudico* for *iudicio*.   [12] Reading *animi* for *animo*.

threaten great and sad things. He comforts the faithful not to fear them, not because they portend nothing, but so that they may trust that they are protected by divine providence among these perils – just as Christ forbids us to fear death, not because it is not harsh, but that we may know that even in death Christ is with us to deliver us. Therefore the mind is to be raised up above this entire corporeal nature; even if the world fell apart, it is not to be allowed that the word of God or the trust in God be driven out of us. Pious minds are fortified by this trust against the present perils, and in the same way they will also have to be fortified against the hostile signs of the stars. Just as other parts of natural philosophy do not harm the Christian religion, so neither does astrology – for we consider that a part of natural philosophy as well – stand in the way of piety, if one uses it in its place.

Beside the two kinds of action that I have recounted, there is a third kind of action, towards the undertaking of which minds are driven against nature by the devil, with great impulse. For the unnatural desires and murders of Nero and similar tyrants are rightly attributed to the devil and not to the stars or other natural causes. And so, since human minds are not moved by one kind of cause only, it follows that the laws of fate are hindered in various ways, at times by divine inspiration, at times by custom, at times by deliberation and that at times they are also turned for the worse by the devil. Therefore Ptolemy says clearly that the decrees of the astrologers are not those of praetors – for the edicts of the praetor force the people to obey. Indeed these signs do not apply violence to men, even though they are active everywhere. History supplies examples of these things.

But this argument is too long to be explained in its entirety here. I have spoken of it at such length so that the young do not altogether condemn this circle of arts, because some inexperienced men mock divinations. For this teaching of the heavenly motions contains a most weighty knowledge which is most worthy of man. And if anyone uses their judgement, they will understand that the other part of the art, that is, that related to divinations, is just as much part of natural philosophy as the doctors' predictions are considered a part of natural philosophy. For one must not think that these beautiful bodies of the stars are made in vain, in particular since their order and course is established with the greatest reason, so much so that it appears that something like a state is depicted in the sky, as if in a poem. For the sun, which appears to rule, is moved to the middle of the orbit, accompanied by senators, a warrior and an orator; it also has stewards, the moon and Venus. These are mainly dominant in putting in motion the humours by which bodies are nourished. Since even here the wonderful order and position, as well as the fixed laws, testify that the construction is established by the highest reason, it is not proper to say that the stars have no meaning and no effects. And it is not in vain that the Holy Scriptures say: 'They will be for signs, seasons and years' [Genesis 1:14]. Here he not only says that the years, the alternating of days and nights and the distinction between the seasons, that is, of summer and winter, are brought about by the stars, but he also adds something about the signs. The agreement of all centuries recognises this, by which it has been ascertained that eclipses have always had sad effects. It is not for the well-instructed man to disagree with the concerted opinion of so many centuries.

Perhaps I have spoken about these things longer than necessary in the preface to this book, but I intended to admonish the young at the very entrance to these arts to think of the entire circle of arts with more respect.

I have written to you, most learned Grynaeus, not because I believed that it was necessary to incite you by this reasoning – you who excel in all of philosophy to such an extent that there is no one among our men whom I could compare to you. But the mention of these arts always renews my memory of you. As a witness of this you have the excellent Jakob Milich who, since he teaches these arts here, converses much with me about them; we usually include you, too, in this conversation. And so there was no one to whom I would rather write about these arts than to you, so that you understand that we connect with them the remembrance of your friendship, although there are also some published works by you which put us in mind of your virtues and beautiful studies. For by your favour we have a more faultless and more refined Aristotle whom you know I admire, love and cherish greatly. But I love him even more now that I have added the name of a man most dear to me in the beginning of his [Aristotle's] works. If only at some time I had the leisure to explain and praise that author as you have undertaken to do with great success. You explained several books far more successfully than had been done by those who, shortly before our time, showed us not the genuine face of Aristotle but barely a feeble shadow. They did not teach philosophy, that is, the knowledge of speaking and judging wisely, but they crushed it by idle and empty subtleties, which were of no use for judging on public and other important matters. But of these things elsewhere. Farewell. Wittenberg, in the month of August 1531.

13 On astronomy and geography (1536)

CR XI, 292–8

Oration on astronomy and geography held at Wittenberg[1]

There is an old story about an oracle of the sibyl concerning Athens – that two banes would be its ruin, namely deceit and the stupidity of its leaders. However, if we consider the everyday life of men and the destruction of realms, the sibyl was prophesying not only for Athens but for all cities and empires. In the past, Germany excelled both in the greatness of minds and in the truth, honesty and faith of its counsels. Nowadays people contend with ruses, righteous intentions are made sport of, and the ancient desire for military glory and courage are extinct. Therefore you can see that there is no help in such public danger, not only in Germany, but also in the rest of Europe. When I think about this, I am distressed in my mind for the Church and for our studies, both of which are particularly threatened with devastation and ruin by the savagery of the Turks.[2] Although dangerous hardship is imminent, as there are many signs not only in the stars, but also in the morals of men, I nevertheless sustain myself by the hope that God will care for the Church, and that the Son of God will defend our assemblies, as Daniel foretold. Therefore, young men, these our studies are not to be cast away in desperation of rewards or of salvation. On the contrary, they are to be kindled even more enthusiastically, so that they may be preserved even in the midst of enemies, if that is what destiny brings. And because these our assemblies are part of the Church, every time we gather together, every time we think of our studies, let pious prayers be added, and let us pray to God, the Father of our Saviour Jesus Christ, that He may protect the Church and honest studies, and save and guide us.

I wanted to say this in advance, because in these assemblies it is most fitting for us to think of our studies as well as of the universal perils, and to join our prayers together. For the saying of Christ concerns these assemblies as well, when He said that He would be there wherever two or three gathered in His name [Matthew 18:28]. As the duty of my office imposes on me the need to speak here, I have decided to speak of the art which I profess, that is, of the science that teaches the laws of the movements of the heavens, and

---

[1] Melanchthon was Dean of the faculty of arts at the end of year 1536.

[2] This probably alludes to the campaigns of Suleiman in 1526, 1529 and 1532 during which Hungary, Transylvania and Moldavia were conquered. In 1529 Ottoman armies even entered Vienna briefly before withdrawing.

indicates the sizes, spaces, distances and boundaries of the regions. Even though I know that in this university these divine arts are not disparaged, it is nevertheless our duty – since they are practised more sluggishly than they should be – to incite and rouse, as much as we can, in every way, the young to study. In this matter I should wish for us to be helped by princes, just as in Egypt the generosity of the kings invited men of genius to practise and explain these arts; and, more recently, 300 years ago, when those in the West had not even a shadow of that refined science, that most ingenious prince the Emperor Frederick II[3] took charge of having it translated into Latin from the Arabic records, and of having it restored in any way whatever at great expense. And there is much evidence which shows that the most ancient kings were devoted to this art, such as Atlas, Orion or Chiron. Therefore grateful posterity assigned their names to stars in order to indicate that they received from them the science of the movements of the heavens and the description of the year. And in Lucan [*Pharsalia* x.185f.] Caesar says about himself: 'In the midst of war I ever found time to study the world above us and the starry and celestial zones.'[4] It is well known that the Emperor Charles V understands the heavenly science almost like an expert, and loves it so much that when he has a pause for rest he does not assuage his mind by games or pleasures, but by discussions about that most agreeable science. I know that, sitting in the baths, when he had to take time for the treatment of his foot, he tricked leisure by skilfully describing clocks. I know that he is most diligent at seeking the longitude and latitude of regions, so that at sea he can direct the course by looking at the sky. What is nobler for a great prince than to refresh the tired mind by such pleasure?

Would that others imitated this most noble example, and offered prizes to men of talent; if they did so, these arts could be preserved and explained more. But it often comes to my mind that the arts, together with the sky, grow old and are extinguished gradually, and that the end of the world is foretold by their ruin. Nevertheless, in the meantime eminent minds, which originate from heaven, should think of their home and should contemplate it now and again, and declare that that most beautiful sight of the bodies and movements of the heavens is not displayed to men in vain. They

---

[3] Frederick II (1194–1250), Holy Roman Emperor and King of Sicily, had a predilection for Arabic philosophy, on which he was probably guided by Michael Scot, the translator of Averroes' translation of Aristotle's *De Caelo* and *De anima* and of Avicenna. See Thomas Curtis van Cleve, *The Emperor Frederick II of Hohenstaufen, Immutator Mundi* (Oxford, 1972), pp. 299–318.

[4] As translated by J. D. Duff in Lucan, *Pharsalia* (Cambridge, MA, and London, 1969), p. 603.

should inquire into the order of these admirable things, which, as it is most suited to the nature of man, also brings great benefits for life. I shall expound some of those briefly, for reasons of time, and I shall speak only of the science of the movements and of boundaries of regions, leaving out the part of divination, lest I attract some criticism to myself.

As it is most befitting in all things to start with God, so, in this consideration of studies, we should be reminded of the Architect when we contemplate heaven itself. We should consider that He neither established this marvellous order in vain nor handed down the knowledge of these movements to humankind without reason. If someone does not think about this, how does he differ from a Cyclops who, spending his life in a cave, neither looks up to heaven nor worships any eternal god? However, if someone, as it is proper for human nature, makes much of God's gifts he must declare that the laws of these motions were established, and the knowledge handed down, for the sake of great benefits.

The usefulness of the movements is clear for all to see. What could be more agreeable for the preservation of living beings than the alternating of days and nights, and what could be more beneficial to the fertility of the earth for bringing forth produce of the fields and for nourishing living beings than the varying weather of spring, summer, autumn and winter? The Maker has put such diligence into them that he not only determined the periods to be measured by the movements of the sun and the moon, but he also added their powers, so that the earth would at times be warmed by fertile warmth, at other times moistened, at others dried out and at others left to rest bound in ice. In order that we would understand that this was done with purpose, he joined to the sun the rising and setting of certain constellations appropriate to the single parts of the year. After the spring sowing the Hyades set, of which Pliny [*Natural History* xviii.lxvi.247] says that it is a violent constellation that causes disorder on land and sea. This is established in such a way, because at that time the earth needs watering. During the harvest dry weather is needed. Therefore the lesser Dog Star then increases the heat. In the same way certain risings and settings are appropriate to the remaining parts of the year. These benefits are known which, as Xenophon says, give evidence that the Architect greatly loves our kind, since he provided for our needs so assiduously; as Xenophon himself says, he is loving of mankind (*philanthrōpos*). However, these things can perhaps be observed without science, although the order is perceived better with the added benefit of erudition.

I shall therefore speak of the benefits which are lost when science is neglected. Moses said [Genesis 1:14] that the seasons, days and years would be for signs. He explained this heavenly oracle to humankind so that they would learn to observe certain boundaries in the year, set up by divine providence, and to consider the periods of the year. This can by no means be done without erudition or knowledge of the movements. Therefore God added a shadow that instructs us, so that we can observe the equinoxes and the revolutions of the sun, He added the science of numbers and measures, which lifts the minds up to heaven, so that we can distinguish the fixed paths of the stars and their boundaries as if with our own eyes. Thus the first ancestors, and then the more educated offspring, and some of them of the greatest talent, always took pains with observing the revolving of the year, in order to preserve a fixed order of seasons. Their service has to be welcome to us, and their ingenuity, diligence, constancy and their wish to do good to humankind must be praised. There are many illustrious proofs of ingenuity and diligence, such as the prediction of eclipses and the description of the year, the revolution of which can be understood with great certainty, at least as far as that is possible.

People have approached this in various ways. The most ancient ancients perceived that the true length of a year was the return of the sun to a certain fixed star. Then, when some centuries later it was noticed that the stars had progressed, another way had to be sought. Therefore Meton, of whom they write that he lived in Athens, an ancestor, I believe, of Empedocles, defined the year as the return to the same point of summer solstice. Since for the Athenians the beginning of the year was the summer solstice, he established that as the preferred mark. Then, after the age of Alexander, Hipparchus preferred to observe the equinoxes rather than the solstices, because the variation, of a few days around the solstices, of the inclination towards the equator cannot be discerned by the senses. Therefore Hipparchus defined the year as the return of the sun to the same point of equinox. Following him Ptolemy, adding his observations as well, nevertheless handed down a computation of the year that was more consistent than the above, that is of 365 days, 6 hours, minus the three-hundredth part of a day. This diligence was not yet satisfactory to posterity, for Albategnius[5] in the seven hundred and forty-third year after Ptolemy, that

---

[5] There seems to be some confusion about dates. Al-Battani (*d.* 929) was usually known in the Latin West as Albategnius. His astronomical tract based on Ptolemaic astronomy was published as the *De motu stellarum* for the first time in 1537: see note 7, oration 29, p. 240.

is, before our times, around the year 600, perceived that there was need for emendation after Ptolemy. Then again most learned men followed the first path with some corrections, and preferred the year to be the return of the sun to a certain fixed star, since in that way there appears less fluctuation of the course of the year over longer periods.

I have recounted these things so that you may admire the diligence of those excellent men who strove to transmit to us a fixed calendar and a fixed description of the year. Just think what a service it is. For if these masters had not preserved this sequence of seasons for us, what darkness would there be in religions and all of history, and what confusion of all life? We would not be able to understand and locate the beginnings of the world, we would not know which religions were earlier and which later; the succession of realms would be unknown and so would the beginnings and propagation of the Church. In order that we may know all these things God enjoins us to learn what the year is, and shows us that the year contains twelve months and establishes the beginning in the equinox. For the first men these things were the seeds of this science. Therefore, admonished by that heavenly voice, let us ponder the benefits, and let us embrace, love and cherish God's gift. The science of the heavenly movements and geography are connected with one another, and they cannot be torn apart. Who is so inexperienced in public life or so without common sense as to believe that life can make do without the art that shows the position of regions, their distances and natures?

No navigation and no slightly longer journey can be undertaken or conducted with certainty by those who are ignorant of this art. What is there in the prophetic scriptures on how the Church wandered and what was done where, from where one could judge, if that skilful description of regions were lacking? Every day, in our prayers, we need to contemplate the land where the Son of God dwelt and was made a sacrifice, and we need to think of the place where the heavenly voice first sounded. For God wants to be invoked so that at the same time we think of His son's sacrifice and of His promises. Since the prayers of the mind need to dwell in these places every day, what sloth not to think where in all the lands they are! Even the uneducated wish to see these in paintings. And if the art of geography did not exist, all men would think that the earth was something infinite, and would know only the size and distances of the regions that are nearby. Many grave errors in life would originate from that. Now indeed, how agreeable and how useful it is to understand in the mind the entire circumference of the earth, comprehended by a determined, easy and short computation. If you consider it in your thoughts as well as with your eyes, you may even be surprised at its smallness, as it is 5,400 in our miles. Without the science of the heavenly movements, this cannot be enclosed in fixed descriptions as within borders.

I would say how much pleasantness and sweetness there is to that science, if I could expound it in words. But these things need to be known by experience. For each one the activity most appropriate to his nature is the most agreeable one, such as swimming for fish or singing for the nightingale; so men are necessarily affected by great pleasure when they contemplate the entire nature of things, when they find the proportions of numbers and magnitudes when they perceive the harmony and agreement of the heavenly and the inferior bodies and when they see that everything is made by a fixed law, in order to remind us of the Architect. If we are born for that contemplation, it must needs be a pleasure to natures that are neither preternatural nor distorted. Although I said in advance at the beginning that I would not talk about the part containing divination, let me add nevertheless that the science of the heavenly movements is in itself an art of foretelling (*mantikē*), and an outstanding and most certain divination ruling all of life. For these laws of the motions are evidence that the world has not originated by chance, but that it was created by an eternal mind, and that this creator cares about human nature. Since the laws of the motions demonstrate this clearly, it cannot be denied that this science is divination (*mantikē*) of the greatest thing. For this notion about God and providence assuredly rouses minds to virtue. The natural philosopher predicts rain when the south and west winds are blowing, clear weather when it is the north wind. How much more profitable is divination for assuring minds of providence, so that they may not imagine that the world exists by chance. It was for a great cause that God displayed to us this evidence of Himself. For, if we learn from it that God is the ruler of all things, we understand that one needs to obey Him, we recognise that order was installed by Him, both in our minds and in political society, and that punishments are set for those who confound this order; not even the Titans could escape them, even if, to entrench themselves, they dared stack Mt Pelion on top of Mt Ossa [Virgil, *Georgics* I.281]. Moreover, the order of heavenly laws also gives us many admonitions regarding God and morals, testifying that the changes of things are made for the benefit of humankind. Therefore Plato said sagaciously that only that man is happy who has learnt this science, and that only he can guide morals, and only he is moderate, just and useful to the citizens. I add Plato's words so that the voice and authority of such a great man may stir you up to the love and the study of these foremost arts. Nature has only one bond, namely the science of numbers, figures and heavenly movements, and if anyone seeks a different way to learning, let him invoke fortune,[6] as they say. For without these no one can ever be happy anywhere. This is the way, the education and the discipline, be it easy or difficult. It is necessary to pass through it, and it is not lawful to neglect God, who, to our benefit, bestowed the tradition about Himself on humankind in these arts. These are Plato's words; think about them, how wisely it is said that the tradition of God can be heard in these arts, which means that in the knowledge of the order of numbers and of the heavenly bodies it is necessarily established for us that the world has been created by an eternal mind. In fact, the very science of which we are speaking is *mantikē*, even if we do not investigate the other kinds of divination, of the alterations of air and of our bodies; not all of this is altogether useless, if it is contained within the right limits.

Since, therefore, the science of the heavenly movements is full of knowledge, it is useful in life for the distinction of seasons and regions, it is most agreeable, it strengthens in the minds the worthy notion of God and, since there is an opportunity to learn it, I encourage good minds to devote themselves to these studies, both for their own sake and for that of the state, for which we must preserve the noble arts that are useful for life. I have spoken.

[6] Erasmus explains that the invocation 'bonae fortunae' (here's luck!) may be more amusing if turned to somebody who ventures something trivial with as much bother as if it were of the greatest importance: *Adages*, I.vi.53.

14 The dignity of astrology (1535)

CR XI, 261–6

Oration on the dignity of astrology, held at the graduation of Masters by Jacob Milich, in the year 1535[1]

It is an excellent institution when on these occasions someone speaks about the dignity of the arts and about the praise of virtues, because that oration has great power to shape the judgement of the young and to kindle in their minds the love of good things. Even if it is usually mainly for the benefit of the young that an oration is employed here, nevertheless for others no other gratification to the ear is more pleasant[2] than the praises of the arts and the virtues; if anyone understands them, he will therefore admire them ardently. Thus, even if our oration will be more appropriate for the young, I am assured nevertheless that it will not be disagreeable to you either; the greater your erudition and sagacity, the more I believe you will be delighted by the very thought of the arts. I shall speak of that part of astrology that discusses the effects of the constellations on sublunar nature – and I have chosen this topic even more willingly, because I am aware that it needs to be discussed among learned men dedicated to philosophy, and not in the crowd of the inexperienced. Just as the Greek orators said with great sagacity in the definition of art that art not only needs to be true knowledge, but they added also that it needs to be useful for life, so I shall show both that the science of heavenly influences is true and that it brings great benefits for life. And I ask you in the beginning (and that would be most benevolent) not to confer the errors of the masters to the art itself; I would have to speak about this at more length, if this oration were not held among most erudite men. But there is another flaw – which even among the learned detracts from the credibility of the art – that is that the art itself does not foresee everything in that infinite variety of human vicissitudes. Therefore intelligent men reject the art, that is, they deny that a universal and lasting science can consist of particular observations of a few events, as if medicine healed all illnesses, or as if political wisdom could provide for all calamities of the state and remedy all troubles. Nevertheless it has to be admitted that either of those arts has many precepts that are true and immovable and useful for

---

[1] Jakob Milich (1501–59) presided as Dean of the arts faculty at the promotion of Masters on 18 July 1535.
[2] Reading *ullum* for *ullam*.

life. In the same way the art of divination has some true and lasting signs – maybe fewer than that of the doctors (and I do not conceal this), for the former deals with things that are far removed from our range of sight; and as it decides on the temperaments and morals of men and predicts the greatest future vicissitudes in the life of things, it appears to be of divine nature. Therefore, although there are not as many proofs for this art as for other less weighty ones, this should be conceded to the greatness of the art. And with all the greater care any aspect, however small, of this art – which the gods have shown to men – needs to be preserved, and with all the greater zeal the mind needs to be turned towards these indications, which are certain, for they have the greatest power and varied benefit for life. Those who attempt to embellish or aggrandise the arts with false opinions are not only impertinent but also wicked. Clearly I do not believe that indications of every event are certain, but I also assert that there are many certain and in only the smallest degree fallacious indications; if someone were to pay attention to them, he would have a great support for ruling nature and for managing most of fortune's onslaughts. Favorinus, too, in Gellius [*The Attic Nights* XIV.1], belittles this art, and says that some few things are foreseen rather broadly (*pachymeresteron*). Not only do I not refute this, but I even applaud it that he said *pachymeresteron*; he gave a splendid commendation to the art, since he says that some extraordinary things in nature or morals can be perceived; and from these, wise men judge many things thereafter. You can see in morals how much is divined from some gesture or laughter. So, if certain marks of the most important things are imprinted in nature, many interpretations can be taken from them later.

Perhaps astrology would not have to be considered an art if it consisted only of conjectures; but it is the art of things that do not fail. Indeed this art itself, like medicine and politics, first consists of certain observations, and then many interpretations proceed from these. At the birth of Catiline the astrologer saw the ominous positions and aspects of the planets which signify cruelty of the mind, audacity, perverted morals and restless and calamitous decisions. It is possible[3] that he could not foretell with certainty that, under Cicero's consulate, Catiline would lead an insurrection, and that later he would be killed in the line of battle at the foot of the Apennines. However, having noticed these unpropitious signs, which are in truth certain, he could conjecture that he would be a disruptive and mutinous citizen and that his life would have a tragic ending. Thus some signs which

3 Reading *Fas* for *Fac*.

do not fail can be judged broadly (*pachymeresteron*) in temperaments and morals. So this art is not to be spurned for the reason that it does not foresee everything. How little is certain in the other best arts, and I am not only speaking of medicine and politics. Is the entire science of meteorology to be disparaged, therefore, because it contains few proofs and accomplishes most things by conjecture? How often do we not err in agriculture; should the fields therefore not be tended? Rather, let us make use of the benefits of the arts, and contemplate how far the human mind can advance. As for me, it is not only the usefulness in these arts that delights me (which I also observe in healing and in other things), but much more the fact that when I contemplate the marvellous agreement of the heavenly bodies with those below, that very order and harmony remind me that the world is not driven by chance, but guided by divine providence.

I wanted to say these things in reply to the abuse of the crowds before speaking of the art. In the beginning we need to establish something like a definition of astrology, in order to distinguish it from the superstitious divinations of which Ptolemy says [*Tetrabiblos* 111] that no cause can be assigned to them (*anaitiologētous*). Astrology is a part of natural philosophy, which teaches what effects the light of the stars has on the elements and on mixed bodies, and which temperaments, alterations or inclinations it contrives. And since morals, studies, decisions and vicissitudes often re-echo inclinations, 'each follows the elements of his nature', as it is said. Therefore astrology shows some of the stars' meanings. If it is evident that the constellations have some effects, it clearly has to be granted that this art is a part of natural philosophy, just as the doctors' predictions are. I shall not be talking at length about that part, but I shall refer to only the one statement by Galen on this point; he not only reproves those who deny that the bodies here below are affected by the heavenly light, but severely rebukes them, saying that it is sophistry to deny manifest experience. Consequently he says also that he was won over by experience, and that he attributes great power over the bodies below to the light, and he most severely reproaches those who disagree.

Or is there perhaps any doubt that the alternation of summer and winter is caused by the approaching and the moving away of the sun, that the light of the sun heats and dries, while the moon humidifies? If these things are evident in these two brightest stars, why should we believe that the others are made without purpose? It is demonstrated by continuous experience that remarkable conjunctions have remarkable effects, and this shows itself plainly in the weather. In the year twenty-four we saw the conjunction of planets in a wet sign, and everywhere all the waters swelled, and for the whole of two years there was wet weather.[4] This summer Jupiter in Pisces and Mars in Taurus brought on, in everyone's opinion, frequent rains and unwholesome varieties of weather. I could quote many more examples if the lack of time did not prevent it. In truth there is no doubt that the light of the sun, moon and the other planets diversifies weather, and afflicts the air and our bodies. The facts themselves confirm that there is the greatest power in herbs, in metals and in the most despised things, and this saying by the ancient poet [Hesiod, *Works and Days* 41] is praised with justification: 'that there is great boon even in the mallow and the asphodel (*hotti kai en malachēi kai asphodelōi mega oneiar*)'. If that is so, why should we believe that these most beautiful lights are made without purpose, given that nothing is more outstanding by nature or more powerful than light? And indeed, do not the laws of the motions themselves indicate that the light of the sun and the moon is modified by the appearance of the other planets?[5] Mercury and Venus never move far away from the sun. The higher planets move away in such a way that they nevertheless always meet with the sun in their epicycles half way to the apogee. Finally, Hippocrates, too, bears witness that weather is brought about and changed by the power of the stars. He teaches that not only the difference between regions has its origin in heavenly causes, but also the difference in customs between various regions [*Airs, Waters, Places*]. If these things are certain, it is manifest that the foundation of the art is true and fixed, that is that heavenly light has great influence in tempering and changing the elements and the mixed bodies. Furthermore, it is also proved by this obvious tempering that the light of the various planets is different: that of Saturn is melancholy, that of Jupiter temperate, that of Mars choleric, that of the sun vivifying, that of Mercury rather dry, and that of Venus and of the moon rather humid. And these, in various combinations, form wonderful mixtures, just as in remedies various herbs are mixed, and voices in song. I have explained these things only briefly, not only because one needs to keep track of time, but also because I thought that they were sufficiently demonstrated for very learned men like you.

[4] In February 1524 all planets moved into the region of the sky known as Pisces, and this 'conjunction' was commonly believed to lead to a deluge. Great pamphlet wars broke out concerning the meaning of this conjunction, one of whose authors was Johannes Stöffler (1452–1531), Melanchthon's erstwhile teacher. For a recent study on the rôle of Lutherans in this pamphlet war, see '*Astrologi Hallucinati*', *Stars and the End of the World in Luther's Time*, ed. Paola Zambelli (Berlin, 1986).

[5] Reading *ipsae* for *ipse*.

Therefore I now come to the other part, that is, to the usefulness [of astrology]. In truth, I do not believe that anyone is so superstitious as to deny that observations of the stars are employed in medicine. Since there are precepts on these things, and they are also known by experience, I shall not discuss them any longer. But how much greater is the usefulness, not only for sick bodies, but much more for the state, of considering the causes or meanings of the greatest changes, so that we can adapt our decisions to them, and mitigate misfortunes by art. For Plato says truthfully that the revolutions of the stars cause various vicissitudes, not only for animated bodies, but also for the entire nature of things, the life of men, empires and states. Just as farmers are enjoined to observe the signs of storms, so the great men in the state must understand and consider the signs of change. And indeed, the signs taken from morals and inclinations are collected in political writings, just as doctors foretell diseases from intemperance or from corruption of the humours. It is of great benefit to a great and wise man to pay attention to these heavenly signs as well, so that he can some-how manage fate and beware savage storms, or at least mitigate them. For it is said rightly that 'He who is prudent, prepares his mind for any fate, and he can ease foreseen calamity by his art.' For if these signs are not meant to be considered, why are they written and painted on the sky by divine providence? Since God has engraved these marks in the sky in order to announce great upheavals for the states, it is impiety to turn one's mind away from their observation. What are eclipses, conjunctions, portents, meteors or comets if not oracles of God which threaten[6] great calamities and changes for the life of men? If anyone spurns them, he rejects God's warnings. That great man in the Holy Scriptures [Jeremiah 10:2] teaches to what extent they are to be feared, and what great store is altogether to be set by heavenly signs, so that the mind be not deceived by impious confidence or despair. Just as in agriculture or in navigation it is not irreligious to follow the forecast of weather, so it is pious and profitable in the administration of things to consider the natural signs which God has set up in order to make us more watchful and to sharpen our attention.

But let us look at individual morals. If someone understands the tendencies of his nature, he is able to nourish and strengthen what is good, and to avoid vices by diligence and reason. For what Ptolemy says is true, namely that the wise soul assists the labour of heaven, just as the best farmer in ploughing and cleansing assists nature. This is evident in the care for one's

[6] Reading *minitantur* for *minitatur*.

health, in choosing a way of life or type of studies, and in undertaking business that is either fitting or unfit for one's intellect. If the parents of the Curiati or those of Anthony had sufficiently understood the character of their sons, they could have bent their wild and restless minds to moderation by extraordinary skill. We have heard that King Philip of Macedon, who was particularly artful, when he noticed that his son Alexander had a nature that was not base, but nevertheless rather harsh and impatient of authority, and when he saw that he would not bear stern control, took the decision of moving him to gentleness and affability by teaching and philosophy. By this procedure he cultivated his nature to such an extent that despite his career of victories there was hardly anyone more humane and more moderate. Thus it is profitable to see where his nature leads a person, so that he may be moved to virtue by the appropriate discipline, and turned away from vice. I could list other economic benefits as well, but it would take too long to pursue those. Therefore you candidates, who already publicly devote yourselves to philosophy, remember that, as you have to embrace, cherish and honour to the utmost of your ability the other parts of philosophy, this part, too, is to be loved. It is not only stupid but perverse to strive for praise of one's intellect by deriding the good arts. For good men have to honour as well as they can the distinguished arts that are useful for life, so that as many as possible be attracted to studying them. I have spoken.

15 On philosophy (1536)

CR XI, 278–84

Oration on philosophy, held when conferring the degree of Master to some learned and honourable young men. Philip Melanchthon, 1536[1]

I hope that my character is sufficiently familiar and well known to all of you so that I can easily convince you that I have not taken on the office of speaking again out of impudence, or confidence in my intellect or meddlesomeness of any kind. For it was because it was allotted to me by that excellent man, Jakob Milich, the dean of our college, who is most dear to me because of his outstanding virtue, and because of our fellowship in studying and many duties, that I was moved by the motive of duty to obey my friend's wish. I am not to such an extent a Suffenus,[2] nor so ridiculously taken with myself as to be unaware that there are many in this university who are both more suitable by their personality, and better prepared for speaking with erudition than I am, and truly I give them plentiful praise for their intellect and erudition. However, I did not want to appear capricious, since a great friend solicits this duty from me. Indeed, I do not want to make excuses any longer, for I believe that my character is sufficiently approved of by you. And they are mainly of the kind where this little verse is appropriate: *Tropos esth' ho peithōn tou legontos, ou logos*, which means that the speaker's character, not his speech, convinces the audience [Menander, *Fragment* 407.7].

It is established with excellent judgement that on these festive occasions there is a speech either about studies or in praise of the virtues. Therefore, in order to contribute a topic appropriate to this occasion, and to say something about the merit and usefulness of the arts which philosophy professes, I have set up an oration in which I shall demonstrate that the Church has need of liberal education, and not only of knowledge of grammar, but also of the skill of many other arts and of philosophy. Since we have established this, even if other subjects present themselves for discussion, good minds must nevertheless give attention mainly and most zealously to the purpose of applying their studies to supporting and honouring the Church; for to the good nothing must be sweeter than the name of the Church, and

---

[1] As Dean of the arts faculty, Melanchthon presided over the promotion of Masters in January 1536.
[2] Suffenus is a character ridiculed as a bad poet in Catullus, *Poems*, 14.19: cf. Erasmus, *Adages*, II.v.12.

nothing dearer than it. This reason must encourage and incite us most to strive, with the greatest exertion of our minds, for perfect knowledge, from which some benefit for the state or the Church may derive. Indeed, for us professors no oration on another subject is worthier, nor is there anything more useful for those who are good and devoted to learning than to contemplate in their minds the aim and the goal of the most honourable course to which they must relate their efforts.

With regard to these things, the merit and power of the arts themselves cannot be observed better in any other way than when we see how much need there is for them in the Church, with how much darkness ignorance overwhelms religion, and how much devastation, what fearful destruction of churches, and how much savageness and confusion of the entire human race it brings about. If anyone considers these things, then he can indeed esteem the great power and dignity of the arts and of doctrine.

Although no oration can be devised that is a match for such great things, nevertheless the young – because base conjectures on this matter are often propagated by the inexperienced – need to be admonished and reassured that, although it is discussed by the teachers in the schools daily, nevertheless the oration held in this place on behalf of the state must have more authority. For it is the common judgement of all the most learned men in this assembly, which it would be extremely insolent to spurn. Therefore, as I shall be saying things both necessary for the state and beneficial for you, and as this my voice sets out the common judgement of all, I ask you to listen to me diligently because of your humanity, and to be warned not only to flee the foolish judgements of those who do not believe that the Church needs liberal education at all, just as the companions of Ulysses sailed past the Sirens with their ears plugged [*Odyssey* XII.158ff.], but also to execrate those people themselves like the most loathesome pests and fearful monsters. Moreover, it should sharpen and arouse the concern for learning that your studies are relevant to the Church and the state, and not only private benefit is sought from them.

Altogether the most prevalent in an Iliad of ills[3] is ignorant theology. For it is a miscellaneous teaching, in which the great things are not explained clearly, things that should be separated are mingled together, and on the other hand those that nature claims should be joined are pulled apart; often contradictory things are said, and things that are merely similar are seized

---

[3] 'Ilias malorum' signifies the simultaneous occurrence of great catastrophes. For classical sources for this phrase, see Erasmus, *Adages*, I.iii.26.

in preference to those that are true and proper. Finally, the entire teaching is monstrous, and similar to the painting in Horace: 'If the painter chose to join a human head to the neck of a horse, and to spread feathers of many a hue'[4] [*Art of Poetry* I.1f.]. Nothing in it is consistent, and neither the beginning nor the progress nor the conclusion can be discerned. Such a teaching cannot fail to produce endless scattering and endless dispersion [Cicero, *Republic* II.4.7], because in such a confusion each one understands something different, and, while each defends his own dream, there are struggles and discord. In the meantime the wavering conscience is forsaken. And since no Furies torture the mind more violently than this doubt about religion, finally all of religion is cast aside in hatred, and their minds become impious and Epicurean.

Since, therefore, ignorant theology has so many ills, it is easy to judge that the Church has need of many great arts. For in order to judge and to explain correctly and distinctly complicated and obscure things, it is not sufficient to know the common precepts of grammar and dialectic, but varied knowledge is needed; for many things are to be taken from natural philosophy, and many are to be contributed to Christian teaching from moral philosophy.

Furthermore, there are two things for the acquiring of which great and varied knowledge and long practice in many arts are necessary, namely method and style of discourse. For no one can become a master of method, unless he is well and rightly versed in philosophy – indeed in that one kind of philosophy that is alien to sophistry, searches for and discloses truth properly and by the right path. Those who are well versed in these studies, and have obtained for themselves the habit (*hexin*) of relating to method everything that they want to understand or teach to others, also know how to represent methods in religious discussions, how to clear up what is complicated, pull together what is scattered and shed light on what is obscure and ambiguous.

Great and abundant knowledge is also needed for another purpose, namely for the shaping of a discourse, as all know who have occupied themselves even slightly with literature. No less study is needed in order to acquire this habit (*hexin*) of shaping method. It cannot be achieved by those who are not versed in most parts of philosophy. Those who have no practice in these would obtain only the shadow of method, even if they acquired

---

[4] As translated by H. Rushton Fairclough in Horace, *Satires, Epistles, Ars Poetica* (Cambridge MA, 1978), p. 451.

dialectic. None produces what is corrupt and sophistic more often than these men. Whereas they consider themselves masters of method, they nevertheless stray from the path, and they are, to use the Homeric word, blind watchmen (*alaoskopoi*).[5] Moreover, there is the need for philosophy not only because of method, or, as Plato calls it, inevitable rules for composition (*anankēn logographikēn*) [*Phaedrus* 264b7], but, as I said before, the theologian needs to adopt many things from natural philosophy, where the relation of the single parts is such that for those who strive for genuine knowledge it is not sufficient to choose a few aspects, but, as far as possible, the entire art needs to be known. The theologian who does not know of these most learned discussions on the soul, the senses, the causes of desires and emotions, on knowledge and on will, lacks a great tool. And he acts insolently who professes himself a dialectician if he is ignorant of those distinctions between causes that are only taught in natural philosophy and can only be understood by natural philosophers. Doubtless there is a cycle of arts by which they are all bound together and connected, so that in order to grasp individual ones many of the others have to be taken on. Therefore the Church has need of the entire cycle of sciences.

I do not believe that anyone is so foolish as not to notice that those who are versed in moral philosophy can practise more easily many parts of Christian doctrine. For if many things are similar, concerning laws, political morals, contracts and many of life's affairs, we are helped, not only by the order and method in philosophy, but also by understanding the things themselves carefully. If some things are dissimilar, then a comparison brings much light. Moreover, one who lacks a knowledge of natural philosophy practises moral philosophy like a lame man holding a ball.[6] Again, history and the exact computation of time periods require mathematics, but that part also needs to be joined to natural philosophy, for from the former, as from a source, many things in natural philosophy take their origin. And it is a form of barbarity, to say nothing else, to spurn the most beautiful arts concerned with the motions of the constellations that bring about for us the distinction between the years and seasons, announce many great things that are to come, and warn us in a useful way.

I am not ignorant of the fact that philosophy is one kind of teaching and theology another, nor do I want to mingle them in such a way as a cook

---

[5] The form *alaoskopoi* itself does not occur in Homer's works, but must refer to *alaoskopiē*, *Iliad*, x.515, meaning a blind man's watch; see also Erasmus, *Adages*, i.viii.41.

[6] A lame man holding a ball refers to somebody who cannot make right use of a thing, as in Cicero, *In Pisonem*, xxviii.69.

mixes together many sauces [Plautus, *Ghosts* 1.3.120], but I want to help the theologian in the management of method. For he will need to borrow many things from philosophy. If anyone does not trust this oration, let him consider the theology of the ignorant, and let him ponder with himself if he wants to let loose on the world such miscellaneous sophistry, and wants doubtful theology to be brought upon the Church. By ignorant I mean not only those who are unskilled in letters, such as the Anabaptists,[7] but also those impertinent men who, although they may declaim magnificently, nevertheless say nothing true, both because they are not used to the method, and because they do not grasp the origins of things sufficiently. Therefore, because they are not trained in philosophy, they do not understand sufficiently what theology professes, or to what extent it agrees with philosophy.

There is no need to recount here the ancients, who thoroughly overwhelmed Christian doctrine by the most foolish subtleties. I am searching for erudite philosophy, not the sophistries where there is nothing underneath. Therefore I said that one kind of philosophy has to be chosen which has as little as possible of sophistry and which preserves the true method; the teaching of Aristotle is of that kind. Nevertheless it still needs the addition, from elsewhere, of that most excellent part of philosophy that is concerned with the heavenly movements. For the other philosophical sects are full of sophistry and of absurd and false opinions, which are also harmful to the character. For the exaggerations of the Stoics, namely that good health, riches and similar things are not good, are altogether sophistic. *Apatheia*, too, a false and dangerous opinion on fate, is imaginary. Epicurus is not philosophising but being facetious when he asserts that everything exists by chance; he takes away the first cause, and disagrees in everything with the true teaching of the physicists. The Academy,[8] too, is to be shunned, which does not preserve method, and takes an excessive licence to overturn everything; those who strive to do this must by necessity conclude many things in a sophistic way. However, he who follows mainly Aristotle as a guide, and aspires to one, simple and the least sophistic teaching, can now and then take on something from other authors, too. For, just as the Muses, when they competed in song with the Sirens and defeated them, made themselves crowns out of their feathers, so it is also with the philosophical sects: even if one is most recommendable, we nevertheless

---

[7] For Anabaptists, see note 2, oration 1, p. 5.

[8] The Academy of Plato became renowned for its adherence to scepticism. See note 3, oration 9, p. 85.

now and then gather from others something true with which to embellish our opinion.

However, there will be occasion elsewhere to speak about the kinds of philosophy and the distinction between the sects. It seems to me that it also contributes to one's character to choose a sect that has the inclination to search for truth and not to disagree with it, and that loves moderate opinions and does not strive for the applause of the ignorant with tricks of reasoning and absurd opinions. This habit of seeking the applause of the unlearned is extremely bad, and those who bring it to the Holy Scriptures in truth cause great commotions there. The simple philosophy of which I am talking should first of all have the inclination not to assert anything without demonstration; thus it will easily escape absurd opinions, because they do not have demonstrations, but are only defended by sophistic tricks. Finally, on account of that, the knowledge of the Church is beneficial in general, because the ignorant are both more foolhardy and more heedless. Teaching puts a curb on oneself and accustoms one to diligence. For many things come to the mind of the erudite that are akin to the matter on which I have to pronounce: they see how easy it is to err and to be deceived, and they are accustomed from the other arts to seek for the sources of all matters, and to explain what appears to be opposed. And studies will be transformed into character; therefore the same diligence that is employed in inquiry creates modesty. Furthermore, it is evident what great danger foolhardiness and heedlessness bring, from examples of all ages and all states and in the Church itself, which has in the past been torn apart often by the thoughtless hastening of the ignorant, and is also being torn apart cruelly in our times.

Thus I first urge you, excellent listeners, to consider that your studies in truth concern the state and the Church, for the purity and harmony of teaching safeguard the welfare and harmony of men, and especially of the Church. Furthermore I entreat you, for the sake of the glory of God, which we must set before all other things, and for the sake of the welfare of the Church, which must be most dear to us, to resolve that the most excellent disciplines that philosophy contains are to be safeguarded, and to devote yourselves to them with greater effort, so that you may obtain for yourselves teaching that is genuine and useful for humankind.

When Epaminondas was asked what had been the most delightful thing to happen to him in his life, he replied that he derived the greatest pleasure from having freed his country from slavery while his parents were still alive, having defeated the Spartans in a great battle [Plutarch, *Moralia* 1098A]. He bears witness that both had brought him the greatest pleasure, the salvation of his country and the joy that the virtue and glory of their victorious son brought to his parents. Would that we were disposed in such a way towards the Church that we considered it the greatest pleasure to see it flourishing and peaceful, which is more truly our home-country than the country and the home that received us at birth, and to take it upon ourselves that the Church – that is the heavenly angels and the entire assembly of the pious, whom one should revere and love like one's parents – may obtain genuine pleasure from our good deeds.

On the other hand, let us resolve that no torment is harsher than to see the Church dispersed, and the angels and the assembly of the pious thrown into mourning and grief by our desires. I am not speaking of rewards here, for we should be moved by virtue itself, and we need to hold dear the love of the Church and the regard for the duty that is due to God. However, for those who learn properly rewards will not be lacking, for God says: 'For them that honour me I will honour' [1 Samuel 2:30]. If we are Christians, we have to do our duty in the hope that we may feel that God cares for us, so that we and our children be not needy. Indeed, you should know that it is because of our cause, and not that of the tyrants or of those who hate pious studies, that the entire nature of things is safeguarded by God: the sun rises and the changes of the seasons occur in order to make the fields fertile. The Stoics said rightly that all belongs to God, but that the philosophers are God's friends; therefore all belongs to the philosophers. So let us defend with great spirit the study of letters, and let us consider ourselves put in our position by divine providence, and because of that, let us do our duty with greater care, and let us expect the reward for our toils from God. I have spoken.

16 On natural philosophy (1542)

CR XI, 555–60

Oration on natural philosophy, held at Wittenberg[1]

Peace is the best of all things 'that it is given to man to know, peace alone triumphs' [Silius Italicus, *Punica* II]. It is more powerful than countless other things, says the poet, and most of all among citizens. Let us therefore entreat God for everlasting peace, for the sake of the Church that is otherwise quite badly affected, and is retaining only some small remnants of erudition. And let us now give thanks to God, the father of our liberator Jesus Christ, for calming the panic (*panikon*) unrest that has originated nearby;[2] I shall say very little on that, because it is now to be hoped that the whole matter will be forgiven. But let us be warned by that danger, and let us therefore worship God with greater piety and diligence, so that He assist the Church and the studies that are necessary for humankind. We should achieve this more easily if we do not abuse leisure for the purpose of luxury or of vile pleasures, but instead keep in view the goal for which God has granted peace to the state, so that the young be educated and instructed, and ruled by discipline, and that we apply greater assiduity in this our gowned profession.

As it is usual to speak of a variety of either arts or virtues at this point in these assemblies in order to encourage you, so I, too, am going to hold an oration, this time on the science of natural philosophy. It both takes its first beginnings from mathematics, and again and again borrows demonstrations from it. Therefore I have spoken of mathematics often at other times and recently. Perhaps, however, just as soldiers are inflamed not so much by words as by their nature and grief, and by the greatness of the cause – as it is said in Sallust [*The War with Catiline* LVIII. I] – words do not supply virtue. In the same way this our trifling speech for kindling minds does not provide that much impulse. But I nevertheless believe that they are profitable to good intellects for judging on the arts; they show the goals, teach where, so to speak, the hand should be guided in learning, and which subjects should most be chosen. These same admonitions are nevertheless conducive to kindling zeal. Nor do I believe that the habit of leaders is utterly useless,

---

[1] Another version of the *De doctrina physica* was delivered by Paul Eber in 1550: see CR XI, cols. 932–9.
[2] The battle at Wurzen, 1542.

who stir up the soldiers not only by a speech, but also by the bugle. By the kindness of God you have, in this University, most learned lecturers expounding natural philosophy, who are wont to attract eminent minds by the quality of the subject and to promote studies by their discourse. I do not doubt that natures that are not twisted will be kindled both by their judgement and by their authority. Since, then, an oration expressing the sentiment of the entire University is to be held, I reckon that I ought to speak of the same topic, so that you may understand that the sentiments of all agree on this kind of science. Virgil's verse is well known, in which it is said: 'Happy is he who can know the causes of things' [Virgil, *Georgics* II.490]. Even though human nature is weak, and cannot avoid disease or dangerous misfortunes by sagacity or diligence, we should nevertheless not believe that life is provided in vain with so many arts, which are after all shown to humankind by divine providence.

Sometimes the art of sailing is overcome by storms; nevertheless the art of building ships and of rowing is not shown therefore to be pointless. Sometimes the crops either perish from unseasonable heat, or are choked by rainfalls; nevertheless, agriculture is not to be abandoned. One could say the same about all the other arts. Medicine often succours life, and it drives out pernicious diseases, although sometimes the illness is stronger than the learned art. The starting-point of medicine is natural philosophy, which is usually taught to the young because of its many benfits, and of which I am yet to speak.

The knowledge of physicians includes very great learning that is salutary for human life. But not all can practise the same art: Aristotle says that the state consists of farmers and doctors, that is, the state has need of various arts.[3] Therefore the beginnings of natural philosophy are taught not only for the purpose of knowledge or pleasure, but in order that they may be of use for many aspects of life. Although not all practise the art of healing, nevertheless all who do not live like barbarians need some kind of general knowledge of the seeds of the body which we call the elements, of the temperaments, of the function and nature of the limbs and organs in humans, of the causes of diseases, and, I add further, of the movements of the heavens and the various effects that accompany the motions. I bear in mind that this is also knowledge for mothers of families, because it is necessary for the protection of health and for education. All have need of some kind of household science for protecting their health and for

[3] See note 3, oration 2, p. 10.

managing their way of life. And it is proper for the educated to know the sources of arguments which, although they appear trifling, can nevertheless teach the studious many things. Varro was not a doctor by profession, but nevertheless, by his reason and diligence, he protected himself and his company in a province that was infested by a destructive plague. He ordered that all windows be barricaded, especially those on the north side from where the harsher winds blow. As you can all understand, he had taken this advice from the basic precepts that are taught in natural philosophy on the difference between the winds.

Galen recounts that the Emperor Antoninus[4] usually rid himself of repletion of the stomach by fasting for a day and taking one *cyathus* of wine, into which he had sprinkled some pepper. These are household remedies, but we cannot use them correctly without knowledge of natural philosophy. For one needs to ask Antoninus the reasons why he used substances that are almost inflaming: he had noticed that for him the repletion originated from the cold in the stomach. How many ancient and recent leaders could I recite who, although they did not practise medicine, nevertheless by this philosophy took care of their own health and that of others. Alexander had extraordinary eagerness in this field, knowing that Achilles, too, had learnt medicine from Chiron, as we read in Homer [*Iliad*, XI.831f.]. Now I am not speaking about the entire art of physicians, but of the general and household science that we cannot do without, if we do not want to live like wild beasts.

Let me also add some examples from the Church. Noah, Abraham, the Prophets and the Apostles commanded the same science of natural philosophy. For, in order that they would stand out from among the other men by their dignity and could also bind many to themselves by their services, it was God's will that they join the medical art to the profession of God's Gospel, and He directed their hands towards healing. Do not consider it unseemly for yourselves to imitate the studies of such great men, who – although they upheld other difficult duties – inquired into the workings and temperaments of the human body, and into remedies for diseases; some perhaps more studiously than others, but nevertheless they all understood that general kind of natural philosophy that cannot be taught without letters.

It may be the foremost benefit that it is a small part of medicine, but there are many other reasons why natural philosophy is taught to the young. A

---

[4] Reading *Antoninus* for *Antonius*, which refers to the Emperor Marcus Aurelius Antoninus (160–81 AD).

great part of ethical disputations spreads from it, because the causes of the virtues are to be sought in the nature of man. And so in civil business, too, often something can be gained from the science of natural philosophy. And Plato says [*Phaedrus* 270] that Pericles surpassed other orators to such an extent because he had listened assiduously to the physicist Anaxagoras. Well-informed natural philosophy also strengthens worthy sentiments on God and on providence, for from the teaching of the causes we infer that there is an eternal, single mind, of great power, wise and the best, and, as Plato says, the cause of the good in nature. It is of no use for instruction to strengthen weak and listless minds by these arguments. Not infrequently I weigh in my mind all the reasonings of the natural philosophers concerning God, so that I can more clearly refute the tricks of false opinions, which the Epicureans or Academics spread over the eyes of men. We learn from the natural philosophers that nature that has understanding cannot originate from the irrational, or be produced by chance. The human mind is an understanding nature, and indeed in being born it brings with it some unchangeable distinction between what is worthy and what is vile. Therefore it has to take its origin from some more outstanding and eternal mind. Who does not see that the reflection on other arguments is of great benefit? But I agree that the reflections need to be led by a heavenly voice, in which God reveals more clearly both His nature and His will.

Therefore I come to the doctrine of the Church. While I know that in the past the Manicheans and several others, bewitched by fanatic madness, brought about great upheavals in the Church by badly constructed opinions of natural philosophers, there is nevertheless no doubt that the Church has need of well-informed and genuine natural philosophy. If some have foolishly made a disturbance one should execrate the madness of these men, and not censure the art which they themselves have shamefully perverted. And they can be more easily refuted by producing true demonstrations. Examples also show that the ancient commentators could not do without natural philosophy. Thus Gregory of Nyssa published a long commentary on the parts of man.[5] And how much physiology is there in other authors, when they discuss the parts and duties of the soul! So many times, in most serious theological controversies, one has to speak of the causes, the variety of which is taught learnedly only in natural philosophy.

---

[5] The *De natura hominis* of Nemesius of Emesa circulated under the name of Gregory of Nyssa in this period: see H. B. Wicher, 'Nemesius Emesenus', *Catalogus Translationum et Commentariorum* 6 (1986), 31–72.

As for maintaining a distinction between the parts of the soul, when there is such discord between them, the mind retains God's law engraved on it, it shows God's kindness and teaches that punishment threatens for disobedience. However, the other part of the soul, which is called the appetitive soul, the seat of which is in the heart, is neither moved by kindness to love God constantly, nor does it tremble when it is admonished by horrid examples of all ages to fear an angry and avenging God. Often one has to speak about the origins and seats of the affections, and one has to distinguish learnedly between affection (*storgas*) and corrupt emotions. One who is not versed in the natural philosophy that is taught in the schools will never explain these things skilfully.

Sometimes we also see ancient writers who are not vulgar get stuck in these subjects as if in mud,[6] because of their ignorance of physics. Many times in the Church a dispute about fate is begun. How will one who is inexperienced in natural philosophy speak about this, how will he overthrow the axioms of the Stoics or the Peripatetics, which he does not know? It is not only in the matters of which I have spoken that natural philosophy is of use; in the explanation of the science of the heavens one often happens upon natural-philosophical passages, where a knowledge of these elements is a great support for the expounder, just as a certain ability to paint is for the architect or the sculptor. Erudition that includes not only the knowledge of words, but also some variety of things, is a great ornament for the Church. For it is neither possible to form a judgement without the consideration and comparison of many things, nor does one's oration have vigour or strength if it does not arise from good things. For the verse is well known: 'Knowing is the beginning and source of writing properly' [Horace, *Art of Poetry* 309]. Therefore natural philosophy is also to be embraced, if we do not want the Church to be ignorant, and in this matter we have to give attention to many things. Because they do not restrain their minds with the fixed limits of the sciences, the ignorant stray easily from the path, and it is more difficult to correct them, because they neither know nor observe the laws which one has to follow in teaching like a pattern, and they do not have true hypotheses. If we want to avoid these disadvantages there certainly is great need for us to improve and refine our minds by true erudition. You know what the vagaries of the Anabaptists[7] are like, which, it is evident, have originated only from the illiterate and are propagated by them. If the light

---

[6] For this saying, see note 4, oration 11, p. 102.   [7] For Anabaptists, see note 2, oration 1, p. 5.

of erudition became extinct in the Church, various kinds of madness would ensue, as has happened before. The rulers would need to foster the study of letters, but since few are affected by this care, let us exert ourselves all the more strongly, so that we may protect this embellishment of the Church as much as we can. This is the proper duty for our rank, which God will assist and honour with rewards, even though we are disregarded by the Centaurs,[8] and much hardship is to be borne. But you know that it is the duty of virtue to do what is right and be of use to others, even though the multitude may be ungrateful. We most need to be strengthened in this way in the Church, where hatred against the well-deserving is sharp and violent. What thanks were rendered to Isaiah or Jeremiah for the highest and divine services? Let us rouse ourselves by their example to preserving the beneficial teaching for posterity, and let us acknowledge that God will not fail His army, nor will He permit that the heavenly teaching be utterly destroyed. Let us sustain and encourage ourselves by this hope in the tribulations that accompany our profession. I have spoken.

[8] Centaurs were considered barbaric and savage: see, for instance, the entries on centaurs in Erasmus' *Adages*.

17 Dedicatory letter to Melanchthon's *Epitome of Moral Philosophy*

CR III, 359–61

Greetings from Philip Melanchthon to Christianus Pontanus of Wittenberg[1]

Among other crimes, Socrates was reproached with mocking the inquiry into nature and rejecting physics, since he had transferred the studies of men to discussions of morals. Xenophon most weightily refutes this false accusation, and gives evidence that Socrates did not lure men away from physics, but rather he added to it that more learned teaching of morals, which was neglected by the others, since that part, too, being most useful for life, had need of method and art [*Memorabilia* 1.1.11–13]. Common precepts on morals are known generally, and some are born with us, but, nevertheless, there is doubtless the need for art and some more learned teaching for the purpose of deliberating on many duties, of grasping the true distinction between just and unjust actions and of understanding their origins. The nature of man needs to be examined; thought needs to be given to what is the order of the parts and what duty is ascribed to each by nature; furthermore the proper causes of actions are to be investigated. Socrates himself, discussing providence in Xenophon, assembles and points out the traces of divinity in nature in order to show not only that there is a god, but also that the god cares for human affairs [*Memorabilia* 1.4]. The origins of these disputations lie in physics. Just as Xenophon absolves Socrates, so, when we teach this part of philosophy concerning morals, we too do not want the young to be lured away from the rest of philosophy, but rather we want them to be attracted to it; I thought that by this beginning of the work readers should be enjoined to consider that there was also a need for art in teaching about morals, and that this art is like a small brook flowing from natural philosophy. Therefore they should not reckon that anyone can become a master in this field without the other parts of philosophy.

One needs to take pains with this part which contains the origins of the laws and of justice – from which not only lawyers borrow many precepts, but also theologians, whenever they discuss morals and the civic

---

[1] Christianus Pontanus was the son of Gregor Brück (1483–1557), jurist and chancellor to successive Electors of Saxony. For Melanchthon's oration on the life of Gregor Brück, see CR xII, cols. 350–60.

customs of life – as certainly its great usefulness demands, if we strive not for a shadow of the art, but for a firm knowledge, and therefore it will truly be necessary to join it to the rest of philosophy. Accordingly, although I did not want to stray too far afield, I related many topics in this *Epitome* to reasonings of natural philosophy for that purpose, so that the examples might show that these discussions of morals are mutilated and maimed without the rest of philosophy. I also declare that the customs will not become milder, nor can what is properly called moral (*ēthikon*), that is, moderation and gentleness, be achieved, unless liberal teaching is added to the common precepts – a teaching by which those of us who are accomplished and inured can discern the causes of duties, moderate all actions through reason, and temper them by some gentleness and elegance. The power of this matter is such that, if a person of mediocre disposition were instructed and inured in this way, he would not only be gentler in private company, but he would also be more moderate and diligent in the most important business of the state. For how many storms and how many tempests do foolish men not set in motion occasionally for no other reason than that they are not polished in this kind of learning, or, as the Greeks say, they are unprincipled (*anēthopoiētoi*) [Cicero, *Letters to Atticus* X.10.15]. Therefore, since I expounded Aristotle's *Ethics*,[2] I have added this commentary in which I follow not only Aristotle's meaning, but also his method. It is true that I have added some disputations that are more suited to our times, which I have collected because I considered them to be beneficial for morals, because they form one's judgements on much public business, and they prepare the students for civil law and for that part of theology that contains precepts on civic duties. I know that some admire other sects. For some look up to the Stoics as if to demi-gods. Valla attacks the other philosophers furiously, while he nevertheless gives Epicurus obvious approbation.[3] I, however, who have been engaged in these disputes among the sects for a long time and often at length turning them upside down (*anō kai katō strephōn*), as Plato enjoins one to do [*Gorgias* 511a], urgently admonish the young to reject Stoics and Epicureans and embrace the Peripatetic school. For even if Epicureanism and Stoicism are defended zealously and, so to speak, advertised, in order to do so it is necessary to mix

---

[2] Although the *Eudemian Ethics*, *Magna Moralia*, and *On Virtues* were available in this period, the *Nicomachean Ethics* was considered the central text of Aristotle's moral philosophy. C. B. Schmitt, 'Aristotle's Ethics in the Sixteenth Century: Some Preliminary Considerations', in his *The Aristotelian Tradition and Renaissance Universities* (London, 1984), VII, p. 94.

[3] See note 5, oration 3, p. 25.

in much sophistry, according to the saying by Euripides: 'The unjust word, sick in itself, needs wise remedies (*ho de adikos logos, noson en autoi, pharmakon deitai sophon*)' [*Fragment* 354]. Furthermore, false beliefs also harm morals, and the very habit of sophistry is destructive in many ways: it corrupts one's judgement, lures minds away from the love and study of propriety and simple truth, and accustoms the intellect to loving monstrous beliefs, and to striving to obfuscate rather than to explain things. In Aristotle, however, method governs the disputation and, so to speak, forces it within boundaries, so that it does not stray from demonstrations and the right path. For that reason it elicits true opinions and explains them in order and properly. Therefore Peripatetic philosophy is more useful, because of both the true opinions and the example of method. Aristotle himself said that beliefs that have no usefulness for life or morals should be rejected. Many Stoic ideas are of that kind, namely those on freedom from emotions, on fate and several others. When someone boasted that he had heard Carneades'[4] lectures for many years, someone else replied that one needed to bear in mind not for how long he had heard him, but whether he heard him when Carneades was an old man, as then his disputations were not prepared for idle show and for attracting applause, but for usefulness and the explanation of things – or, as Plutarch says: 'For what is useful and sociable (*pros to chresimon kai koinonikon*)' [*Moralia* 791B]. Therefore, since in choosing a type of teaching one has to choose what is correct, true, simple, steadfast, well ordered and useful for life, I believe that young minds need to be instructed chiefly with Aristotelian doctrine, which in these qualities surpasses all other sects. Why? Because Aristotle's *Ethics* should also be loved, because he alone saw and understood that the virtues are middle states. By that description he instructs us most learnedly that the impulses of the mind must be bent to moderation and held back. Although I lacked the time for perfecting this little book, since I included very useful things, I nevertheless did not resist those who were demanding its publication. However, since in disputing I have always imitated limited and trivial dialectical forms, I made the decision to set out examples of method and of dialectical precepts also in these more pleasant subjects. And I reckon that this system of teaching is useful for schools. For it accustoms the mind to accuracy in expounding, which is particularly necessary in great and serious matters.

---

[4] Carneades of Cyrene (214–129 BC), a Greek philosopher of the Academy who argued that certain knowledge was not attainable but conclusions of varying degrees of certainty could be drawn. See, for instance, Cicero, *De natura deorum*, I.ii.4; I.v.11f.

To you, however, my Pontanus, I have dedicated this short treatise – first, because I owe much to your father, a most illustrious man, I thought that this expression of my fondness for you would please him; furthermore, since I also think well of your intellect, I particularly wanted to write to you in order to advise you and your peers, our students, that this kind of teaching particularly concerns the young. For truly, it cannot be understood what honour and what beauty there are in that moderation in morals, which we accurately call ethical (*ēthikēn*), unless our minds are imbued from adolescence with that liberal teaching, and they learn to curb and rule their impulses. Furthermore, the beauty can be understood more easily if, put in mind of the precepts, we also understand the examples in which uncommon virtue shines. And you have been given a most perfect example in your family, that is, the outstanding moderation and virtue of your father in every duty. Since in him to the excellence of his intellect were added the knowledge of many great arts, eloquence rewarded with every oratorical praise, and the knowledge of guiding the state, what great honour does his action, if I may say so, add to these qualities? For in him there shines a special modesty and elegance in the performance of every duty, because of which the other ornaments of his intellect have more dignity and grace. Even though his nature has great power, nevertheless without a variety of knowledge or erudition he would not have achieved this moral (*ēthikēn*) elegance. You see how he is on fire with enthusiasm for what is greatest. To the knowledge of law, in which he excels, he also joins the study of Christian doctrine, in order that he may understand it exceedingly well, and cherish it with the greatest piety. What eagerness he has to know the history of all ages! Just as Homer proclaims the fluency and richness of Ulysses' speech so much that he compares it to the snows of winter, so the eloquence of your father, Gregor, equipped with great fluency and variety of knowledge, is held in the greatest admiration among all the intelligent. The harmony and modesty in his behaviour, which we call moral (*ēthikēn*), wonderfully adorns these many successes. Whenever I look at him, it seems to me that I see one of these ancient heroic men who, because of their wisdom, knowledge, eloquence, political knowledge, seriousness of behaviour and elegance, held the first place in the state – as we read that Laelius, Crassus or Cicero did in Rome and Pericles and some others in Athens.[5]

---

[5] Gaius Laelius (*b. c.* 186 BC), a soldier who achieved heroic feats under Scipio in the Third Punic War. He was also a learned orator: see Cicero, *De amicitia*. Lucius Licinius Crassus (140–91 BC) was an outstanding orator and a supporter of aristocracy, and Cicero's exemplar: see Cicero, *De oratore*; Marcus Tullius Cicero (106–43 BC), Roman orator and statesman, supporter of Pompey the Great; Pericles (*c.* 495–429 BC), Athenian statesman who dominated politics.

Therefore, my Pontanus, look at your father with all your mind and all your heart, and when you learn to understand the beauty of his behaviour, attempt also to fashion it for yourself. For although his example is common to all nevertheless, since it touches you more closely, it must move your heart more powerfully. May the authority of your father's name spur you on! I believe that some seeds of these virtues continue in you, too, which it behoves you to cherish with art and reason, and to rouse and form. At the same time you should consider also that your father could not have achieved such honour – however powerful his nature – if he had not perfected it by erudition and a variety of knowledge. For that reason devote yourself, with all the powers of your intellect and your mind, to this discipline, the most perceptive study of which you see at your home. The state, too, should encourage you to do so with great concern; since it has need of the erudition and art to which your father has destined you; prepare yourself with all the effort of your mind, so that some time your intellect may be of use to the state, and you may add to your father's great offices. Farewell. In Wittenberg, 1537.

18 Preface to the *Commentary on the Soul* (1540)

CR III, 907–14

Greetings from Philip Melanchthon to the most honourable and outstanding man, Dominus Hieronymus Baumgartnerus, Senator of Nuremberg[1]

Some criticise and deride the titles which we have given to the little textbooks, although they were sufficiently substantial – on the world, the heavens, the nature of animated beings, on the soul – saying that these textbooks contain wholly trifling and trivial knowledge, and that they barely represent a shadow of these greatest things. For that reason they disdain most arrogantly these wretched writings and discussions. Although it has to be admitted that textbooks do not correspond to the vastness of such great things any more than the painting of the Roman state on the shield of Aeneas corresponded to the greatness of the deeds, virtues and power of the Roman people, nevertheless that knowledge is very necessary for life. Some elements and first principles are handed down in order that they stir up minds to ponder nature in some way. And we advance as far as we can, for God, too, has commanded us to contemplate His work, and He assists our study, for He has repeatedly disclosed many things that are useful for life. At the same time we notice the traces of God pressed upon nature, by which He wants to be known, and we learn the origins of worthy actions, and discover much help for life. It is profitable to know the disposition of bodies, the causes of diseases and some remedies. It is useful to comprehend the size of the Earth in one's mind, and to have a sequence of seasons, so that we grasp the distance of places from each other and the sequence of time, in religious doctrine as well as in all of history.

Socrates used to say that men know either nothing or little. I therefore have to admit that the subject that I relate is extremely uncertain. But let us consider what barbarity in life and what darkness in the Christian religion would follow if that faint and uncertain knowledge were lost and annihilated; thus manifold learning is needed for expounding it. Therefore let us not be deterred by the judgement of those who mock the schools from defending our Sparta to the utmost of our ability and from praying. Yet

---

[1] Hieronymus Baumgartnerus (1498–1565), senator of Nuremberg, who had also studied at the University of Wittenberg and knew Luther and Melanchthon personally. He promoted the Reformation in Nuremberg, helped establish the school of St Aegidius and founded a town library.

why is it that they despise us? Or rather do they hold some more outstanding kind of wisdom, or do they, by their own shrewdness, find ways
for accumulating riches or increasing their power? They practise tricks by
which they strive for the favour of the mighty, they are intent upon their
competitors and, as if in a wrestling-school, they watch where they could
overthrow them, or trip them up (*hyposkelizein*), as they say commonly.
They prefer that sophistry to our books and discussions. But I shall lay
aside this comparison. Let us draw – from these very books which they
mock – that moderation of the mind so that, as we know that God wants it,
minds may be improved by these, however slight, elements of the arts, and
that we may guard this moderation seriously and constantly.

Therefore the good will of those good men is to be praised who strive
to the utmost of their ability to bestow care on this matter of the greatest
usefulness for life. The kings and rulers of human affairs ought to rouse,
assist and guide the studies of citizens in this course of studies, and also to
add men capable of judging who should choose the most useful writings,
so that the young be accustomed to the best writings from the start. But we
see how lightly this concern touches the minds of the mighty, and the facts
show that the preservation of the arts is the favour of God alone, who
rouses the minds of citizens to this toil and this matter and service, while
those who excel in power search for pleasure and domination.

It is customary in the schools to teach some descriptions of the soul, and
to distinguish between their powers and functions. I praise this custom, and
I certainly do not fear the jeering of those who, believing that perhaps souls
are nothing, laugh at us who appear foolishly to put forth a teaching about
a thing unknown to us, and then say only commonplace things, which can
be grasped even without writings: namely how many senses there are,
which are the organs, which are the objects, and where the seats of the
organs are. Let them diminish and degrade these things as much
as they like, but nevertheless there is need for this basic knowledge. And
if they can grasp a part without writings, they themselves being already
improved by habit and by abiding among the learned, nevertheless many
other things have been examined by the masters and shown by divine
providence, and they cannot be known without writings. How great is the
benefit of knowing the distinction between the parts of the body in some
way? Since God employed so much skill in constructing the human body,
He certainly willed that such a wonderful work be contemplated, in order
that we consider that machines made and arranged so skilfully could in no

way have originated by chance, but that there is an eternal constructing mind. Indeed the skill of the workmanship cannot be described without writings nor recognised without knowledge.

Already in the explanation of religion there is the greatest need for having learned the distinctions between the powers of the soul. If the soul had kept that light and harmony which are bestowed upon it in its creation by divine providence there would be less need for other learned men, and it would examine its nature by its own sharpness of vision. However, now that – like some outstanding picture by Apelles[2] bespattered with mud – it lies in the body, buried in hideous darkness, there is the greatest need for knowledge that should bring it forth and put it in our view, and show how great a wound the enemy inflicted on it, who overthrew the first ancestor of humankind, and show also the traces of the divine image on it, and the remains of the heavenly gifts. While there is a need for erudition in order to expound all these great things in the Church, there also survive the commentaries on the soul of the ancient theologians, such as Gregory of Nyssa, who was the brother of Basil of Caesarea.[3]

This knowledge of the soul leads to piety. If we consider that the notions of the distinction between what is proper and what is vile are innate, it is necessary to acknowledge that this nature does not exist by chance. Again, the recognition of our misery curbs unruly minds if we consider that our souls, which God loved so much that He painted His knowledge and His image on them, have been torn away from, and deprived of, the heavenly light by the ruses of the devil, and that they are surrounded by frightful darkness, doubts about God, scorn of God and other horrid banes. Furthermore consider that they are subject to the cruelty and fury of the most haughty tyrant, the devil, who, out of savage hatred against the Son of God, drags with him as many souls as he can towards various disgraceful acts and into eternal destruction.

Whenever I think of this darkness of the soul, this weakness and sad servitude, I am almost[4] out of my mind with horror. But with what grief and commotion of the mind need we reckon that the first ancestors thought the same; since they had seen the earlier light and harmony of nature and were endowed with the greatest excellence of intellect, they could reckon

---

[2] Apelles (4th century BC), the most famous and greatest painter of antiquity.
[3] Gregory of Nyssa (335–94) was the younger brother of Basil. The *De natura hominis* of Nemesius of Emesa circulated under the name of Gregory of Nyssa in this period: see note 5, oration 16, p. 136.
[4] Reading *paene* for *bene*.

more correctly the greatness of their disaster, and judge to what a cruel tyrant they were subject, both on account of their own fights and of the murders of sons and grandsons, and other disgraceful acts. Nor do I believe that any ancestors ever lived in greater and harsher sorrow and sadness than those first ones who, seeing these great ills, would have perished from grief if some sign of divine goodness had not lifted them up again. They had heard the promise of a victor over the most arrogant tyrant, and they realised that they were not rejected by God when they saw the sacrifices burn. By that consolation they sustained themselves in so many tribulations.

This somewhat basic teaching of the soul brings much weight to such great things, in order that we may contemplate them with more attention. One should not reckon that those who spurn this teaching, that is, those who do not want to behold their minds, are either troubled by these great tribulations or seek divine consolations. On the contrary, just as Psyche in the stories, who, having inquisitively touched[5] Cupid's arrows and wounded her finger, was aflame with love for him, and, out of her mind, followed him as he fled, so these people are carried away, blind, by their desires, and delight in their own error.

Since therefore the young have to be attracted to the teaching of the soul, I encouraged Doctor Jakob Milich[6] to select other parts of natural philosophy as well as this one and, having shared the work, we have prepared a small book, which we are now publishing – by no means as polished as I would wish it to be. For you know that these turbulent times do not grant me the leisure for cherishing these studies. There are many, fairly well-written, books on this topic, and therefore perhaps some may criticise our decision to publish this disordered hodge-podge, but I believe that the studies of the young also need to be encouraged by new writings. And as I have made an effort as best I could so that we would collect useful things, so I wish from my heart that others may defeat us and publish better works.

Moreover, it is useful for the young, for the purpose of sharpening and strengthening their judgement, to compare two or three works. For this reason I encourage them to examine a sample of earlier writings. I approve of the acumen of Vives, the diligence of Velcurio and the

---

[5] Reading *contrectatis* for *contractis.*
[6] Jakob Milich (1501–59) was born in Freiburg i. B. and attended the University of Vienna before arriving in Wittenberg in 1524. He became lecturer in mathematics in 1529, and obtained his doctorate in medicine in 1536 and became professor of anatomy at Wittenberg. For further information on his life, see Eusebius Menius, *Oratio de vita Jacobi Milichii* (Wittenberg, 1562).

abundance of Eisennach,[7] but I believe that this little book will be useful for understanding the others. For I have expounded some passages which were lacking in others, even though this entire discussion strikes against many subjects which are beyond human comprehension, and often suggests to moderate minds that, despite the great darkness of the human mind, they should desire to be ruled by heavenly doctrine and should embrace with all their hearts the saying: 'Thy word is a lamp unto my feet' [Psalms 119.105].

I preserve several opinions accepted in the schools, as well as the customary form of teaching, and, since we have to say some things slightly differently in the Church than they are said by Aristotle, I ask to be granted forgiveness if now and then I depart from an Aristotelian phrase. I would like the elegance of the language to be greater, for I do not feel that these things cannot be said elegantly. No part of nature affords a more magnificent discourse than the parts and actions of the soul. I pass over other reprimands, because whatever is in this I have undertaken intentionally for the good of the work, and I request that it be received with the sincerity which becomes the good and the learned. Nor will I bear it ill if someone corrects the faults courteously, mindful of the precept which is in Aristophanes: 'Question him gently. It is not proper to slander men who are poets as if they were bakers (*elenche, elenchou, loidoreisthai d'ou prepei/andras poiētas hōsper artopōlidas*).' [*Frogs*, 857f.]. If I live to do so, I shall myself alter some things. I earnestly request Joachim Camerarius,[8] an excellent man, that when this little book will be in the hands of the students, he may call it back for revision and criticism, in order that it profit the students.

I considered that this commentary should be published under the guidance of your name – for many other reasons, as well as because I wanted a token of my continuous love for you to exist in a written work which I judged would reach the hands of many. For as an individual I love you so much because of your outstanding virtue and erudition that I would not prefer anyone to you, and I also judge that the state owes much to you who protect with great faithfulness the Muses, sad because of the present storm.

[7] Juan Luis Vives (1492–1540), *De anima et vita* (Basle, 1538); Johannes Bernhardi Velcurio (lecturer in natural philosophy at Wittenberg, *d.* 1534), *Epitome physicae libri quatuor* (Basle, 1537); Jodocus Trutvetter von Eisennach (*d.* 1519), *Philosophiae naturalis summam* (Erfurt, 1517). For Velcurio, see Kusukawa, *The Transformation of Natural Philosophy*, pp. 110f.

[8] Joachim Camerarius (1500–74), a close friend of Melanchthon, who became the rector of the new Latin School, St Aegidius, at Nuremberg. He then taught at the universities of Tübingen and of Heidelberg. Melanchthon had corresponded frequently with Camerarius over his commentary on the *De anima*: see Kusukawa, *Transfomation of Natural Philosophy* pp. 83f.

While I was writing this and considering the disorder (*ataxian*) of the soul with diligence, I often thought about the disorder (*ataxiai*) in the realm which takes its origins from nowhere else than from this darkness of the soul and the obstinacy of its parts. And not infrequently I have lamented with tears the miserable condition of good men: in what difficulties and calamities are they when they are holding the reins of the state? Having spurned the authoritative part of the soul (*hēgemonikon*), the other powers rush where their blind desires drive them, and the poet says: 'The chariot is carried away by the horses, the team does not obey the reins' [Virgil, *Georgics* I.514]. In just the same way, the tyrants in one place and in another the masses – who, as Herodotus says, are also tyrants – do not often allow their impulses to be curbed by lawful advice or the heavenly voice, which in truth must be the authoritative part (*hēgemonikon*) in every rule, in private and in public. For so many years the good have been praying that the Churches be lawfully counselled for, and that those who are sitting at the helm may provide, so that scholarship may not perish entirely, and that religious doctrine not be extinguished. And we urge strongly that harmony and discipline be restored. But it clearly happens to us as is said in the Greek verse: 'Man is like a ship beseeching a rock'(*anēr eoike naus hiketeuein petran*) [*Suida*] or even more as it is said in the *Apology* of Antisthenes, where the hares who form an assembly with the lions receive a very sad teacher's fee (*didaktra*); for they are devoured for their service.

Although that is how things are, my Hieronymus, let us nevertheless by all means do what the authoritative part (*hēgemonikon*) commands; as much as we can, let us attempt to counsel the Church and posterity, each in his place, and let us not desert our posts. Therefore, do not weary of encouraging scholarship, which – if ever it did – truly has need of the protection of excellent men. Erudition is such a great ornament for the Church that, once it is lost, it is impossible for the most impenetrable darkness not to follow. Even though there are other, more outstanding, qualities, such as the true practice of faith, scholarship nevertheless sheds great light on the Gospel, particularly if the Church has sane judges and arbitrators (*agōnothetas kai brabeutas*) of studies, who should rule the impulses of minds and prevent that they be carried beyond the limits. For many and great disputes are held in the Church, which cannot be expounded without erudition. Who would not deplore human impiety? With what solicitude are riches and pleasures acquired, and with what diligence! An apprenticeship of how many years is needed for learning despicable tricks? This great matter is neglected, namely that we are born and reborn for the one purpose of transmitting, correctly and clearly, the heavenly teaching to others. While this criminal negligence is to be abominated in everyone, in the rulers it is truly the murder of the Church not to support the studies of scholarship; and God will punish this with great public misfortunes. Now Christ, suffering hunger and thirst, goes from one to another and requests that the studies of His Church be preserved, that men capable of teaching be supported and that worthy minds be encouraged and favoured. But all too few in the state are moved by the complaints and by the voice of Christ. Scholarship is held in hatred by the mighty everywhere, for the reason that it is considered an opponent of tyranny. Uneducated and Epicurean men enjoy the riches of the Churches. In all realms monstrous cruelty is deployed against men who are learned, pious and upright in their sentiments. Everywhere poor scholars are neglected, and this is done intentionally, so that studies be destroyed. Therefore one needs to pray to God that He stir up the minds of some who are in command to the solicitude that they do not abandon studies, and that He strengthen the scholars, lest they be weakened in their minds and desert the warfare for which they are chosen by divine providence.

You, however, my Hieronymus, may you be – as you already are – one who provides encouragement and support for your citizens in striving for a knowledge that is useful for life. In this matter, consider that you are doing a duty that is most pleasing to God, and that you are doing a service not only to your country, but – what is greater – to the Church and for posterity, and that your service will be extolled, in the presence of Christ and in the assembly of the angels, prophets and Apostles, with true and eternal praise, which I do not doubt you will prefer by far to any trophy made by human hands.

But I have gone on for longer with this exhortation than I intended, since there is no need for it with you, who by your sagacity and erudition can see best of all both the diseases of the state and which parts particularly have to be healed and protected by politicians. I believe that I have already said enough of this little book. It is a feeble gift, not perhaps appropriate for your person. For, if the nature of the soul could be disclosed to a sufficient degree, a picture in which the soul, depicted in vivid colours, would be set out before the eyes would be a most magnificent and splendid gift. But in this darkness of the human mind its feeble shadow can barely be seen. Nevertheless these commonplace descriptions are to be handed on to the young, as I said, and I do not doubt that you approve of this use of this kind of teaching.

But there remain other schools for us, my Hieronymus, in which we can again philosophise about the soul together, when we enjoy the eternal fellowship of Christ and of that venerable assembly of the angels, prophets and Apostles, as well as of the other faithful. There we will not ask Democritus if the soul is made of atoms, or Aristotle if it is a complete reality (*entelecheia*) [*On the Soul* 412a27], but the Architect Himself will show us the nature of the soul, at the same time the Archetype and the copy – that is, He will show us His nature, of which He willed the human being to be the image. In these schools we shall achieve complete knowledge of the soul; however, in order to reach these schools, the soul needs to be ruled and refined with some discipline. For that purpose this commonplace teaching is handed on. But then we shall reap the most splendid reward of this our study. We shall rejoice for having refuted the Epicurean ravings. We shall be glad to have defended what is true and pleasing to God. And for this duty we shall be adorned with prizes. The Epicureans, however, who in this mortal life have defied God, and, untroubled, have scorned God's proofs of immortality that were handed on, will receive just punishment for their madness. But although this disorderly lucubration does not in fact satisfy me everywhere, nevertheless we have attempted to pass on what is right and useful. Nor shall I bear it ill that I do not appear sufficiently sharp while I mainly follow the opinions sanctioned by the consensus of the learned. For I believe that religion needs to be applied in teaching, in order that we do not wantonly overthrow what has been taught correctly by others – as some believe that it is the greatest success of [their] intelligence to overturn craftily what others have said correctly, and they do not consider that they have God as observer and judge of their wantonness. Since He has ordered: 'Thou shalt not bear false witness' [Matthew 19:18], He will also severely punish sophistry by which the arts are thrown into disorder, a matter from which great calamity for morals follows. These games and the tricks of sophisms give me no pleasure, and I do not wish to be a 'lover of horses' as much as a 'lover of truth'.[9] But I leave the judgement to the readers, and I request that they apply frankness in judging as it is worthy of good and learned men. Live well and happily, farewell. At Wittenberg.

---

[9] 'Lover of horses' is a play on the name Philip in Greek: Phil-ippos (love-horse).

19 Preface to the *Book on the Soul* (1553)

CR VII, 1125–8

Greetings from Philip Melanchthon to the most illustrious Hieronymus Baumgartnerus, son of Hieronymus Baumgartnerus who excels by his wisdom and virtue[1]

The divine voice has prophesied both that in this languid and deranged dotage of the world there would be greater commotions of humankind than there had been before, and that nevertheless the Son of God, our Lord Jesus Christ, who was crucified for us and resurrected, would gather to Himself the eternal Church even among the ruins of empires. In this hope He wants us to cherish the study of doctrine, and He promised a home for the Church. Strengthened by this divine prophecy, let us prepare our minds to bear wisely the most saddening lacerations of realms and the frequent panic commotions, and let us hope nevertheless that the Church will not perish. Let us cherish the study of doctrine, encouraged by this consolation, and let us serve public society, each in his place. This consideration keeps old men in government so that they do not, in such violent storms, throw away the oars, so to speak. It must also rouse the younger to study more eagerly the doctrine necessary for the Church and for public life, because the divine word promises us that these labours will not be without effect. Therefore Paul says: 'in the Lord your labour is not in vain' [1 Corinthians 15:58]. That is, God will attend to preserving the Church and some abodes for you, and that your labours in teaching, ruling and studying be prosperous and beneficial for yourselves and for others. You can often hear that your father is strengthened by these divine admonitions in the most difficult labours, and it is proper for you, too, to consider them in order to rouse yourself for studying the discipline necessary for life.

However, I have again compiled the teaching on the distribution of the powers of the soul which needs to exist in the Church. When I published it earlier I sent it to your father, who had no need of these books, but I wanted there to be a testimony of his continuous good will towards me, as well as of my love for him. Now I convey this gift to you because it adds to these initial causes, since your age is already appropriate for learning the first principles of the discipline that I have described here. By sending you

---

[1] The son of Hieronymus Baumgartner, the addressee of the previous oration. See also note 1 of oration 9, p. 84.

these gifts I wanted to encourage you to proceed to the first principles of philosophy, and I strive, as much as I can, to show you and others the way in this part of philosophy.

I am certainly not ignorant of the fact that many mock this entire kind of teaching of natural philosophy. They say that the titles promise great wisdom about God, the world, the soul and the causes of changes in all bodies, but that then, once one has looked into the books, one finds only childish first principles. I acknowledge by all means that this knowledge is very thin and within narrow limits, and that it shows only a shadow of divine wisdom from afar. However, we who assent to the divine disclosures, and believe that there is an eternal life to follow after this mortal life, should reflect that we have two places of learning, and that they are made in that order.[2] And there is another eternal one, where God will be all for all, and will impart His wisdom and justice to us, where we shall see Him in person, and in the Son, the Word (*logōi*), we shall behold not only the ideas and causes of the workings of the world, but also the wonderful joining of divine and human nature, and the plan for the restoration of mankind. There we shall behold the Maker and contemplate the causes of things, and we shall have complete insight into nature. Thus, and not in any other way, the path is open to that companionship with God if first, in this mortal life, we begin with the first principles of that knowledge which He has handed on to us – and how much in it has He set before us that is incomprehensible, which He nevertheless wants us to consider in our foolishness? What wisdom of angels or men perceives of what kind the covenant is, so to speak, and the joining of divine and human nature in the Mediator? And nevertheless very frequently the divine voice addresses us[3] on this great matter. Indeed, in our greatest suffering it wills us to be cheered particularly by the contemplation of that covenant. This entire human nature would have perished utterly if the Son of God had not joined to Himself a fleshy mass of our kind, in which He, so to speak, carries us wretches resting on His shoulders and saves us. Therefore you are not destroyed, therefore all of mankind is not annihilated, because the Son of God joined this physical mass to Himself. Devout minds know that this is the true and greatest consolation, and they ponder the many causes of that wonderful covenant, although they do not

---

[2] According to the editors of the CR, there seems to be a lacuna here, since the sentences do not make clear sense here. Melanchthon seems to mean that there are two places of learning; one, the universities on earth, where the elements of knowledge are taught, albeit imperfectly; the other, in heaven, where complete insight into the workings of nature is possible.

[3] Reading *nos* for *nobis*.

understand all the causes of the divine plan, nor the way in which this wonderful joining is done.

Therefore we do not have insight into the nature of the soul, nor do we completely understand, in this life, its wonderful actions, the shaping of images in thinking, its reasonings, memory, recollections, choices, or the impulses of the heart that result from thoughts. Nevertheless, we need to lay the foundations of this knowledge; and the foundations are necessary for understanding the doctrine of the Church and for the guidance of life, as we frequently demonstrate later in the entire book. Much is learnt that is necessary for life, even though it is not possible to investigate the entire art that God employed in the construction. There will be another university in the heavenly companionship, where this wisdom should be learnt for all eternity. Now, however, the beginning is necessary. There is nothing in this entire working of the world in which so many manifest proofs of God and such evident admonishments are set before us as in the soul of man. In it the numbers, knowledge of order, reasoning and an eternal and fixed distinction between what is proper and what is vile demonstrate that this nature of things has not flown together by chance from Democritus' atoms, but that it was made by an eternal constructing mind. Therefore the soul of man teaches that God is the Maker of things, and that there is an intelligent being. And it teaches us what it should be like, that is, what fixed law there is in us; and it proves that God is just and an avenger, because He has established the order in us which cannot be destroyed, so that crimes are followed by cruel and horrendous torments of the heart. Such manifold wisdom shines in the contemplation of the soul, and it becomes even more manifest when we carefully behold the order and actions of its powers. But the benefits are mentioned frequently in the book, although no one has sufficient eloquence to set forth the greatness of the benefits provided by this knowledge of the soul, which I do not say is a perfect knowledge of the soul, but a beginning which beholds it from afar.

I recite the teaching customary in the universities, and collate it with the beliefs of the Church. I do not produce paradoxes or monstrous conjectures, nor am I so shaken and frightened by the trembling, however terrible, of the Baltic coast[4] as to consider it vile to survey what are the beliefs received from those who were more rational, and to contemplate the perversity of nature in those who – out of ambition or from malice – corrupt what has been handed down correctly, and invent new and monstrous beliefs. And I

---

[4] It seems that there occurred an earthquake on the Baltic coast around 1550.

have modestly followed the consensus of the more reasonable. Indeed, I strive to follow it in such a way that I should also like worthy and learned men everywhere to be censors and correctors of all my works – in particular your father and Joachim Camerarius. Many know what confusion of beliefs there was thirty years ago, when first the pile of monks,[5] if I may say so, was cleared away. I declare, with an excellent conscience, that I wanted to search for simple and correct beliefs in such a variety; nevertheless it is not surprising that I or others have slipped somewhere in so much darkness, particularly since debates about many and the greatest and most weighty matters are set in motion at the same time – as when, in a fire in some town, several buildings catch fire at the same time in different places. And it is very true what the wise poet said: 'No man is wise in relation to all things' (*Oudeis anthrōpōn estin hapanta sophos*). However, God wants there to be judgements in the Church; therefore I never shunned the judgements of our Churches, and I should not want to live like Timon,[6] separated from the learned and those who fear God. Therefore I have always declared that I would willingly listen to and follow the opinions of the learned, and would that I could often discuss doctrine with many of them.

I remember someone who said that he wanted to be a Stoic, and he only proclaimed this about himself with contentiousness (*philoneikiai*) in order to show that he professed a philosophy opposite to mine, and therefore he spread about in the court, very pleased with himself, some of his sayings which were not only paradoxical but also absurd. Although he was fatuous and both a knave and a fool (*kai mōrokakos*) by nature, he nevertheless kindled a fairly tempestuous loud applause (*krotothorybon*), as the Greeks say. But I have learnt often enough that the old saying is true which is quoted from Aeschylus: 'Folly is most often the sister of knavery' [Sophocles, fr. 925]. I did not reckon that, because of censors of that kind, I needed to desert these labours, since I believed that they were useful for those studying the proper arts.

To speak of this little book, I believe that the form of this work is properly designed for the use of universities, and I do not doubt that most things are handed on correctly. However, I have woven in some descriptions of the principal parts of the human body. For certainly the powers of the soul

---

[5] 'Lerna monachorum' may well be a play on the phrase 'Lerna malorum' (an accumulation of ills) where the lake Lerna (where the Hydra lived) is taken as a place where everybody pitched their refuse: see Erasmus, *Adages*, I.iii.27.

[6] Timon of Athens (5th century BC), a misanthropic figure. See for instance, Cicero, *Tusculan Disputations*, IV.8.9.

cannot be discerned unless their locations or machines in the body of man are shown in some way. For what silliness is it when someone speaks of local motion and cannot distinguish between nerves on the one hand and veins and arteries on the other? Furthermore, since throughout life, for protecting one's health and for judging about many actions in the body and in morals, it is useful to know the construction of the human body in some way, other writers before me have also judged that these foundations have to be laid straightaway with the very young, particularly in these elements of natural philosophy. Therefore, although complete anatomical knowledge cannot be contained in these little books, and the young must not be burdened suddenly with the descriptions of the smallest parts, it is nevertheless very useful for all men to know the principal, and larger, parts. I have followed the best writers, namely Galen, Vesalius and Leonhard Fuchs, and occasionally I have added friends, namely Jakob Milich and Peucer, my son-in-law.[7] But since I was not intent upon only this one work with nothing else on my mind, and since our travels often interrupted the design which I preferred to weave, diligence could be found lacking in some places. Therefore I beseech those who will expound these first principles to others to emend the errors frankly, particularly since the pictures by Vesalius are already available, as well as his excellent descriptions, of which Paul Eber[8] says: 'Just as by night the moon habitually defeats the other stars, when it finishes its course with its brother's light, thus Vesalius alone strides ahead of the other books: bodies teaching by what art they are made.'

Although, Hieronymus, I leave it to your father's judgement whether he wants to set this my book or others before you, I nevertheless know that his judgement on the matter itself agrees with mine. He knows that what the wise historian Thucydides wrote is very true: 'The strongest thing is to be educated in the most indispensable' (*kratiston einai en anankaiotatois paideuesthai*) [*Histories*, 1.84.4], that is, that the most necessary things need to be studied. As in all of life the chief wisdom is to do the necessary, thus in studying, too, one needs first take care that what is necessary be learnt.

---

[7] Galen's *De usu partium* and *De administrandis anatomicis* were the authoritative texts on anatomy in this period. Andreas Vesalius (1514–64) published in 1543 the *De humani corporis fabrica*. He was followed by Leonhard Fuchs (1501–66), Professor of Medicine at the University of Tübingen, who published the two-volume *De humani corporis fabrica epitome* (in which he praised Vesalius) in 1552. Note that Melanchthon frequently uses 'humani corporis fabricationem' to refer to the structure of the body. For Jakob Milich, see note 6, oration 18, p. 147. Kaspar Peucer (1525–1602) married Melanchthon's daughter Magdalena in 1550, and began his medical studies while teaching mathematics.

[8] Paul Eber (1511–69) taught astronomy, mathematics, classics, natural philosophy and eventually theology at Wittenberg.

And your father declares truthfully that the knowledge of the doctrine that God has handed on to the Church by manifest testimonies is necessary for man, and he judges that these descriptions of the powers of the soul are a preparation for that. This knowledge also throws light on the laws by which the morals of men are to be ruled. For it shows how which parts can be curbed. Therefore in life and in the sciences these things are not secondary, but orientated towards the subject, and useful (*parerga, alla kai pro ergou kai pro hodou*) for understanding the doctrine of the Church and for the guidance of discipline and morals. Therefore, Hieronymus, learn from the judgement of your father, a wise and learned man, some such descriptions of the parts of man. Not only in these studies, but in other actions as well, give attention to your father's example. For just as in the mechanical arts no one becomes a master unless he constantly reflects upon the examples of his kind of art and attempt to imitate them, so, in shaping one's judgement on scholarship and in decisions on guiding one's life it is certainly of great use to choose certain and proven examples which you want to follow and represent. In fact God has set before you examples worthy of praise at home, your father and your uncle, whom you should chiefly strive to resemble. I pray to the Son of God, our Lord Jesus Christ, who was crucified for us and rose again, who truly is the protector of His Church, and said: 'None will rob my sheep from my hands': may He protect and guide you and your local Church. Farewell. Wittenberg, first of November of the year 1552.

20 On anatomy (1550)

CR XI, 939–46

Oration given by Jakob Milich, Doctor of Medicine, in announcing
the degree of Doctor of Medicine for Paulus Vadianus, for the
study of anatomy. Wittenberg, 6 November 1550[1]

Human gatherings have been established for mankind by God's wonderful
wisdom for the purpose that one teach the other about God and about the
nature of things, and God wants the voice of doctrine to ring out in public
among men, good things to be praised and evil ones to be disparaged. He
wants mankind to be ruled by those agreeing on correct judgements, and
He does not want dispersed and straggling individuals to invent their own
beliefs, whose variety overwhelm truth. God is afflicted by insult, and end-
lessly grieved by mankind. Therefore the assemblies of students and
teachers and public meetings are established not only for shaping judgements, but also for curbing and subduing the wantonness and vanity of
people's characters. Thus, in order that the young see and hear what kinds
of subjects and which arts and masters are approved of by the judgement
of the elders, it is the custom to declare our testimony in public. At the same
time, orations are also given in these meetings – not out of empty display,
but in order to advise the young about what knowledge of arts should be
sought and which beliefs are to be avoided, so that God be worshipped in
the right way, and also human nature be preserved as joined to the laws and
true arts. Therefore the young should not believe that they are gathering for
useless spectacles or for games, but for a proper and salutary admonishment.
Indeed, we are gathering in the temple by the altar because an oration on
good things is a sacrifice most pleasing to God. And at the same time we
must join our prayers here that God, the Maker of mankind and the fount
of wisdom, protect and guide us, that He Himself dwell willingly among
us and indeed that, as the Son of God demands, we be one in Him.

The contemplation of nature is often discussed here, and the scope of the
argument exceeds the eloquence of all angels and men, for only then will
nature be more properly known, when, in that heavenly school, the Architect
shows us the image of the entire workings; therefore we shall discuss a
different part elsewhere. But now I shall address the young and urge them
to study the first principles of anatomy. Those who support or encourage

[1] Jakob Milich was Dean of the faculty of medicine in 1550.

the study of it are truly doing mankind an admirable service. For this wisdom is both useful for morals and necessary for protecting health and driving out diseases. Therefore that wise antiquity was most studious in regard to this discipline.

As you know, natural philosophy has many parts. Some introduction is usually taught in the schools on the elements, on the fixed number of the primary qualities – by which God in His wonderful wisdom has, so to speak, put boundaries around roaming matter – on place, motion, time, the mixed bodies and on the differences of causes. It is necessary to become acquainted with all this introductory matter. However, these things must be taught in order and the deceptions of empty disputations must not be mixed in, such as those ancient ones of Democritus' atoms,[2] and many recent ones, such as whether the whole is different from the parts taken together, and others. For, through people's vanity, it happens in this kind of discipline that – leaving behind the necessary matters, because they appeared to be known – far-off subtleties are pursued which are supposed to give rise to admiration because of their novelty, while in truth the moderate contemplation of things that God has made in nature, in which He willed His wisdom to be seen, is by far the greater wisdom than these empty discourses of words, which are of no use in life.

From these beginnings of natural philosophy the young are soon led to the observation of the human body, so that we may begin to recognise ourselves, who are indeed the principal work in this visible nature. And although the sweetness of knowledge in itself attracts good minds, let us nevertheless also be moved by the greatness of the usefulness which is indeed before our eyes. The method of protecting one's health cannot be sought daily from the precepts of the doctors, but in some ways it must be known to individuals because of daily perils. In order to get to know it, it is indeed necessary to know the position, substance, qualities and functions of many parts of the body, and to observe which of them are assisted or harmed by what. This knowledge, however slight, is useful for avoiding many diseases. Often recently originated diseases can even be driven out with philosophical diligence before they take root, while later the doctors apply remedies to them in vain. This cannot be done unless one has some knowledge of the structure of the human body. Often in sudden dangers,

---

[2] Democritus was a Greek philosopher (*c.* fifth century BC), who propounded that the world was made up of indivisible atoms. His views were influential for the atomistic theories of Epicurus and Lucretius.

accidents befall the orifice of the stomach, which can be prevented easily when noticed in time, but bring death when neglected.

It is evident madness not to be moved by concern for protecting one's life and health, which concern God both enjoins and supports. For He wants humankind to exist and men to be prepared in this mortal life for the eternal fellowship of the heavenly Church. He does not want all men to be annihilated suddenly, but He wants some to be left for the sake of the education, instruction, protection and governing of the young. This will of God should often be reflected upon, both in order that we bear the burdens of life and the universal toils better, and that we assist these fragile bodies with greater diligence for the sake of the will of God and the need of others.

Since this first benefit of the contemplation of the human body is well known, I enter upon the others. The very sight of the structure of many parts in us is the nurse of many virtues. And since the foremost virtue is the recognition of the Maker God, the assent to providence is much strengthened when we contemplate the wonderful skill in the entire construction of man. It is not said at random about this latter that man is a small world, because the mind is the image of God, and man's summit, the brain, nerves and spirit – which govern all actions – reproduce celestial nature; the stomach which produces nourishment is more like earth and water. I reckon that the heart, which is the source of life and life-giving heat, is most rightly compared to the sun. Moreover, the individual parts of the body are so fittingly distributed by locations, and distinguished by material, shape and properties, that we are shown clearly by their order and skill that this nature of things has by no means emerged by chance, but that there is a creating mind that wants evidence of itself to exist in human nature, and wants us to recognise and understand it. It is true that this entire beautiful machine of the world is a temple of God, and that the traces of the Architect are engraved in many parts of it, but even more so man is the temple of God, because the other bodies, being without a mind, do not recognise the skill and the Maker. The human mind recognises the skill and the Maker, and it sees in itself, as the most explicit evidence of God, the notions of numbers and of order, and the distinction of worthy and vile actions, which in the human mind are set apart as if by an eternal wall. It is impossible that such great things are brought together in such a way by chance, out of atoms. And thus often, when I look at man, so to speak, and observe these traces of God in ourselves, I shudder all over my body, and I grieve that such neglect of God has come upon us, since He has engraved upon us such clear and unconcealed evidence of Himself; the assent to providence would be stronger, and our respect towards God greater, if we beheld this structure often and with attention. Indeed, how much more wonderful is it that the Architect included the most diverse things in man, as if in a small world, such as the stomach and the mind.

Since man is made in the image and for the worship of God, and so that he may enjoy His wisdom and goodness for all eternity, what need is there for the stomach, which will be idle in that fellowship of the eternal Church? But without doubt the joining of these completely dissimilar things, the stomach and the mind, was made for the very reason that God wants the beginnings of that eternal light and life to be kindled in this life. Now, too, He wants us to be His temples, and therefore the studies that show the way to the recognition of Him should be more enthusiastic, and our concern for guiding our morals should be greater, just as that very voice of God ringing in our minds enjoins us. Not only does this order overwhelm us, so that we are forced to acknowledge that there is a God, but it also instructs us what He is like, and we carry around in us the image of divine guidance. All of antiquity distinguished the powers of man in that way; they said that in us there is the authoritative part (*to hēgemonikon*), the passionate part (*to thymikon*) and the nourishing part (*to threptikon*). The authoritative part (*hēgemonikon*) contains notions that rule our lives. Since they distinguish between worthy and vile things, they show us what God is like, that is, wise, truthful, good, generous, just, pure, acting in the most unconfined way and the avenger of crimes – thus we understand what that most excellent constructing mind is like, which certainly wants us, too, to agree with the Archetype.

And in order that this distinction between worthy and vile actions be stronger, He added the passionate part (*thymikon*) in the heart by eternal and unchangeable order, and deadly pain in the heart follows the violation of that distinction, so that the annihilation of nature show the Architect's judgement. For you see that the form of justice is depicted in man, the right notion shines forth in the authoritative part (*hēgemonikōi*), and its companion is a most just avenger, and unappeasable pain in the passionate part (*thymikōi*), which destroys nature by horrible punishment because of its crimes. Although nowadays, amidst this depravity of nature, other vicious impulses are also kindled in the heart, nevertheless, whenever this happens, the last and strongest companion is always the avenger who is the guardian and executor of divine judgement. These traces of God are so well expressed in us and so clearly visible that it would be more than cyclopic madness not to want to recognise them, and those who behold themselves are forced to acknowledge that what we have said is absolutely true.

In God there is also the glory that is a free agent, and He also willed the image of His goodness to be seen in us, which is useful for the governing of morals, too: the nerves and the tools of voluntary motion obey the authoritative part (*tōi hēgemonikōi*), so that it can set in motion the outer limbs by its decision. The authoritative part (*to hēgemonikon*) restrains Achilles and hinders his hands so that they do not kill Agamemnon, but return the sword to its sheath [*Iliad* I.190–221]. This freedom has remained in us both in order that it be a curb to desires gone astray, and that it admonish[3] us that God is in truth a free agent – for from slavish nature, like the God the Stoics imagine, a free agent cannot be made.

Besides, there are other images of God in us, engraved upon us, so that they would be reminders of Him as well as being seeds and incitements of virtues, that is, affection (*storgai*): the parents' love for offspring, the offspring's good will towards the parents, compassion towards those who are unfortunate, protection of petitioners, friendship between equals brought together by worthy duties. Even though it seems ridiculous to the Stoics to attribute emotions to God, nevertheless, whenever parents feel the wounds of love and grief in the misfortune of their offspring, they should consider that God has similar love towards His Son and us, for He said clearly about His Son: 'This is my beloved son in whom I rejoice; listen to him' [Mark 9:7]. In God there is true love, neither cold nor feigned, towards those who duly invoke Him, and great anger which is the avenger and guardian of justice. In some men there are also heroic flames, either of wisdom – as in those who prophesy, and outstanding masters whose judgements are similar to prophecies – or of courage, as in Alexander. These impulses also show God's friendship with men. Since we perceive in ourselves so many proofs of God, there is no doubt that the assent to providence is strengthened; and this assent is the source of many other virtues. It is necessary to ponder the structure of man, so that one can perceive and understand these proofs in one way or another.

Since we recognise this wonderful likeness of notions in human minds and in God's, let us contemplate that God truly cares for us, since He poured into us the best things in Himself, that is, the rays of His wisdom.

---

[3] Reading *commonefaciat* for *commonefaciant*.

That our minds shape images by thought and that the spirits that are born in the heart spread the flames of the emotions are also shadows of divinity in us. These things are arranged so that when we hear the Son of God being called the image of the eternal Father, and the Word (*kai logon*), we understand that He arose from thought, and that the spirit is the flame of divine love. We have to acknowledge that in the contemplation of these greatest things we are assisted by pondering on the nature of man: for many traces of divinity are engraved upon us in order that we recognise the Architect, and that our entire life agree with the pattern of the divine mind, the semblance of which is poured into us. The nourishing part (*threptikon*) is added to the higher powers, and by this action it is proved that the Architect also has regard for the life of the body, and that He wants to nourish and support humankind. Thus divine providence and His love for us can be perceived in all parts of the structure.

Once the assent to providence is strengthened, then the other virtues follow, whose rules shine in the mind. Let us strive to protect this temple of God, let us not violate it with slaughter or intemperance, and let us not pollute it with the disorder of desires. Let us see that the individual parts are made for a fixed order and measure. Let us understand that it is justice to guide them as their nature demands it. If I had to speak here about the individual parts which serve the functions of various virtues, the oration would not be much longer, but nevertheless I recommend that your minds observe man himself, and that you contemplate the difference in the substances of the parts. The brain stands firm as the summit, and its cavities are filled with spirits, just as the heavens encompass the entire remaining mass.

The nature of the brain, too, is similar to that of the heavens, and in it wonderful actions are produced: cognition, reasoning, the conservation of images in memory, and recollection. There is no doubt that these actions are produced by the work of the spirits, and that they are, so to speak, pulsations of the spirits against the body of the brain. The spirit originates in the heart, and then it receives new powers and new light in the brain. Even though we do not yet examine these things, there should nevertheless exist in us wonder at such great works, and at the same time reverence towards the Artisan and Creator should be kindled. Neither the purity of the heavens, nor the glitter of the stars, nor the brightness of the sun surpasses that flame, which is called vital or animal spirit; let us recognise that most noble thing and abode of God within us, which is the author of the most outstanding actions, and let us cherish it by our attentiveness as much as we can.[4]

But it is troubled in many ways: by a bad way of life, by intemperance, the conflagrations of desires, the immoderate ardours of emotions – anger, hatred, love or grief – and the afflation of evil demons. Marius burns with the desire for vengeance, and with the hatred of Sulla and the other leaders.[5] The spirits set aflame by this ardour of disordered emotions drive him, so that he preserves order neither in thought nor in action, and he rushes furiously and gluts his cruelty. And the devils fan this turmoil and fury of the spirits even more, like storms. In that way the rage that is originated and increased destroys all peoples. These perils need to be understood so that, in nourishment and in all impulses, we apply greater care, contemplation, hesitation and moderation. And, indeed, let our prayer rise to God also, that He govern His abode within us.

The recognition of the frailty of this structure of the human body is also very beneficial for the care for one's health and for guiding morals. The fineness of the eyes is there for everyone to see, and in the same way nerves, veins, extremely thin fibres and extremely soft bodies are spread throughout the body, which are nevertheless the tools and channels of the principal actions, and can easily be harmed. How easily the harmony of properties in the members can be troubled, too. The heat of the stomach can be quenched by a slight accident, and then there follow faintness, obstruction and putrefaction of the liver. And indeed many destroy the power of these parts of the body by intemperance and the inability to restrain their desires. In many men hearts are destroyed by anger, hatred and sadness. Nor can the stronghold of the brain remain unharmed when the powers of the stomach, the liver or the heart are extinguished. Even though the frailty of our bodies can be known also without knowledge, by sad examples, nevertheless those who are forewarned by knowledge are less imprudent. The knowledge of anatomy also shows the connections of the parts among themselves.

Since therefore the usefulness of knowing the structure of the human body is remarkable, anatomy is by no means to be neglected. It is a matter

---

[4] For an excellent study of theories of medical spirits in this period, see D. P. Walker, 'Medical Spirits and God and the Soul', in *Spiritus. IVº Colloquio Internazionale Roma, 7–9 gennaio 1983*, ed. M. Fattori and M. Bianchi (Rome, 1984), pp. 223–44.

[5] Gaius Marius (157–86 BC), a successful commander, clashed with Sulla (138–78 BC), leader of the aristocratic party for the command against Mithridates. By popular resolution the command was transferred to Marius, but Sulla marched to Rome with six legions and Marius fled to Africa, and vowed to return: see Plutarch, *Lives*.

altogether worthy of man to behold the nature of things, and not to spurn the contemplation of this wonderful work of the world which is made with so much skill that it can be beheld like a theatre, and it should remind us of God and of His will. But it is nevertheless most fitting and beneficial to see in ourselves the sequence, shapes, combinations, powers and functions of the parts. They said that there was an oracle, 'Know thyself' (*gnōthi seauton*),[6] which admonishes us about many things, but is also adapted so that we examine with zeal the things that are worthy of wonder in ourselves and are the sources of several actions in life. And since men are made for wisdom and justice, and true wisdom is the recognition of God and the contemplation of nature, we should acknowledge that we need to know anatomy in which the causes of many actions and changes can be observed in ourselves.

No one can deny that this our exhortation is sincere. We do not cry out for you to learn useless disputations or slyness which corrupt the powers of judgement, and later harm life and morals. But we lead you to the discipline that strengthens assent to providence and stirs up caution lest we upset the appropriate order of nature. And since it shows the dignity and frailty of man, it admonishes us to treat with more respect our own life and the lives of others, and to love and cherish this weak species. Indeed, since we see that we are made in such a way that we prepare ourselves in this life for the eternal fellowship with God, the zeal to know the true doctrine about God should also be kindled. There is no doubt that those who study the first principles of anatomy will understand straight away that they are helped by this contemplation, however slight, in protecting their health, and that they are admonished of many virtues, and taught about the parts of the human body, whose knowledge is necessary in other arts and in all of life.

I pray to the eternal God, Father of our Lord Jesus Christ – who without doubt is both the Maker and the preserver of humankind, and has made us for that very wisdom, so that we may behold the theatre of the world, and recognise Him, admonished by the traces which He engraved upon nature – that He mitigate the harshest punishments which are diffused throughout humankind, and that He protect the Church in these lands,

---

[6] For the proverb 'know thyself' see Erasmus, *Adages*, i.v.95. For the proliferation of this phrase in anatomical literature in the sixteenth century, see W. Schupbach, *The Paradox of Rembrandt's 'Anatomy of Dr. Tulp'* (London, 1982), and Andrea Carlino, '"Know thyself", Anatomical Figures in Early Modern Europe', *Res* 27 (1995), 52–69.

in which He is truly worshipped, and that He do not allow studies and proper discipline to be annihilated. Make this prayer with me with sincere lamentation, and I pray with all my heart that the eternal Father will grant it for the sake of His Son Jesus Christ, our highest Priest. I have spoken.

The higher faculties

21 On the merit of the art of medicine (1548)

CR XI, 806–11

Oration on the merit and usefulness of the art of medicine, held by Doctor Melchior Fend, when the degree of Doctor was awarded to Petrus Sibilenus Torgensis on 7 August 1548[1]

In the beginning, I thank the eternal God, the father of our Lord Jesus Christ, the maker of humankind, together with His son, our Lord Jesus Christ, and the Holy Spirit, for protecting His Church in violent storms, and picking out the pieces of our shipwreck with wonderful goodness, so that the voice of the Gospel may still ring genuine in public assemblies, and in the prayer of all the faithful in their chambers, and in the education of children at an early age, and that the study of true philosophy be cherished not only with some attendance and diligence, but also without perverse beliefs. And I pray to God, the source of wisdom, that He continue to protect you, and that He grant lasting peace to the study of erudition.

Today the attestation of erudition is to be given to a man learned in the art of medicine, and it is the custom in such assemblies to say something on the same art. Although no one's eloquence is a match for the greatness of this art, it is nevertheless necessary to admonish those who are younger by some kind of oration. Therefore I shall not resolve upon a eulogy, since the art's usefulness is clear for everyone to see, and there is such authority in contemplating nature that it cannot be demonstrated sufficiently by any oration. But I shall rebuke, not only the young, but all of us, for our ungratefulness and sloth which are both most disgraceful for many reasons.

The hardness of human hearts is such that it is not surprising that the ancients imagined that men were born from stones. From the hour in which the midwives' hands first draw us out of our mother's belly, through all stages of life, we all make use of the countless benefits of the art of medicine. Although this is so, many do not consider the art the gift of God, and they do not give thanks to God as the maker of remedies and the teacher of the art, nor do they feel respect towards the art or speak respectfully about it. The mothers themselves are subject to countless diseases once the child has been born, and cannot be protected without medical help. And very often experience shows that, in their dangers, the remedies are applied not

---

[1] Melchior Fend (1486–1564), professor of medicine, was the Dean of the medical faculty in 1548, when Petrus Sibilenus of Torgau obtained his doctorate in medicine.

only for the sake of idle show, but they are truly efficacious and beneficial. Often the breasts have to be cured, and often sleep has to be counteracted by the art. The dangers to the womb are almost countless. Furthermore, ulcers are common to all children, which would not soften and would bring on other illnesses, unless the art brought help.

But I pass over this enumeration, which cannot be contained completely even in great tomes. I direct the young to the first beginnings of life so that, if they think that they owe gratitude to their mothers, they consider at the same time that they owe much to the art of medicine, which is needed for women in childbed and for the offspring. And in this consideration they should not only understand the diligence of men or the remedies, but they should also recognise the goodness of God, who both made the remedies and showed their use in order to assuage the miseries of this life in some way.

It is the voice of a Cyclops, and unworthy of man, that says that he fears neither Jupiter's lightning nor rainfalls, nor the infertility of the earth, because the rocks protect his cave and in his cave he has a flock of sheep on which to feed. Similar to this is the utterance of many uneducated and barbarous men who spurn temperance in maintaining their health, and all remedies when in danger. And they do not even think that remedies and the art are the gifts of God, but these Cyclopes wage war against God and nature.

However, worthy minds should know, first, that all of nature bears witness that this world has not emerged by chance, but that it is made and shaped by an eternal creating mind. Furthermore they should know that there are notions implanted in man which show the choice in things as being in accordance with the divine mind; and that, in nature and in morals, our judgements need to accord with the divine mind. God declares that life, good health and the protection of life are good things and are made by Him, and He commands us to enjoy these divine gifts.

Let us therefore recognise these gifts, and love them and give thanks to the maker. So it is written in the maxims of Sirach: 'Honour the physician, for God has created him for the sake of our need' [Sirach 38:1][2] This maxim confirms that the use of remedies and of the art is necessary, as examples show every day. And Sirach adds expressly: 'The Most High created remedies from the earth, and healing is from God' [Sirach 38:4]. Not only are the remedies distinguished by the maker's counsel in such

---

[2] Sirach is one of the apocryphal books of the Old Testament, also known as The Wisdom of Ben Sira or Ecclesiasticus. In Roman Catholic editioins of the Bible, it is located among the Wisdom Books of the Old Testament. In Protestant editions, it is included among the 'Apocrypha', placed between the Old Testament and the New Testament, or at the end of the New Testament.

a way that different ones drive out different diseases, or are helpful for different parts of the body, but the physician's judgement is ruled by divine providence, and his efficiency is supported by God. Since this is the case, let us be moved, by the usefulness for us as well as by the maker's goodness, to honour the remedies and this discipline.

I believe, however, that worthy minds are delighted by the contemplation of nature not only because of its usefulness, but even more by the fact that all this variety of nature is like a theatre, in which the evidence of the creator God can be perceived clearly. To begin with, it is clear that the appearance of His abode, that most beautiful machine in which the constellations move, is made with skill, so that the days, months, years, summers and winters be distinguished in order that the nature of the seasons be dissimilar from each other, and that every year the earth bring forth produce at a fixed time.

Furthermore, how much art is there in the entire nature of man! The distinction between light and dark, and between knowledge and ignorance as well, is the highest part in the brain, closely resembling heaven, in which knowledge shines and is stored and kept. And some light of God is implanted, and many other notions are added, which are the precepts of life showing distinction and order, such as the numbers, the understanding of order and consequence, and the distinction between what is proper and what is vile, distinguishing by an eternal and immovable division between what is to be done and what is to be avoided. It is impossible that these things have emerged by chance, or only out of matter. The nature of things itself cries out that there is a God, and that He is wise, good and kind, the avenger of crimes and the protector of human society.

I shall not speak now about the entire construction of the human body, nor of roots or plants, but I shall only admonish the young to contemplate the variety of use and of virtues in such multitude. Agrimony and endive are beneficial to the liver, hart's-tongue, spleen-wort, tamarisk and tree-germander to the spleen. Saffron, dates, rosemary, thistle, corals and gold to the heart; mugwort, balm, feverfew, pennyroyal and centaury for the womb. Liquorice-root, iris and white horehound are good for the lungs, hyssop, elecampane, maidenhair and pine-thistle for the chest. Sage, marjoram, rose and marigold are good for the brain; fennel, swallow-wort and bugloss for the eyes; mallow, clover and pine-thistle for the nerves. Scammony and rhubarb excellently draw forth yellow bile. Agaric, trefoil and aloe draw forth phlegm. Fern and sallow draw black bile.[3] But this is not the occasion for a longer enumeration. It is by no means proper to say that this almost infinite distribution of virtues, which remains continuous in various species, has emerged by chance. And in order that it be evident that a Creator understanding human nature has added these things as a help to man, it is necessary that He be affected by care for humankind.

What is more proper and more appropriate for man than for those who search for traces of the divinity in nature, in order to establish as true the idea of providence, to recognise God as the maker and protector of humankind? Or to understand that God's mind and will are such as He Himself represented in the light which He has poured into us, and to distinguish Him from evil natures, in whom there is confusion of His order, and to guide one's judgements and morals according to that precept that harmonises in the mind with the divine precept?

All who are sound in mind understand that these things are most in accordance with nature, and not those Cyclopic ideas, which the Epicureans defend wildly, namely that all things are brought together fortuitously from atoms, that all things are moved and joined without order and without a guiding mind, and that continually other worlds and other species come into being. It is not only [a sign of] wisdom to oppose such madness, but also outstanding virtue that is pleasing to God, and for which rewards are given by God. The falsehood of the Epicureans can be clearly refuted and their madness, too, by greater steadfastness of the mind. At the same time, the conviction of providence needs to be assiduously strengthened in the mind by observation of the most beautiful order in nature, and the parts of nature are to be contemplated often, as well as the construction of the parts of the body, and experience reflecting the teaching on the use of remedies. Just as men often carelessly attract to themselves deadly danger by a slight mistake, so, on the other hand, the wise physician often disperses deadly dangers by wholly common remedies. I could list many examples, but I believe that most of you have read or heard many yourselves.

There is no doubt that the art is most useful for life, for the preservation of health, and that it has great merit because of the knowledge of the greatest things, that it is praised by divine laudations, that it shows illustrious

---

[3] Classical sources for the medicinal uses of plants were Dioscorides, *Materia medica*, Galen, *Faculties of Simples*, and Pliny the Elder, *Natural History*. Melanchthon's student Valerius Cordus (1515–44) had lectured upon and commentated on Dioscorides' *Materia medica* at Wittenberg: see his *Annotationes doctissimae in Dioscoridis De medica materia libros* (Frankfurt 1549).

testimonies for providence, and that it needs to be aspired to, known and revered. Since this is so, honour is also due to the good and learned men who are the guardians and propagators of the most renowned discipline, and often succour the lives of men.

The possession of the eminent parts of philosophy has always been in this rank. And I believe that since the first fathers – Adam, Noah, Abraham and Joseph – the teaching of the movements of the heavens and of remedies has been spread in distinguished families. Then, later, it was upheld by those who were physicians by profession.

It is in itself a great virtue to have knowledge of so many things about the movements of the heavens, the construction of the human body, and the causes of changes in the body, as well as of diseases and remedies. However, it is a much greater virtue to apply this knowledge for the welfare of men. Therefore God has bestowed wisdom upon humankind: first, so that He be known, and, second, that it be beneficial to as many as possible. In those who practise this art honestly, many virtues need to be united: erudition, diligence, honesty, constancy, sagacity and endurance in bearing much that is troublesome. It is most just to recompense such a physician by any kind of favour.

But ingratitude in this aspect is not only great among the masses, but also among the mighty, and there are hardly any who more often than the physicians experience the truth of the familiar saying: 'After the service, gratitude ages immediately.' Worthy minds should nevertheless consider first what they owe to God, the creator of life and remedies, then how much they should be in awe of the teaching and finally what is due for the physician's toil, honesty and services. Since wise rulers reflected upon this, they kept physicians in great honour, such as Hezekiah did with Isaiah and Darius with Democedes, whom he sent back to his country on a ship laden with gold and silver.[4] Alexander honoured Philippus, Antigonus Diocles, Antiochus Erasistratus, Augustus Antonius Musa, Antoninus Galen and others other physicians.[5]

---

[4] The prophet Isaiah cured Hezekiah's sickness (Isiah 38.1–6); Democedes (6th century BC), a physician from Cnidus, was sent to Darius, King of Persia, as a prisoner, cured the king's foot and received a chestful of gold (Herodotus, *Histories*, III.129f.).

[5] Alexander the Great honoured Philippus, a native of Acarnania and physician, who had cured him of a fever just before the battle of Issus; Erasistratus of Ceos (*d.* 257 BC), grandson of Aristotle and celebrated physician, was rewarded with 100 talents for the cure of Antiochus by the latter's father Selecus, King of Syria; Antonius Musa, freedman and physican to Gaius Julius Caesar Octavianus Augustus (63 BC–14 AD), cured his master of a dangerous disease by use of cold bath. Galen was physician to the Emperor Marcus Aurelius Antoninus.

Just as the discipline that we cherish is an eminent part of philosophy, so our inclination, too, should be philosophical. This means that, although many are ungrateful, we should nevertheless, for the sake of God and for virtue, protect the possession of the discipline and be of use to many. If this is our inclination, our toil and our families will be dear to God.

I encourage you who are younger to rouse your minds to the love of the discipline by thinking of the usefulness and merit of our art. And, by observing nature, earnestly contemplate the signs of God (which, as Paul says, show Him to be so close that we can almost touch Him with our hands), so that you may fear Him as an avenger and call to Him with a good conscience.

I want you, too, to join your prayers to mine: 'We call to you, all-powerful God, eternal father of our Lord Jesus Christ, maker of heaven and Earth, of men and of your Church, of one being with your son, our Lord Jesus Christ, and your Holy Spirit. And we pray that, for the sake of your son, our Lord Jesus Christ, whom you wished to be the victim for us, mediator as well as suppliant (*kai mesitēn kai hiketēn*), you may guide us by your Holy Spirit, and lead the study of this discipline and instruction, and grant us peaceful reception. Assemble an everlasting Church for yourself among us, now and hereafter.' I have spoken.

22 On the merit of laws (1543)

CR XI, 630–6

Oration on the merit of laws

It is the custom, on this occasion and in these ceremonies, to say something about the merit of the laws, and it is surely most useful to incite men to respect them. I, too, wish to speak about the same topic, but the more frequently I think about realms, about the management of life and about laws and judgements, which are the nerves of government, peace and discipline, the more difficult it is for me to choose what to say from such a multitude of things. For, first of all, how difficult is it to respond to the belief of Cyclopes and Centaurs, who say, amidst such turmoil of human affairs, that all that we call law and political wisdom is just an empty name, for as long as it is understood that realms are ravaged by force of arms, and ruled by the whims of the mighty. Without mentioning ancient examples, does the ferocity of the Turks care for any laws? They advance as they can, and command the oppressed by force as they wish. One hundred years ago there was a most flourishing school of our laws in Constantinople; now that teaching has been driven far away, and everything is ruled by the nod of one tyrant or of some barbarous ruler.[1] Thus, when the world was torn apart by the retinue of Alexander was the voice of laws or political teaching ever heard? Therefore, what place is there for wisdom and for our political art, when everything is governed rather by the fury of tyrants and by the whims of the mighty? For one must not imagine that our art is similar to that of the military, which serves now the enemy, now the citizens, and lends its service to wrongful desires on both sides. This political art, or teaching of law, is a different thing, and it has its place only in a peaceful city, and in a council that adapts its judgements to the precept of justice – just as the authority of laws was intact in Athens as long as Solon was at the head of the city. In Rome, respect for the laws was upheld as long as Augustus lived, but in both places the citizens were oppressed by tyranny soon thereafter, and the laws fell silent. Just as Peisistratus grasped the power while Solon was still alive, soon after Augustus several tyrants raged most cruelly in the state.[2] These

---

[1] Constantinople fell to the Ottomans in 1453.

[2] Peisistratus came to prominence in a war against Megara, and gathered allies from Athenians dissatisfied with the settlements of Solon (640–558 BC), who had introduced the constitution to Athens in 594 BC. Peisistratus occupied the Acropolis and became Tyrant. After Gaius Julius Caesar Octavianus Augustus (63 BC–14 AD), Rome suffered in succession the neglect, abuse and tyranny of Tiberius, Gaius Caligula and Nero.

examples often induce even great men to believe that our teaching is either of no or of very little use, and indeed Cicero's saying is in their mouths: 'Amidst weapons the laws are silent' [*For T. Annius Milo* 11]. Marius said that he did not hear the voice of the laws amidst the battle-signals and the sound of war-trumpets. And Gregory of Nazianzen says of Julian that the prince's will is an unwritten law. I am set to refute this vituperation of our discipline in order to strengthen my own spirit, and perhaps some others. I shall demonstrate that there is and will be a use for this art, even though there are and have been great changes in human affairs, and there will be more, and that we must not reject these studies, but cherish them all the more, so that they be preserved.

Let us first establish that it is a political art, for it was not in vain that God instilled the laws of nature into human minds. He wanted their explanation to be visible in the writings and works of the sages, and He wanted these to be the rule for realms and judgements; it is not without value just because other matters cause disturbances in the government. The medical art is true and taught by divine providence, and beneficial for humankind even though human bodies are not ruled by the precepts of the medical art only, and are often harmed by hidden or sudden causes that cannot be foreseen. In the same way our art is true, shown to humankind by divine providence, and beneficial, even though other matters happen which often curb this wisdom. Now and again realms are torn apart by punishment brought about by fate, or by the rage of the devil, or by the greed of tyrants; at such times political wisdom gives way.

For what place was there for good men, when the thirty tyrants[3] held Athens in their power? Since violence often rules, and there are many sudden and unforeseen changes, the Epicureans believe that human affairs are moved by chance, and that each can obtain as much as he is worth in power. We, however, who are educated in God's Church, and know for certain that God is the observer and judge of all of humankind, must know that realms neither originate nor perish by chance. Furthermore, let us sustain ourselves greatly by this consolation: even if God strikes or overturns realms, He nevertheless does not allow His Church to be entirely destroyed. And, in order that it endure, He gives us a home, He preserves

---

[3] In 404 BC, at the end of the Peloponnesian War, Athenian democracy was overturned by Athenians supported by the Spartan general Lysander. They introduced an oligarchic constitution and a commission of thirty which set up a council, abolishing law-courts, exterminating enemies and confiscating their property.

wedlock, procreation, education, contracts, writings and the teaching passed on to us from heaven. Therefore, it will be necessary that there be assemblies joined to laws. There are many times when there is too little place for political wisdom, just as in very fierce storms experienced sailors are overcome. Nevertheless, as long as the Church exists there will be assemblies joined to laws; if these were ruled by the ignorant, without a fixed law, literacy or erudition, what darkness would life be?

But I shall return to the examples above. Solon transmitted laws to the city of Attica [*sic*], which may not have borne up under all vices, but nevertheless guided contracts and judgements with some humanity, and united the purposes of the citizens. The city used these laws for more than 500 years, until Roman times. Although, in the meantime, the city was set on fire and destroyed in the Persian War, while the citizens were on their ships and they were hiding their wives and children among cliffs by the sea, the Solonic laws were not useless because of that; earlier, in times of peace, these laws had kept up serenity, and some time later they restored the city. Not even the conflagration of the city, although it consumed the wooden tablets [on which the laws were written], could destroy the laws, which had become all the stronger, inscribed in the citizens' hearts. The citizens educated by that instruction would know that barbarous customs must not be permitted, and that one has to fight with joint forces for the defence of freedom, that is, of instruction and of honourable condition. For that reason they desisted from private strife, and upheld harmony among themselves. The laws continued to exist, and their examples could be seen every day in the deeds of Themistocles, Aristides, Cimon and other worthy citizens.[4] In this manner, when Rome was taken by the Gauls the state was not destroyed, even though the buildings were set on fire: the virtue and custom of the citizens, based on the laws, survived. These are of assistance and of benefit to the citizens. Even though for some time Nero practised robbery among the citizens, and, suppressing the laws, tore out the eyes of the lawyer Cassius Longinus, and although Bassianus, having murdered his brother, also killed the lawyer Papinianus, who refused to contrive a pretext for absolving him from murder, nevertheless the laws were not abolished in

---

[4] Solon (*c.* 640–*c.* 558 BC), aristocrat and statesman who introduced the constitution to Athens. Themistocles (*c.* 524–*c.* 459 BC), Athenian statesman and commander achieving military success in the second Persian War. Aristides (*d. c.* 468 BC), democratic leader of Athens who was one of the strategoi at Marathon. He came into conflict with Themistocles. Cimon (*c.* 510–450 BC), was an aristocrat and distinguished Athenian commander, and rival of Themistocles. The lives of these people were available in Plutarch's *Parallel Lives* and Nepos' *On Illustrious Men*.

general because of these facts.[5] God still protected political order in some places so that humankind would not perish utterly; there were some ordinary magistrates somewhere in the provinces who listened to the voice of the laws. Therefore the acknowledgement of the discipline must not be abandoned, even if for some time wars or despotic regimes hinder its use.

Indeed, good minds must fight eagerly for the defence of the true laws, because they see that amidst such human weakness and such disorder their authority is often either neglected or suppressed. God gave humankind the political art, and this teaching, so that as far as possible, they might bend those who can be improved towards justice, and curb wrongful impulses. It is not surprising that those who do not know the causes of this disorder in the realms, and have not learnt from the heavenly teaching how to strengthen their spirit, have always violently hated the realms where rarely the good are leaders. If they are of ordinary ability, but good and wise, nevertheless the quantity and variety of affairs does not allow them to be attentive to everything. The provinces loved the justice and integrity of Pompey;[6] when he took with him many rapacious companions, they would nevertheless conceal their wrongdoings out of kindness towards Pompey. From David there are also complaints about his son. In short, it is insanity to demand in one's heart a state without vices or flaws, amidst the weakness of human nature and the great cruelty of the devil.

Just as those who do not know the causes of disorder hate the realms, so they spurn the laws as well when they see that these do not remedy many great ills, and they believe that this entire discipline is useless for life. But heavenly teaching reminds us that much great disorder in life originates, either from the devil or from human negligence or wantonness, and that the madness of all cannot be restrained or set right by the counsels or laws of the rulers. Still, despite these difficulties, the rulers must not desist from their care, nor is their diligence useless, but it restrains or mitigates some ills. The heavenly teaching commands us to invoke God, so that He assist this most difficult task, and reminds us that without God's help that political wisdom is often only dreamt of, and pernicious for the cities. Many who were endowed with the greatest intellects, although they loved their country, nevertheless overturned the state by their counsels, because, relying

[5] Cassius Longinus (213–73), a Neoplatonist, was executed for his loyal support for Queen Zenobia by Emperor Aurelian, not Nero. Aemilius Papinianus, a renowned jurist under Marcus Aurelius, was put to death by Bassianus Caracalla when Papinianus refused to defend his parricide.
[6] Reading *multitudo et* for *multitudo est*; *Pompeii* for *Pompeius* and *amabant* for *amabat*.

on their wisdom, they set in motion things that were not necessary. Pericles, Demosthenes, Pompey and Cicero are examples of this.[7] We err all our lives if we believe that there is prosperous wisdom without God. Let us strengthen ourselves with this consolation, particularly amidst these dangers in the world, and let us be aware that while the entire machine of the world is tottering, and human affairs are tumbling down, nevertheless the ruin is supported by God. Worthy men must exert themselves, each in his place, in order to benefit the common good.

I believe that these things need to be remembered here. For often, when I look at law books, knowing the dangers for Germany, my entire body shudders when I ponder what misfortune would follow if, because of the wars, Germany dismissed this accomplished discipline of law and this ornament of the court. Tyrannies would grow, all erudition would be held in greater contempt, the Church would be neglected even more, and manifold barbarism would ensue. Let us therefore pray to God, first that He grant us peace, and then that He protect these studies. But we shall obtain this even more certainly, if we ourselves honestly employ our judgement for representing the glory of God and for the common good. Let us therefore not be deterred by the dangers, and let us not become disheartened, even if, again and again, pious, moderate and beneficial counsel is prevented by the injustice of men, or by the usual disorder of human affairs. And let us not abandon the occupation of our study, us in particular, if the work of many of our rank in public counsils serves the Church of God as well; and if God preserves the Church, He will also preserve the political arts serving the Church. The art of architecture is not to be abandoned, even if many castles are overthrown, either by the disasters of war, or in other ways. The good arts need to be protected and cherished, and we need to beseech God that He direct our studies and give His Church useful solutions. What did Daniel, Ezra and Nehemiah do when they were in exile? They saw the temple that God had ordered to be built utterly destroyed, and they saw the queen of all cities, to which God had promised sovereignty, razed to the ground, and yet they did not cast aside their studies, broken by despair. Indeed, they both studied and taught their followers with even greater diligence, so that the true teaching of the Church would not perish in exile

---

[7] Pericles (*c.* 500–429 BC), a statesman who dominated Athens, pursued imperialistic policy which led to the Peloponnesian War. Demosthenes (383–322 BC), statesman and orator, in his famous speeches (the *Philippics* and the *Olynthiacs*) urged Athens to take up arms against the threats of Philip of Macedon. Marcus Tullius Cicero (106–43 BC), Roman orator and statesman, was a supporter of Pompey the Great (106–48 BC).

and in the scattering of their people, for they knew that God's Church would not go to ruin. In the same way let us attach our prayers and our hope to God's Church, let us contemplate it and let us cherish our studies by this hope.

This ship carries our discipline, and will carry it without doubt if we strive to embellish the ship. Men of our rank can do very much for the Church if they influence the minds of the rulers by whom they are asked for advice towards care for the protection of pious studies and of arts that are beneficial for humankind. I have said little about the teachers, but, before I finish, this scholarly assembly, too, needs to be warned of its duty. Often, in holy assemblies or in lectures, divine sayings on discipline, good manners and the punishment following the violation of discipline are set before you. And the punishments are before our eyes: the Turks ravage with impunity nearby,[8] and the intentions of the princes are divided. Germany is not protected and even wages or prepares a fairly cruel inner war. If all these reasons do not induce you to live more moderately and to take refuge in God, what good can my oration do? What can we say publicly about the merit of the laws in front of those who, like the Cyclopes, care neither for God nor for any laws? I am ashamed to say such things in a university, which should not only listen to, but also cherish the teaching of virtue.

If you deem that God is the maker of things and the judge of our deeds, and you are influenced by the heavenly admonitions, acknowledge Him as the creator of things and as your judge, and obey Him in the duties which He requires by the word of the laws. You can see that the alternating of day and night and of summer and autumn is ordered by God; you all acknowledge that these alternations are fixed. Then why do you doubt the rewards for those who have acted rightly, and the punishments for evil-doers? All the impious are overwhelmed by punishment by God's fixed law. Or do you think that it is by chance that the world has already been subjected to the barbarous tyranny of the Turks, unlike any other before? This has not happened by chance at all, but this miserable prison has to restrain and hold in check the madness of men who do not allow their behaviour to be curbed by any laws, and who want to be licensed to prac-tise wantonness as they please, like wild beasts. Oh deplorable negligence of the princes! They should have remedied these ills in order to call the unrestrained crowd back to moderation by the most severe punishments.

[8] By 1541 most of Hungary had fallen under Ottoman rule.

Nevertheless, if they do not do this, God in His wrath would oppress these peoples by servitude to the Turks.

But I shall return to the scholars: this entire assembly of your teachers entreats you, and instructs you by divine voice, to worship God, to live with more moderation, and to be mindful, in this matter, both of your own and of the common welfare. For, unless your behaviour becomes more moderate, you will assuredly lose all the good things, namely the light of the teaching about God, the Church, the laws, erudition and all the other embellishments of life. How many good things did Adam lose by his one fall? How long did the pagans live in darkness and with horrid crimes, because their leaders rejected the teaching of the first fathers? Rouse yourselves to piety and moderation by these examples. If you do so, you will not only understand in truth the merit of the laws, but you will also be fortunate in ruling, for God promises His followers wisdom and success. So you understand that the laws are God's word, and that this political order both has been established by God and is protected to some degree by Him, in order that He become known in human society, and that, united by mutual duties, we show proof of our notion of God and of the Son of God, and mutual benevolence, and that we incite each other to virtue by mutual example. For understanding these things there is, as I have said, assuredly the need for some study of virtue, for fear of God and for moderation and diligence in ruling one's behaviour. I have spoken.

23 On the merit of studying theology (1537)

CR XI, 324–9

Oration on the merit of the study of theology, given by Doctor C. Cruciger in the year 1537, at the graduation of Master Peter Palladius[1]

Our elders have imposed on me the function of speaking on this occasion and, since we must honour them with the greatest piety and respect, it was not in my power to refuse their authority. I therefore beseech all of you not to assume that I step forward in this place out of confidence in my wit, or by my own decision, but to know that I am brought here by duty. For that reason it is just if you, too, take my oration in good part; I have prepared it for admonishing the inexperienced young, so that they may learn to think with respect about the study of the Holy Scriptures and the theological profession. Certainly in these times, among such twisted judgements and such great hatred against the doctrine of the Church, this oration is particularly necessary. Although my person does not bring enough authority to such a great cause, nevertheless, since the oration is given officially, I shall recite only the opinion of the Holy Scriptures, and since the entire cause pertains to the merit and the usefulness of the Church our admonition should not be disdained.

Therefore, let me come to the point. Just as Paul says: 'I am not ashamed of the Gospel of Christ' [Romans 1:16], so it is proper for all the faithful to be disposed in such a way that they love the word of God with all their heart, acknowledge that it is the highest of all God's favours, and respect with great piety its ministry, that is, the public office of teaching, bestow honour upon it, assist it for the sake of its calling, and defend and adorn it. This must be the chief concern of all the faithful – but let us compare the judgements of the world to that saying of Paul. The majority of men openly despise and hate the Gospel; they also judge that the ministry, that is, the office of teaching, is the cause of the discord and destruction of all humankind, and Paul himself described in clear words the harshness of the hatred among men against the teachers of the Gospel, when he said that the Apostles were considered outcasts and scapegoats, that is, detestable criminals, against whom God is angered implacably, whom the entire nature of things abhors, and whose shadow, like a pollution, harms the

[1] Caspar Cruciger was Dean of the theology faculty in 1537.

entire society of men. 'Already the sun halts, stunned by the greatness of the crime, and, growing pale, checks its chariot; and it denies light to the Earth, the earth denies its fruits, and nature is thrown into the old chaos.' For it cannot be but that there is hatred of a terrible harshness in those who consider the Gospel either blasphemy or an imaginary fable which overthrows realms, laws, established states, governments and the peace of humankind.

While the majority of the world burden the Gospel with these enormous crimes, Paul nevertheless cries out with a great heart against these false judgements: 'I am not ashamed of the Gospel.' He strengthens us by his voice, so that we declare that certainly the Gospel is true and powerful, that it is the eternal will of God, and that the office of teaching is the most sacred veneration of God, which He chiefly demands from men. But in truth, even in those who are not openly ungodly (*atheoi*) or defenders of impious kinds of worship, there is such weakness that they are moved only by the judgements of the world, so that they have less reverence for the ministry of the word, that is, for the public office of teaching. Add to this, that – given that the teachers of the Gospel are despised, hated and live in constant dangers, and many even perish from hunger – men are deterred from the ministry of the Gospel by the fear of dangers and misery, and since honours and great rewards are in store for those who practise other, gainful, arts, very few devote themselves to this study of the Holy Scriptures or the ministry. Many also believe that this kind of teaching can be understood without teachers. Therefore the rank of ministers lies in contempt.

Although this is how things stand in general, nevertheless the pious young must impress upon themselves this word of Paul: 'I am not ashamed of the Gospel', and understand how much dignity there is in this ministry, and prepare themselves for it, so that they can serve the Church when there is need. For this is the highest worship of God, as Christ teaches when he says: 'Herein is my Father glorified, that ye bear much fruit; so shall ye be my disciples' [John 15.8]. Here he clearly testifies that the Father is glorified, if we teach the word to others whom we have received from Him as disciples, as it were; and the prophet says how beautiful are the feet of those proclaiming peace [Romans 1:15]. For this means that these messengers please God and the Church, even though the world hate them, and curse them like monsters. Paul calls the office of teaching itself a sacrifice, just as elsewhere, too, the Scriptures call it that. For that reason we should realise that this worship in particular is required from us, and that it is an office most pleasing to God. By this consolation the good and pious who lead the Church, should sustain themselves against unjust judgements, and know that they perform the office of teaching that is most important and sacred to God. May this worship attract many to prepare themselves for these celebrations, and may they know that they, too, by teaching the doctrine, bring a most pleasing sacrifice to God.

But someone may ask: 'How does this oration about the ministry concern the schools, and the degrees in the schools?' But I have spoken at such length about the ministry in order that you contemplate with what intention the Holy Scriptures are taught, and for what purpose these degrees are established. For these studies in the schools pertain properly to the preservation of the Church ministry. With that intention schools were established in the past in Alexandria and in several congregations, so that teachers and ministers of the Church could be taken from there. For Christ gives the Church ministers, prophets and teachers, He wants the Church to be established and taught by them, and He wants those who are to be placed in authority over the Church to be prepared, and He does not want men who are utterly unlearned to be put in authority, or inexperienced men who consider themselves self-taught (*autodidaktoi*) and invent beliefs from themselves, without any spiritual practice. Therefore, in the beginning there were schools in the Church; if only they had preserved the pure teaching passed on from the Apostles. But this was restored later by a great and wonderful favour of God, and God gave a prophet again to these last times, so that others be educated, and certainly the Church must again attend to preserving with the greatest zeal that favour of God, that is, the pure doctrine of the Gospel, and to passing it on to later generations.

Accordingly it is of great importance in turn whom we have as teachers, and to whose judgements on the greatest things and on dogmas we listen. Thus the holy fathers often adduce partly the Apostles and partly those of the generation following the Apostles. For Irenaeus cites Polycarp, who had been a disciple of the Apostle John, and Valentinus opposes Polycarp's authority to Florinus.[2] Basil studied with Gregory of Nyssa whose authority was distinguished when the impiety of Paul of Samosata was condemned. There is no other testimony about the Trinity after the writings of the Apostles, which is older than that of Gregory. Basil had such a high

---

[2] Details of the life of Polycarp (69–155) may be found in the tract *Peri Monarchias*, written by his follower Irenaeus, which was addressed to a Roman priest named Florinus. Valentinus is a gnostic theologian of the second century.

opinion of him that he said that his ears resounded with Gregory's[3] voice, and Sabellius opposed his testimony to those troubling the church of Nyssa. Jerome heard Epiphanius and Gregory of Nazianzen, and I leave out many others.[4] I have only called these to mind in order that listeners reflect that it is an extraordinary favour of God to hear the doctrine of the Gospel from such teachers, whose judgements we can safely follow. Therefore the schools belong to the ministry of the Gospel in the Church, and for that reason attestations of knowledge are bestowed upon good and learned men, so that it be evident which teachers they heard, in order that the doctrine be propagated to later generations with firm authority. This was a very ancient custom in the Church, but later uneducated men were admitted to leading the Church, without attestation of the teachers, and, as Gregory of Nazianzen said, they were immediately made teachers, just as in stories giants are called giants as soon as they are born. From that practice a great confusion of doctrine originated.

Therefore, since God in His great mercy has restored the light of the Gospel for us, let us give thanks to God, and let us preserve this favour with the greatest zeal in the churches and schools, and let us attend to it that those who are to undertake the Church ministry be honestly instructed, and that neither the uneducated not the self-educated (*autodidaktoi*) be received. For we see that in our age the fanatical beliefs of the Anabaptists originated only from the uneducated and the self-educated (*autodidaktois*).[5] How much do we owe God therefore, who gave us a leader[6] and teacher excelling in faith and correct judgement, by whose teaching we were protected against these fanatical beliefs whose founders often disturbed our Church! However, since many who are educated in this school preside over our Church, who gladly admit that they are not self-educated (*autodidaktous*) but students, the experienced leaders established their Church sagaciously, and – assisted by the divine help which protects pious teachings – they preserved them in office. Therefore the schools belong to the ministry of the Gospel or if you will, they are an essential part of that most sacred

---

[3] Gregory of Nyssa (335–94), the younger brother of Basil, defended the doctrines of the Trinity, Incarnation and Redemption and wrote polemical tracts against Eunomius and Apollinarius; Paul of Samosata (3rd century AD), held heretical views of the Person of Christ and was condemned at the Synod of Antioch; Sabellius (*fl. c.* 220) espoused the trinitarian heresy of monarchianism.
[4] Jerome heard Epiphanius (315–403) defend Nicene faith against heresy. After meeting Jerome in 382 he attacked Origenism. Gregory of Nazianzen (329–89), whose preaching restored the Nicene faith in Constantinople.
[5] See note 2 oration 1, p. 5.   [6] Reading *gubernatorem* for *gubernatorum*.

office; for it is necessary first that those to whom the leadership of the Church is to be entrusted be trained long and diligently.

Then, the degree is the attestation, so that it be evident from which teachers they have received the teaching. Just as at the time of the Apostles, now, too, this is of great importance. For when there is great discord about doctrine, or when there are great struggles about religion, it is necessary to see whose authority they follow. John says: 'If there come any unto you, and bring not this doctrine, receive him not' [John 2:10]. The Scriptures often command in the same way elsewhere. For that reason the kind of teaching must be considered diligently, and one must look from which sources it is taken; therefore the teachers in the schools carry a heavy load. It is necessary to know from which authors they have received the doctrine, to preserve its purity, and to take heed lest new and improper beliefs be added. Thus, when Paul of Samosata began to spread his poison in the Church of Antioch, Malchion[7] as the only one among the teachers understood that something new was being disseminated by that tenet, and the old purity was being corrupted, and he was the first to cry out; and he notified the nearby bishops of Alexandria and Jerusalem how much danger there was. Thus the madness of Paul of Samosata was checked and eradicated by Malchion's faith and diligence.

Therefore the ministry of the Gospel must be kept and protected with equal care both in the schools and in the Church. Pious princes must not only establish schools, but they must also choose the kind of teaching, as if it were a nursery-garden that is approved by a certain and strong authority, and pay attention that the nursery be not corrupted. This attention is necessary in the schools in order that posterity know what kind of teaching it has received. God demands this diligence from princes and the Church, and for the purpose that He commands, so that all honour and adorn this ministry for the sake of its calling. You who engage in studies, consider in particular that we are not placed in this position only by the private calling of our elders, but by the official calling of the entire Church, in order that you study the teaching of the Gospel in particular, and that many prepare themselves for the ministry. In this matter most weighty divine threats and promises should move you. Christ says: 'He who receiveth a prophet in the name of a prophet shall receive a prophet's reward,' [Matthew 10:41], and: 'Whoever gives to one of these little ones even a cup of cold water because he is a disciple, truly, I say to you, he shall not lose his reward' [Matthew

---

[7] Malchion was the presbyter who interrogated Paul of Samosata at the Synod of Antioch.

10:42]. For that reason, those who do good to the ministers of the Church may in turn expect from Christ protection and many other favours. One cannot say with what great hatred against the Gospel the popes and many kings and princes were burning, and how often they have already declared war against our princes whom God called to grant some shelter to pious teachers. Among these perils, I only sustain myself by these promises, by which He testifies that He is concerned that those who strive to honour the ministry of the Gospel and protect the pious teachers be not oppressed or destroyed. How beautifully did Christ paint us an image of the Church in Lazarus who, sick and afflicted with ulcers, lies in the entrance to the house of the rich man, by whom he is neglected and left to starve. And yet God testifies that He cares for him by sending angels to him. Thus lies the Church in the realms of kings and princes, and it is not only neglected, but also trod under foot; and yet God has regard for it and sends angels and princes by whom it may be protected, and He does not allow it to be oppressed or destroyed.

The widow of Zarephath received Elijah as a guest, although there was a great scarcity of food; for this kindness God kindly provided for her in those very hard times [1 Kings 17:10–16]. So all should know that it is a duty pleasing to God to support and honour the ministry of the Gospel for the sake of its calling. On the other hand, the tyrants and impious men who either scorn or even hate the ministers of the Gospel, and attempt to oppress them, will receive the harshest punishments – just as in the fourth book of Kings the Lord says: 'I may avenge the blood of my servants the prophets and the blood of all the servants of the Lord' [2 Kings 9:7]. The contempt for the ministers of the Gospel will not go unpunished, and some time the tyrants who attack the pious will receive punishment for their cruelty. I judged that this admonition is necessary for the young in these times, because we see many being corrupted by the examples of the impious and feeling no respect for the ministry of the Gospel and the study of the Holy Scriptures. They need to know that it is part of their worship of God that they should love and revere the ministry of the Gospel. Also they need to know that it is piety to prepare one's intellect so that some time it could be of use to the Church. For that reason the young should learn to under-stand and perform their duty. I pray to our Lord Jesus Christ that He may set alight all our minds by His Holy Spirit, in order that we may truly understand His Gospel and obey it, so that the glory of God is always adorned and honoured by our studies. I have spoken.

Authorities

24 On Plato (1538)

CR XI, 413–25

Oration on Plato, held by Conradus Lagus, when conferring the title of Master on some students, in the year 1538[1]

In a very serious deliberation in Thucydides, the Spartan king Archidamus said that the discipline of his country was such that the citizens did not study the laws with eagerness, in order to win or to overthrow, but that they obeyed them without subterfuge [*History* 1.84.3]. I believe that respect for the laws is beneficial not only for the Spartans, but for all states anywhere in the world. Since this is so, it is honourable both for me and for you to preserve the degrees established in the schools, so that we may obey the laws which have been passed on to us by our ancestors not without serious reason. Therefore I praise your courtesy for having come together here in order to preserve public morals, and I entreat you to listen to my oration with a favourable mind, especially since I have not taken on this rôle out of confidence in my intellect, but the nature of the office imposes upon us the necessity of speaking on this occasion. I do not know how others are affected, but I can declare it of my own mind that these scholastic assemblies and gatherings are most agreeable to me for many reasons. For it delights me to see, so to speak, the protection of the state, that is, the elders, who are already leading the state by their counsel and authority, as well as this flower of youth, who will guide succeeding generations. We must supplicate well on their behalf in these gatherings, and make our prayers that God may preserve these ornaments of life: education, laws and religion. It also comes to my mind, when I behold the teachers of all disciplines, what an embellishment the complete multitude of the arts is for life. Therefore let us remember that these assemblies are to be celebrated in such a way that they may put us in mind of the gifts of heaven, of the state and of our duty.

What is more appropriate in the company of the learned than to speak or hear about good things? Since the nature of my office demands that I deliver an oration here, I greatly wish that I could satisfy you in this matter. But it is convenient if you give permission to those who speak, if nevertheless they make an effort to recommend their study to you, and to bring to it arguments that are proper and useful to scholars. Furthermore, it is greatly beneficial to know the stories of learned and excellent men, for

---

[1] Conradus Lagus (*d.* 1546) was Dean of the arts faculty in 1538.

their examples and dangers and various fortunes admonish us of life and of morals, and their beliefs shape the judgements of those who study them. I commend therefore the counsel of those who have told the stories of most learned men here before. In order to imitate them I have decided upon an oration on Plato; it is truly beneficial to know about his studies, travels and advice on the state, and to see somehow what kind of philosophy he deals with, and what benefit it brings to those who learn it. I shall, however, omit the vulgar praises, which are called for by the renown of the topic and by the love for one's country. For if this oration is to be held for the benefit of the students, I have to speak extensively about his type of teaching.

But let me first expound his life briefly: Plato was born in Athens, in the month of March in the year in which that most eloquent man, Pericles, died; that year was the third of the destructive war that the Greek cities waged among themselves, which was called the Peloponnesian War.[2] On his mother's side he descended from Solon. He possessed great wealth, and was therefore educated in a manner befitting a gentleman. He studied letters, arithmetic and geometry, for in Athens these arts were taught to boys early. Since he had a powerful intellect he wrote poems and tragedies, inspired by admiration for Euripides, with whom he was acquainted, for Plato's adolescence coincided with a time which was not quiet for the city, but yet not sad. For although the beginning of the war had been inauspicious, and great misfortunes were endured, nevertheless after about twenty years many favourable events followed and raised up the city again. Later, when Plato was almost of adult age, the changed fortunes of the city, both in military and civil matters, prevented him from having a political career: at home destructive discord had broken out among the citizens. This was followed by disaster abroad, where the Athenians were defeated by Lysander. Then the city was taken, in the year in which Plato was twenty-three years old. At that time his country was oppressed in sorrowful servitude by the Spartans and by the thirty tyrants, and since Plato had an intellect which abhorred civil discord and fighting, and was fond of erudition, he reckoned that he had to leave the country, because he could neither bring succour to his country which was going to ruin and perishing, nor would he be safe amidst the monstrous cruelty of the thirty tyrants and the unremitting disturbances. It is said nevertheless that he served in the military before his country's overthrow and the civil discord but, since it

---

[2] Around 427 BC. The main source for Plato's life seems to be Diogenes Laertius, *Lives*, III (pseudo-) Plato's *Epistles* and Ficino's summary in his translation of Plato's works, *Opera*, 1517, fols. iii^rf.

was a brief first campaign, it is not necessary to relate it. While away he heard Euclid in Megara; the one whose geometry is extant. Since at the time the teaching of the Pythagoreans flourished in Italy, and Archytas of Tarentum was much admired, he then sailed to Italy, where he heard Archytas and Timaeus discussing the beginning and workings of nature and other topics of physics. It is possible to estimate what these topics were from the book which he called the *Timaeus*; they are some basics of physics, on the origin of the world, the double motion of the heavens, on who made, as he himself says, the letter X in the order of planets, on the sequence of elements, the generation of man, on the nature of humours, the parts of the human body, the soul and God the Maker of nature. These are briefly contained in the *Timaeus* [36C]; although there are some arithmetical riddles in it, Galen nevertheless considers that the remaining physics is taken from Hippocrates, and that these discussions are incomplete in Plato rather than finished – for neither is the reason of the motions of the heavens explained, nor is the anatomy unimpaired.[3] I nevertheless praise the beginnings, and I believe that the kind of physics that describes the nature of humours and the parts of the human body is useful. And so Galen often borrows Platonic descriptions.

Plato remained in Italy until Thrasybulus regained his country, and Conon rebuilt the cast-down country, after the power of the Spartans had been shattered. Therefore Plato returned and began to listen to Socrates, captivated, it seems, by his political disputations. For Socrates had seen terrible changes in the Attic city which give much food for thought to an ingenious man who thinks deeply about the morals of men and about the strange vicissitudes of life. After the restoration of the country's freedom and the victory of Thrasybulus, Socrates lived for about thirty years. He prophesied Plato's future greatness clearly when he said that, the day before Plato came to him, he had dreamt that he held a swan in his lap; it then flew high up, singing most sweetly. He said that Plato would be that swan for the Greeks [Diogenes Laertius, *Lives*, III.5].

When he had heard Socrates for some time, and was not content with these popular discussions on life and morals, but believed that the teaching of the nature of things needed to be added, he made for Egypt; his travelling companions were Eudoxus and the poet Euripides. And I do not doubt that these things happened by divine providence, so that in that way the old and erudite philosophy of the movements of the heavens be spread further. For

[3] See Galen, *On the Opinions of Hippocrates and Plato.*

although Thales had passed on to the Greeks a small part of that knowledge, it had been consigned to oblivion again. Therefore Plato and Eudoxus did a great service in not only bringing it back to Greece again from Egypt, but also in teaching it to their listeners in order to spread it. Indeed, Eudoxus also left tables of the motions and an order of the year. The knowledge that was founded in this way was preserved for a long time by the studies of the Greeks. If, as we must, we esteem its merit and usefulness, we must certainly render thanks to these first founders. Also worthy of admiration is the virtue of those who did not hesitate to undertake such distant journeys amidst great toil and danger, in order to search for the truth. What sharp goads were there in their minds, what enthusiasm for investigating things that were worth knowing?

We, by contrast, should be ashamed of our sloth, neglecting the arts given by divine providence and discovered by great toil, and allowing them to perish. Let us therefore be roused by Plato's example, first to love truly the noble arts, and not to shrink from the dangers and toil involved in obtaining them, and then let us imitate his decision. As he did, let us add that secret knowledge of the motions of the heavens to the moral discussions. And see[4] for what purpose he sought after these arts. He listed the public benefits elsewhere: in this civic life there is need for a sequence of seasons and a description of the year, but the true purpose of learning is that the investigation of nature may lead us to a knowledge of God, and show human minds that a light is given to us by divine providence, by which life is guided, so that it may obey God, and that the minds of those who, recognising God, submit to Him, will live with God in a wonderful and eternal[5] light after they have departed from this life. These are Plato's words in the *Epinomis* [989D].

Are these not most weighty words, young men? I do not want them to be part of the Gospel, but they should have their place. It is a knowledge of reason, which leads to the boundaries set up by divine providence, if it applies itself to philosophy correctly, if it seeks for the traces of divinity in things and if it considers the nature of the human mind. For the ravings of Epicurus stray far from the path, take away physical principles and consign to oblivion the knowledge of God imprinted on to human minds.

But let me return to history. When he had returned from Egypt, Plato stood by Socrates in his trial. When he began to speak for him in public, he was prevented by the noise of the opposing faction; he was therefore forced

---

[4] Reading *videte* for *videre*.　　[5] Reading *aeterna* for *aeternae*.

to desist, since he was not heard, but in some other services he manifested towards Socrates faithfulness and steadfastness worthy of a good man. The Apology, which still exists, indicates with what dignity he would have defended Socrates had he been permitted to do so: in it many things are said with great wisdom against the arrogance of the men who despise God and deny the existence of providence. He then goes on to say many things about immortality, and that it is a great pleasure to the sage to depart from this life, and join those men where he can learn about the highest things with certitude.

After Socrates had been killed, when those who had indicted him lay in ambush for his friends, Plato again resolved to leave the country. Thus he travelled to Sicily, and came to the tyrant Dionysius, the father of the younger Dionysius – who were both expelled from rule shortly thereafter – for the Sicilians had frequent commerce with the Athenians, and they imitated their laws and studies. The tyrant himself was of a powerful intellect, and he delighted in Greek studies. There was a citizen of Syracuse of the highest merit, Dio, who received Plato as a guest in order to hear him speak about nature and about the state. However, just as there is a natural discord among many things, and of animated beings between each other, such as between wine and hemlock, or the swan and the eagle, there is also an innate and implacable hatred between the nature of tyrants and that of philosophers. Therefore, when Plato openly rebuked Dionysius' violence in some matters, the tyrant was going to kill him. However, upon Dio's plea he granted him his life, but in such a way that he was given as a slave to some Spartan, whom Dionysius commanded to sell him. Thus Plato was taken to Aegina, and was bought back by Dio for 30 minas, that is 300 crowns, as we would now say.

When the father died and the young Dionysius succeeded him, and was guided mainly by Dio's counsel, Dio wanted to bend Dionysius' youthful intellect towards virtue, justice and moderation, and decided that Plato should be called. Although Plato had been warned by the earlier example that there is no friendship between philosophers and tyrants, he was nevertheless overcome by Dio's exhortation and returned to Sicily. The beginnings were favourable for the companionship at court, and the citizens all foretold a golden age for themselves, when the youth began to be led by Plato. For he listened to the philosopher treating with great enthusiasm of God and of immortality, as the letters prove that are still extant. These are the foundations of true virtue, to hold a correct belief concerning God and the immortality of the soul; this is a philosophy worthy of kings. Therefore Plato accomplished so much that the horrid form of tyranny was utterly removed; the king went forth in public and engaged with the citizens, surrounded not by a tyrant's attendants, but by the most learned and noblest citizens. Not only was the youth's private life without baseness, but he busied himself also with the most excellent studies. In his rule, nothing was done cruelly, unjustly or without the counsel of the good men Dio and Heracleides.

These many good things were not to be spoiled by Dionysius' nature, as much as by the common plague of courts, envy. Some base men, who desired the condition of tyranny, so that they might have licence for their crimes, attempted to draw to themselves the reins of affairs, expelling Dio. It is not unknown how powerful false accusations are, not only in the courts of princes, but also among private persons. Since Dio had Dionysius' sister for his wife, it was whispered to the king that he should not grant too much power to a relative lest he might at some point covet his kingship. When deceit got the upper hand Dio was driven from the kingdom, while Plato exerted himself in vain in various ways lest something unjust be decreed against such a citizen endowed with the greatest virtue and merit.

After Dio had been exiled, for a short while the power of the base men grew, and the king's mind began to be depraved. By chance, at that time Plato predicted an eclipse. At that point Aristippus, who was present, said that he would divine its meaning, and jokingly said that it portended enmity between the king and Plato. By this joke he wittily rebuked the change at court, but he should have added that, because of his change in morals, Dionysius would lose his kingdom. Although the tyrant attempted by cunning to detain Plato, Plato nevertheless suspected – and rightly – that there was some danger to him because of Dio, and removed himself from Dionysius in any possible way. He was released, therefore, not without gifts: they write that 80 talents were given to him, that is, 58,000 crowns.

He returned to Athens therefore and had disciples. Dio stayed with him, as well as many noble Syracusan youths, among them Aristotle's friend Eudemus. After Plato had been expelled, the tyrant began to proceed with all kinds of crime. He forced Dio's wife to marry another. This led to Dio starting a war, in which he was greatly helped by noble citizens, Plato's pupils. Thus Plato's school inflicted the just punishment upon the tyrant. For, as Plato had predicted, the tyrant lost his kingdom.

Later Plato aged, not in leisure, but – as is most virtuous – he encouraged the study of the best arts by teaching and writing. Here you have the history of a philosopher which contains a truly philosophical course of life. Out of desire for learning he went to many distant lands, brought the best arts to his country, encouraged studies and came into conflict with tyrants – for that, too, concerns a philosopher. He left behind not only writings, but disciples, who educated later generations and preserved the arts that are useful for life. What kind of life is preferable to this? Or what office in life is more useful for human society than the office of teaching? And so it is said rightly that even though philosophers do not hold a civil office, and although they abstain from public occupations, they are nevertheless just, for the reason that they inquire into and teach arts that are useful for life. An aedile who builds some building certainly does not do the state a better service than a learned man who guides religious [scruples], who shows what is just, who discloses the nature of things and shows to men the necessary remedies. Therefore, although Plato by his own decision did not hold a civil office in his country, he nevertheless did a great service to its citizens and indeed to later generations by a more outstanding kind of office. He himself mentions the reason why he abstained from the administration of the city: because he did not approve of the present state of affairs, but nevertheless felt that it had to be tolerated, because the behaviour of one's country has to be endured, like one's parents', even if it is not very appropriate. But I believe that the first reason for which he did not accede to public office was his country's misfortune and servitude, then the study of knowledge led his mind away from other occupations; in this he accomplished a much greater task for the state and for all later generations.

Now something had to be added about his writings: first of all, his eloquence is such that he excels by far all Greek and Roman orators whose writings are extant. No one's speech is richer or more splendid. In some we particularly praise the propriety, in others the elegance and the charm of the figures of speech; what Plato wants to express properly, he says so clearly that it is impossible to think of anything more appropriate. Again, when he wants to add splendour and embellishments he defeats by far all orators in the variety of his elaborate descriptions and the beauty of his figures of speech. Therefore some have said that if Jupiter were to speak Greek he would use Plato's words. Gorgias and Thrasymachus were slightly superior to Plato as orators, as well as some others who practised public speaking in their youth – for it was considered then that the young had to be prepared for the state by that discipline in particular. Plato rails wittily here and there that they passed on nothing other than booklets of rhetoric, and accustomed the young to an empty talkativeness without the knowledge of things. Since nothing is more dangerous for the state than for young intellects to become accustomed to sophistry, Plato justly raged against the orators of that age, whose schools nourished only sophistry. Having curbed their studies, he roused up and appealed to those who practised rhetoric later, first to flee sophistry, establish the arguments of their subjects by some true reason and to take the topics from the sources of the business, not exotic and poetic ones, but such as are appropriate and fitting for the things about which one needs to speak.

These form the vigour of an oration[6] and without them, even if beautiful and variously depicted things are said, the oration is nevertheless both empty and inept. In oratorical delivery, too, many eminent virtues follow this vigour, such as dignity and brilliance. Thus Demosthenes' oration is by far superior to the writings of the older writers both in content and in delivery. Gorgias' little speeches have some meretricious ornament and flowers without true arguments, brilliance or disposition. Lysias' arguments may be appropriate, but they are feeble and without beauty. Even though Plato's disposition and manner of embellishing first appears borrowed from Isocrates, who was slightly older than Plato, it seems that nevertheless Plato's delivery, too, was of some use to later generations. The advice for finding the vigour, and the elaborate descriptions in Demosthenes, are without doubt redolent of Plato's teaching. For Demosthenes does not seek far-away arguments that are foreign to what has been established, but he takes his matters from the origins of affairs, as behoves an educated man, and he weaves them together with great skill by dialectic, almost as it is done in school, and, often striving, he utters sentences that are not common but, so to speak, scholarly, that is, drawn out from some very weighty knowledge. Why should we doubt, therefore, that Demosthenes was accomplished in that more erudite knowledge, and not in the pamphlets of rhetoric? And he himself indicates that he was a pupil of Plato, about whose philosophy he writes the following to a friend: 'I see that you cherish the discipline, and indeed that of Plato, that truly abominates vile profit and deceit, and that commands that the aim of all actions be virtue itself and justice. That those instructed by this teaching cause crime and deceit for others, and are not just towards everyone' [*Letters* V.3]. These are

[6] For 'vigour' (*nervus*) as essential for a succesful orator, see Cicero, *On the Orator*, III.xxxi.80.

the words of Demosthenes, in which he gives a testimony that does honour to Plato.

It was indeed not simply a matter of common sagacity to see what faults the earlier sophistic of Gorgias and the like had, and to alter wholly the course of studies of his entire century. This matter was the sign of a great and heroic mind. He saw that the young were given weapons to move the state, when their minds were not curbed by a more weighty teaching, but the only action considered praiseworthy was to throw into disorder and to disturb the laws and other matters. Therefore he became the one to exhort the Greeks to cherish a different kind of teaching, which was useful for morals and for peace.

He demonstrated his belief clearly in his interpretation of the Delian oracle.[7] For the Greek cities were tired of the continuous and grievous war that they were waging among themselves, and consulted the oracle at Delos, how the god was to be placated, so that he would free Greece from its present ills. When the god answered that the entire Delian altar – which was of cubic shape – had to be doubled, the Greeks added a mass of equal size and created a rectangular shape (*tetragōnon*) in which the length was greater than the width. When they asked afterwards whether they had obeyed the oracle in a proper manner, Apollo denied it. Therefore they were struck with consternation, and suspected that something hidden was signified under this guise, and resolved to seek an interpreter for the oracle who was outstanding in intellect and knowledge. They therefore related the oracle to Plato, who demonstrated to them the error in doubling the altar, because they made a rectangular shape (*tetragōnon*) instead of a cube, and he taught them how to double a cube by determining its diameter. He admonished the Greeks, however, that the god did not care greatly for the bulk of the altar, nor would he be placated by a pile of stones, but that the hidden meaning was that the Greeks should cultivate other, better studies, that is, philosophy, which would be useful for curbing people's minds, for moderation, justice and the love of public peace. Plato never failed in his effort to kindle these studies. In order to admonish the young who were desirous of eloquence that it was not to be employed for causing public disturbance, but for a different, more honourable use, he said that the goal of eloquence is not to delight men, but to say what is pleasing to God.

If only the young imprinted these precepts in their minds. That way, when they think that there is such a great goal set before them for their

[7] For the Delian puzzle of doubling the cube, see Vitruvius, *On Architecture*, IX.13.

studies, namely to elucidate the glory of God by their speech, they will prepare themselves much more diligently for such an excellent task. They should also see how vile it is to devote oneself to eloquence for parasitical and facetious abuse, for deprecating the honourable arts, and for inflaming hatred against Christ. Since those who do so by that very act imitate the devil, they are by right to be called followers of the devil, and not eloquent. And in truth there are not a few of them in these public dissensions, for it is more than true what Menander says: 'Life delights most in those who are worthless: the flatterer fares best of all, the swindler second, and the malicious man third.'[8] Those who should most restrain these plagues nourish them, but perhaps this is not the place for this complaint.

I return to the established topic, therefore. As Horace says in praise of Pindar: 'A mighty breeze uplifts the Dircaean swan / Antonius, as oft as he essays a flight / to the lofty regions of the clouds' [*Odes*, IV.2.25 ff.].[9] So certainly this swan, that is, Plato, singing some divine song, defeated all orators in eloquence. Here and there in Cicero, not only in the philosophical writings, but also in his lawsuits in the forum, many embellishments were plucked from Plato. Indeed, Cicero announces that he was made an orator at the Academy; we, too, can therefore borrow many embellishments from him. However, I shall stop speaking about eloquence, which is sufficiently celebrated by the testimony of the greatest orators – but eloquence is a great ornament for a man.

Concerning the things themselves and the type of philosophy, the controversies among the learned are great. First of all, it is well known that Plato did not write in order about all of the arts, but he demonstrated in more unrestrained discussions here and there what he approved of and what he did not. Befitting an ingenious and eloquent man, who was also by nature given to mockery (*skōptikos*), there are also many ironical and figurative discussions, as for instance when he jokingly argues that all great men who are of service to the state are justly punished by its citizens, because, by their services, they increased the people's passions and licentiousness. The *Republic* (*politeia*), in which he imagines the common use of things, is certainly ironic, for he wanted to censure wittily and figuratively the infinite greed of the mighty. The uneducated have pretended that these ideas were ravings, as they did not understand the type of greater discourse in Plato, and did not see that he himself called the ideas images

---

[8] This is very similar to a passage in Menander, *Theophoroumene*, fr. 1. (223), but without the first line.
[9] As translated by C. E. Bennett in Horace, *Odes* (London and Cambridge, MA, 1968), p. 289.

and notions which the learned conceive in their minds, that is the definitions or demonstrations.[10]

Since he does not often employ the method which he proclaims so many times, and sometimes digresses freely in his discussion, and wraps some things in images and conceals them deliberately, and, furthermore, since he rarely announces what one should notice, I agree that it is rather Aristotle who should be presented to the young. He explains completely the arts he teaches, and employs an easier method, like a thread for guiding the reader, and most of the time announces what one should note. There are many weighty reasons why this is necessary for those who teach. For just as from the dragon's teeth sown by Cadmus a crop of armed men sprang forth, who fought among themselves, so, if one sows ambiguous opinions, various destructive disputes will spring forth.

Not long ago, Bessarion and Trebizond disputed among themselves in a hostile manner, when the one preferred Plato and the other Aristotle.[11] Theodorus Gaza resolved this strife by saying that each had to be attributed his place. Thus the perusal of Plato would be very profitable, if one had been correctly instructed in Aristotle and read Plato afterwards. For if the reader brings the Aristotelian method to it, he can easily, as if within fixed limits, enclose the things that are widely scattered in Plato. I believe that this was Aristotle's reason for striving for such a concise method, that he could pass on in its entirety to following generations what he had received from Plato, collected and divided with some economy and order. Although he even wished to polish and correct some things, there is no great difference on any of the issues. And it is not difficult for the experienced to see which of the two excels in which part. Although I may be called impertinent, daring to judge the two most excellent philosophers, just as Midas presumed to judge between Apollo and Pan, it is nevertheless useful to show the young what the authors profess, who are usually presented to them.

What Plato has written about the management of cities is more copious, and it is embellished by wonderful splendour of speech. Since he wrote

[10] Note that Melanchthon equates Platonic ideas with Aristotelian definitions: see *Enarrationes Aliquot Librorum Ethicorum Aristotelis*, CR XVI, 290.

[11] Johannes Bessarion (1403–73) wrote the *In Calumniatorem Platonis* (1469) against George of Trebizond (1395–1484), who in his *Comparationes Phylosophorum Aristotelis et Platonis* (1458) attacked the philosophy of Plato on moral grounds and criticised attempts to revive Neoplatonism as subverting Christianity proper. Theodore Gaza (1400–76), who belongs to the circle of Bessarion, is best known for his Latin translations of Aristotle's *De Animalibus* and *Problemata*, based on earlier translations by Trebizond; the best account of the conflict is in John Monfasani, *George of Trebizond: a Biography and a Study of His Rhetoric and Logic* (Leiden, 1976).

differing books, the *Republic* and the *Laws*, he joked in the former, but in the the *Laws* he explained his purpose simply and without riddles, and he brings together useful precepts for the leading of cities, from which the Roman lawyers drew many things as from sources. For it is manifest that in many laws the authors almost copy Plato's words. Concerning rape perpetrated with violence, Plato ordained that it was lawful to kill the rapist, not only for those to whom violence had been done, but also for their father, brothers or sons. The law on abductors, imitating this, gives the power to kill the abductor not only to the father, but also to other kinsmen. But the mentioning of examples takes longer than it would be convenient at this point. Indeed, the lawyers conceded so much to the authority of that writer that they inserted his words even into the laws; for example, in the section on trade a sentence is quoted which confirms an honest negotiation as a retail trader's (*kapeleutiken*). Furthermore, Cicero quotes several sentences from all of Plato's discussions of the vicissitudes and ruling of realms.

Aristotle, too, has gathered many embellishments from Plato, which he explains by applying his method. For he took from Plato the divisions of justice, which are greatly useful, and he included them more strictly within dialectical boundaries. The distinction between types of justice is also Plato's invention, together with its arithmetical and geometrical proportions. Still, in Aristotle the dialectic is complete. Physics, too, is more learnedly begun in these dwellings, so to speak, that is, from the first beginnings, and continued to the description of the natures of animals. Ethics as well is taught more simply. Let us therefore love them both, and when we are reasonably versed in Aristotle let us read the other for the sake of political matters and of eloquence. He has certain passages with which he can give pleasure to the learned. For he discusses quite weightily the immortality of the human soul, and he everywhere establishes as the goal of philosophy the recognition of God, as he says in a letter: 'We philosophise correctly, if we recognise God as the father, cause and ruler of the entire nature, and obey him by living justly' [*Letters* 6, C–D]. He says that this alone is not education without refinement (*amouson paideian*),[12] and true philosophy. And since he saw that this was ridiculed by the atheists, he encourages the reader, saying that it is not enough to think like this, but that the mind has to be so strengthened and corroborated that we can spurn those who deride us for thinking that way. For he could see that the philosopher has need of

[12] See note 12, oration 7, p. 68.

that strength, so that he would not allow himself to be deterred from the correct belief by the judgement of the impious. Although I myself, too, love and admire these thoughts of Plato's, nevertheless the error of those is to be rebuked harshly who, as a result, confuse Platonic philosophy and the Gospel. This confusion of types of teaching has to be avoided and abominated by the learned, and one needs to see what place is to be granted to philosophy. All good arts are gifts of God, but the individual ones should have their place. True philosophy, that is, one that does not stray from reason and from demonstrations, is some notion of the divine laws: it recognises that there is a God, it judges on civic morals, it sees that this distinction between worthy and vile acts is implanted in us by divine providence, it considers that horrid crimes are punished by God, and it also has some presentiment of immortality. It nevertheless does not see or teach what is proper to the Gospel, that is, the forgiveness of sins to be given without recompense, for the sake of the Son of God. This notion has not sprung from human minds, indeed, it is far beyond the range of human reason, but the Son of God, who is in the bosom of the Father, has made it manifest, as is said at length elsewhere. Therefore sagacity has to be applied in distinguishing between types of teaching, and those impudent people are to be rejected, who pour darkness on the Gospel; indeed they consign to oblivion and destroy the Gospel, when they transform it into Platonic philosophy. Even more to be reproached are those who do not even understand Plato and generate monstrous beliefs by distorting his forms, and spread them in the Church, such as Origen and many others after him did. For the Christian doctrine was shamefully defiled in these old times by the impudent mingling with Platonic philosophy. I have added this briefly, for, while the comparison of teachings brings some light to scholars, the Church repeatedly warns us to be careful not to confuse the types of teaching. I have spoken.

25 On Aristotle

CR XI, 342-9

Oration on the life of Aristotle, given by Philip Melanchthon at the graduation of the Masters, 1537[1]

Your attendance at this graduation ceremony is most delightful to me, and, while I am delighted by your observance, I also approve of your judgement that you indicate that you think well of this public custom. Although this ceremony contains some childish games, you know nevertheless that the degrees themselves are established by very weighty counsel, so that the order of studying be appointed and the young be attracted to a fixed order of studies. Certainly for us in this school it happens that those who strive for a degree dedicate themselves with greater diligence to the study of philosophy; for that reason we gladly preserve degrees. Furthermore it is proper for a mind which does not shrink from humanity to esteem and love the harmony of orders, which also brings the greatest benefits to the state. Finally, what is more beautiful than the multitude of the assemblies in which men of outstanding intellect, learning and virtue get together to hear in what studies the young are engaged and what progress they make, and the young are advised on many great things whose knowledge is most useful for life? If there were gladiatorial games, or exotic merchandise, or if wild beasts were displayed for show, what assemblies of men would there be in the whole town? And in truth there is no more beautiful sight than an assembly of good and learned men, for the state has no greater ornament. And since nothing is more admirable than virtue, it is a great pleasure for a worthy mind to see such men in which it shines forth illustriously. Therefore it is proper for you to disagree with the opinions of the Cynics who foolishly criticise these customs. Nothing is more fitting in an assembly of the learned than to have some discussion about good things.

Since accordingly the nature of public office requires me to speak in this function at this time, even if I realise how much I am lacking, by right, in what pertains to the success of eloquence, nevertheless, since it behoves me and others to preserve this custom, I did not wish my effort for the state to

---

[1] Melanchthon, as Dean of the arts faculty, presided over the promotion of Masters in January 1537. A slightly different oration on Aristotle was delivered in 1544, also translated by R. Keen in *A Melanchthon Reader* (New York, 1988), pp. 78–87. For a comparison of the two versions, see further, R. Keen, 'Melanchthon's Two Lives of Aristotle', *Wolfenbütteler Renaissance Mitteilungen* 8 (1984), 4–11.

be lacking. In turn, it will be a token of your humanity to take my oration in good part, which I urgently beseech you to do. Since on this occasion one often speaks about the merit of the arts and the true virtues, I believe that history should be brought to mind, namely that of the life of Aristotle. Not only because greater enjoyment can be conceived from history – for the variety of matters and events delights the mind – but also because for many reasons it is beneficial for us to know the counsels, utterances and deeds of great men.

For the mind is roused to virtue by contemplating their example. Furthermore we are advised on many things. A general can imitate many of Scipio's or Caesar's decisions, and in the same way we, in our studies, can judge about many things more correctly when we consider the sagacity and reason of the most learned men in searching and teaching the arts. The comparison of the outstanding masters is of great profit for sharpening and shaping one's judgements. I shall therefore speak of Aristotle, not as it is done in eulogies, but I shall recount briefly what we know of his life. Then I shall add something about his kind of philosophy and his writings in order to advise the young that his kind of philosophy should be most esteemed and aspired to, and show how useful it is to be versed in Aristotelian reasoning and method. For indeed I consider that no one can become a master of method of any kind without it. Those who are ignorant of that path of teaching that Aristotle indicates cannot but mix together many things in a sophistic manner. Again, how many errors and upheavals does this sophistry give rise to in the Church and in the state? It is written in the stories that, when Ixion approached Juno, a cloud in Juno's shape was cast in his way, from which it is said that the Centaurs were born [Pindar, *Pythian Odes*, II.21–48]. In the same way the uneducated, by their false and sophistic beliefs, produce rifts that are pernicious for the Church. But these things will have to be discussed later, for first his life must be surveyed briefly.

Aristotle was born in Macedon, his father being the physician of King Amyntas. It is well known by the testimony of many that his family descended from Hippocrates; for the descendants of Hippocrates continued to live in Thessaly, and they kept hold of the art of medicine for a long time, since the parents passed on the art to their children in turn, from their hands, so to speak. So Aristotle, too, from his early years, was instructed, by family custom, in the best and purest teaching of Hippocrates, of which his writings are redolent in many places. Here and there he borrows not only ideas from Hippocrates, but also words. For I consider that Aristotle's entire teaching is simpler and more methodical for the reason that he was made accustomed to the philosophy of Hippocrates when a boy. For at the time there were other physicists as well who followed Democritus as a founder, whose teaching was full of monstrous beliefs and obscure arguments. Had Aristotle imitated them, he would by no means have obtained that most elegant thread of method or propriety. What great concern and ingenuity the descendants of Hippocrates employed in that instruction within the family can be inferred from what Galen says, namely that at first anatomy was not written down, because it was known from instruction within the family – for the descendants of Hippocrates used to dissect the bodies of living beings and men at home, and set the individual limbs in front of their children for them to look at from the earliest age. And thus, since Aristotle was accustomed from earliest childhood not to empty and obscure disputations (*logomachias*), but to the recognition of things and to searching for causes, he obtained from this childhood habit two outstanding virtues particularly worthy of a learned man, namely diligence in searching for a method and love of truth; for studies turn into character [Ovid, *Ep. Sapph.*, 83]. Therefore, diligence in unravelling obscure things in turn and properly brings forth a certain zeal and love for wisdom in all aspects of life.

When he was seventeen years old, he was sent to Athens to study with Plato, who flourished at the time with great success of both his acumen and teaching. Since it happened that Aristotle was by disposition talented in all subjects, it was a great good fortune that his intellect was first kindled and prepared by instruction at home, and that he was then taught by that most outstanding teacher, who would perfect his most fortunate disposition. As I judge it, God guided these things in such a way that we would have a perfect master of that part of philosophy in which Aristotle exerted himself.

He studied with Plato for twenty years then, that is, almost until his fortieth year. In the meantime he did not have disciples, but he trained himself in all subjects. He searched, read and examined all authors; so much so that, because of the variety of his reading and knowledge, he was called 'the Reader' by Plato. On this occasion it seems appropriate to admire the sagacity of Aristotle, who stayed so long with his teacher, and did not think that his teaching could immediately be exhausted. His seriousness is also worthy of praise, in that he began to teach very late; for during Plato's lifetime he did not have disciples. There are many testimonies by Plato honouring his talent. He called Aristotle the philosopher of truth, and, comparing him with Xenocrates, said that Aristotle needed a curb and Xenocrates spurs [Diogenes Laertius, *Lives* IV.2.6]. If Aristotle, on the other hand, had not thought highly of his teacher, he would not have thought that he needed to study with him for so long. It is also said that he put up an altar for Plato and added an epigram, in which he honours Plato with the greatest praise. For even this one verse indicates how much he attributed to him, when he said: 'no future centuries will bring such a man'. Indeed, it is a silly belief that inexperienced men think that some rivalry developed between them, because Aristotle sometimes disagrees with his teacher. For just as in speaking their opinion in the senate, great friends often disagree with each other without vexation of their minds, so good and learned men have differing opinions without harshness of their minds. But I shall speak of this difference of opinions a little later.

After Plato's death, when Aristotle's house was already frequented by the most noble men aflame with the desire to learn, Philip king of Macedon approached him and entrusted his son to him for teaching [Diogenes Laertius, *Lives* V.4]. Furthermore, had King Philip, who was able to judge people's intellect with the greatest acumen, not esteemed both Aristotle's[2] teaching and his character, he would by no means have committed to his care his son who was of such promise and such excellent talents. Thus Philip's testimony on Aristotle is to be considered most weighty. Nor would the pupil himself, being of heroic and noble disposition, have loved his teacher so greatly if the latter had not combined his knowledge with integrity and pleasantness of manners. Alexander often proclaimed that he loved Aristotle just as much as his father. Aristotle remained with Alexander for about eight years, and during that time he taught him other parts of philosophy as well as the art of healing. In this matter I think that it is not so much Aristotle's good fortune that one needs to wonder at, because it was his lot to educate a king, who alone was by far the most intelligent of all, and whom destiny called to rule the world, but I consider that his sagacity is to be praised for teaching the youth those things that bent his violent disposition towards gentleness, and which he himself [Alexander] felt were of great use to him, and a great credit, in ruling. For Alexander said that he would rather excel in knowledge than in the size of his empire [Plutarch, *Life of Alexander* VI.7].

After Alexander had crossed over into Asia, Aristotle returned to Athens and began to have disciples. And when he saw that eloquence needed to be

---

[2] Reading *Aristotelis* for *Aristoteles*.

combined with the knowledge of things, he devoted the morning studies – *heōthina*, as he himself called them – to philosophy, and the evening ones, or *deilina*, to rhetorical exercises. He alone saw most clearly the kinship among the arts. For he undertakes physics and begins with geometrical demonstrations. On that account he dealt with all the arts; he wrote on the nature of things, on morals, the immortality of the soul and on heavenly things. He wrote many works for Alexander, so that, being victorious, the latter would provide the states with laws, jurisdiction, judgements and discipline. In Athens he wrote those golden books on the history of animals. In that matter not only is Aristotle's diligence admirable, but Alexander's generosity must also be praised. For that, too, is regal – to embellish the state with arts and education. For when it was not possible to explore the nature of animate beings with his own funds, Alexander sent Aristotle 800 talents, that is, 480,000 crowns, for the purpose of assembling hunters and rearing animals, so that their nature could be examined.

Even though some splendid books of his have perished, I nevertheless reckon that those that are left – which at any rate are most fitting for schools – were preserved by divine providence in order that succeeding generations could be taught more correctly. For afterwards in Greece, as it happens, more recent philosophers, namely the Stoics, Epicureans and Academicians, began to be held in admiration, although they were certainly full of absurdities and sophistry; the old and more erudite teaching was neglected, Aristotle's writings were discarded from the hands of scholars, and his books in the libraries of a few men were consumed by age and dry rot. This great treasure would have perished utterly had not Sulla's foresight left behind for us those that we have. For, since the library had been divided,[3] because there were many books by Aristotle there – for in the past generals most sought that kind of booty, in order to preserve good writings – and although it had been almost annihilated, Sulla took charge of searching for books by that author everywhere in Greece, and he published them with Andronicus' emendations [Plutarch, *Sulla* 26]. So, just as, when alive, Aristotle had the greatest king for a friend, so the greatest and most fortunate general called him back to light when he was almost annihilated. Nevertheless, there are still traces of that disaster in the books which remain, where it appears that sentences are mutilated. Again, after Aristotle had been renewed, gradually the more recent sects began to dry up, since those who prevailed in intelligence devoted themselves to the old teaching. But I shall return to the history of his life.

[3] Reading *partita* for *parta*.

He taught in Athens for thirteen years, and he not only made the city more famous by the success of his teaching, but he also obtained great benefits for the citizens from Antipater, who ruled Macedon and esteemed Aristotle to an extraordinary degree as a teacher. However, when later the hostilities between the Athenians and Antipater increased, he himself was not safe in Athens. For when envious men hoped that they could easily crush him who was already hated because of his friendship with Antipater, they invented the crime of impiety, because he criticised the fantastic multitude of gods, and stated that an eternal and infinite mind was the cause of all things, quoting this verse by Homer: 'It is not good to have many rulers; there should be one ruler' [*Iliad*, ii.204]. Therefore, fearing an unfair trial, he withdrew to Chalcis, which was faithful to Antipater.

Neither the calumny nor his flight obscure the philosopher's glory, but this kind of danger – which is common among all those who serve humankind well – adds even more to his praise. For first of all, the very proclamation of the truth is most honourable; but to retain this amidst dangers, and not to be deterred by any threats or torture, or turned away from the correct opinion, that is the dignity and steadfastness particularly worthy of the philosopher. It is therefore a matter of glory for Aristotle to be counted among the great men who are tormented or oppressed by slanderers because of their worthy beliefs and just counsel. And since in all ages the slanderers wage a war without truce (*aspondion*) against truth, let us uplift our minds by the example of these outstanding men, and let us not allow ourselves to be led astray from our duty by the injustices of men. In that exile he died a little while later, in his sixty-third year, a dangerous year, as they say. Although his character shines forth even in his own words, it can neverthe-less be judged from the kindness of so many kings and princes towards him, which he could not have maintained if there had not been an extraordinary dignity in him. His will also makes clear how affectionate towards his family (*philostorgos*) he was, for he diligently entrusts his wife and children to Antipater [Diogenes Laertius, *Lives*, v.13]. There are other things full of humanity in his will, too, which I omit so that I may not be too verbose. You can understand how outstanding is the image set before us of the philosopher, or of the man engaged in studies and relating them to public utility, if you contemplate all of history in your minds, and consider the power and impulse of natural disposition – first his training, the degrees of his studies, his infinite avidity for learning, his conscientiousness and skill in teaching, the toil of writing such outstanding works, the dignity and humanity of his character and, finally, also the wrongs he suffered from the slanderers. Who is not delighted to see and contemplate in one man so many heroic virtues? For since he was to be the perfect master in that profession, it appears that he was sufficiently endowed with a heroic nature by divine providence.

Thus far I have been speaking about his life, much more briefly than the matter required; now I shall speak about his philosophy. This part of the oration would have been much longer if the lack of time had not prevented it. For the sects were to be compared, and something said about Plato as well, but I shall glance over these things briefly. Plato's eloquence is such that without doubt he surpasses all those whose writings are extant. Many very wise thoughts are also scattered in his works, but he did not hand on any art completely or in order. Furthermore, the greatest part of his works is ironical, a form which is more appropriate for mocking than for teaching. Athenaeus writes that one of Plato's disciples, Cheron, having become a tyrant in his city, imitated those absurd discussions about the common use of things and women; for he passed a law that masters and slaves were to have joint use of all possessions and wives [Athenaeus of Naucratis, *The Deipnosophists*, XI.509b]. Thus the misunderstood ironies of Plato made an utter fool of a silly man. Aristotle, on the other hand, wanted to be mindful of the benefit of those who study, and assist schools. Even in a philosopher this wish deserves great praise. He has explained in their entirety the arts of dialectic, physics and ethics, and employs two things that bring light to teaching, namely method and accuracy of speech. Therefore it is useful for the young to become accustomed to Aristotelian usage. Platonic licence in disputing produces uncertain and doubtful beliefs, just as painters as a pastime paint chimaeras and centaurs. But by how much Aristotle surpasses the other sects in the matters themselves can be understood from the fact that no other dialectic was seen worthy of reaching succeeding generations than that of Aristotle, because it most sagaciously deduces physics from the first principles of geometry. How beautiful it is that he alone saw that the nature of virtue is the moderation of emotions! By this advice he indicates most weightily that in everyone's life the mind must be accustomed to moderation. However, in Aristotle the opacity has been criticised, to which he is said to have aspired himself, when he said that his books were published and yet not published [Plutarch, *Life of Alexander*, VII.5]. According to my judgement, this is said with a quite different intention: that most sagacious man saw that the reasoning of his method could not be grasped except by those who had been liberally instructed. Therefore he said that the books were not published, that is, to the foolish who came in contact with them, unprepared by the other arts. The elegance and clarity of his speech in many books are great. Here and there, because of the conciseness of the things which he pursues for the sake of method, the discussion becomes more obscure; but once one has grasped the method, that darkness is dispelled. Callimachus asks the Graces to wash in his elegies their hands anointed with fragrant juices, so that they could be eternal because of their grace and beauty. The sweetness of the contents and the language is such in most of Aristotle's writings – such as in the book on the animals, the *Politics, Ethics* and the letters – that one can assume rightfully that the Graces have sprinkled some juice from their hands on them, to use Callimachus' words. What is it that his books can be for the libraries? For he quotes many things from old writings that have perished, and I believe that it is because of these ornaments that Aristotle is called a golden river by Cicero [*Academics*, II.xxxviii.119]. How much of Plato's words he expounds, for example in the fifth book of the *Ethics*; although he took the comparison of proportions from Plato, he nevertheless adapts it more beautifully. But I shall leave off here, for to pursue all these things would take too long.

I reckoned that these things had to be said, not only so that you love Aristotle more, but also that you ponder why he is to be loved, and to be held in your hands. I certainly think that a great turmoil of doctrines would follow if Aristotle were neglected, who is the one and only master of method. And no one can become acquainted with the method by any other way than by getting some practice in that type of Aristotelian philosophy. Therefore I beseech you, not only for your own sake, but also because of all coming generations, diligently to cherish and preserve this kind of knowledge. Plato says that the spark brought from heaven by Prometheus is method [*Philebus*, 16c5–6]. If this spark were lost, men would again be transformed into beasts. For truly, without the true system of teaching men are not at all different from beasts. Therefore, in order to retain that spark, the kind of knowledge that Aristotle taught must be preserved with the greatest zeal. I have spoken.

26 On the life of Galen (1540)

CR XI, 495–503

Oration on the life of Galen, delivered by Doctor Milich at the graduation of Doctors of Medicine[1]

Rightly Hesiod berates the sloth and stupidity of humankind, saying that stupid mortals do not even know the uses of the mallow and of the asphodel [*Works and Days* 41]. For we men are made to behold this nature of things, and are as if placed in this theatre by divine providence, so that, by understanding the marvellous movements of the heavens and the variety of things that come into being, we may recognise God as the Maker, and seek salutary protection for life. What is more unworthy and vile than if we forget this gift and, like blind men in a theatre, do not behold and contemplate ourselves or other common things that are in our hands? Instead of this most beautiful sight, the rabble prefers bestial and disgusting pleasures or the most squalid and stupid cares, and while they are engaged with these their minds do not allow more worthy thoughts to enter. Even though this indolence, or rather insanity, of men deserves censuring, nevertheless those are even more to be rebuked who are destined for knowledge and philosophy, but spurn the examination of nature.

One cannot demand that all be dedicated to one branch of study, for there is need in life of many and various arts, and each is due its place and its dignity. Nevertheless, it is proper to the human mind first to love and esteem highly this teaching, which sets nature before us to see as if unfolded, and also to gather something from it, and not to wish to be absolutely devoid of the sweetness that this knowledge brings forth, and then to promote the studies of others, and to admonish the young destined for philosophy that they remember that they are called to the consideration and contemplation of nature by divine providence. What is more appropriate for man than to remember that only our species has been placed in the world in order to contemplate this wonderful work? Furthermore, observing the separate things, what is sweeter than to see the order and harmony of bodies and motions? Or to consider the variety of things springing forth, and to see them made for certain uses, so that we can conclude that all these things are distributed by an eternal mind by marvellous counsel and economy? And indeed, nature has implanted in the minds of all sharp

[1] Jakob Milich (1501–59) was the Dean of the medical faculty in 1540.

goads towards that consideration, and this knowledge brings by far the richest pleasures.

Therefore, if some denigrate this study, they either struggle with themselves or have departed from the nature of men, although many beasts and birds knew and remembered certain herbs. Deer seek out dictamum, mules spleenwort, elephants the wild olive-tree, weasels rue, boars ivy, storks wild marjoram, swallows swallow-wort, ravens wake-robin, and swans Abraham's balm, which is generally called chaste-tree. As Nicander writes, the snakes knew that fennel helps them in parturition, and they have shown us its use:

> when the serpent has sloughed off its dry skin and sluggish old age in spring, and coming forth slowly from its cave with dim eyes, searches for the remedies it knows, and when it has fed on the shoots of the fennel, its clear eyesight returns as well as the vigour of youth.[2]

Furthermore there are countless examples of animals that prevail over many men, if I may say so, in their ingenuity in inquiring into and exploring the miracles of nature. It is vile for men not only to be overcome by beasts in diligence and industry, but to add such madness as to spurn also these studies. Therefore I admonish students as much as possible, as all good men have to do, to strive for and cherish this knowledge, which is not only pleasant, but also brings endless benefits for life. Indeed, the examination and consideration of nature directs one towards moderation and piety, and rouses the mind to the admiration of God. Since God has placed us in this spectacle and has commanded us to contemplate and consider His work, let us not judge that this study is useless, nor that it can be scorned without fault.

What shall I say here of those Cyclopes who not only despise the inquiry, but also the use and the remedies? They inflict savagery upon their bodies by enormous gluttony, immoderate vigils and in other ways, and then, like the Stoics, they say that health and life are ruled by fate and that diseases are not acquired by our vices, nor repelled by diligence and remedies, but by fate. Since these words demonstrate evident madness, they are not worth refuting, but nevertheless now and then their examples harm the inexperienced. Therefore I admonish the young to detest these barbarous insults of the art, which attack God with invective. He gave us the laws by which life has to be ruled, as well as adding protection and remedies, in

---

[2] This seems to be Melanchthon's own translation of Nicander's *Theriaca*, 30–4. For the teaching of Nicander at Wittenberg, see Kusukawa, *Transformation of Natural Philosophy*, pp. 181f.

which He implanted admirable and truly mysterious powers for benefiting the body, and He also showed us the art, so that we may make proper use of these gifts. Thus those Cyclopes despise God's decree and God's gifts, if they think that there are no powers in the things made by divine providence for man's health. For example certain foods and drinks are set before the human body, and we cannot say why they are transformed into blood and nourish the body, but a marvellous power is implanted in such things, and an affinity and sympathy (*sympatheia*) with the human body, so that they can be mingled and flow together into one nature. So there is a mysterious sympathy (*sympatheia*) in the remedies with certain parts of the body or humours, the efficiency of which is evident and certain.

Such is the efficacy of terebinth for the healing of simple wounds that the matter forces one to acknowledge that there is some mysterious power in that remedy, and that it is given to humankind by divine providence for the healing of wounds. How efficacious and thankful do you judge the use of balm to be? It often comes to my mind that balm and myrrh were given to the Hebrews so that they would have an efficacious and instant remedy for wounds at home, since the people was destined for continuous warfare, and would not use foreign things. It is ascertained that scorpions are immediately killed if one puts radish on them. It would take long to speak of the remedies for the individual parts of the body, but just consider the daily benefits of medicine; these testify that the remedies are most efficacious. In a violent catarrh, the slow, sharp and persistent phlegm cannot be drawn out from the lungs without medical help. Specific things are destined for this use, and one is not at liberty to use remedies at random without discrimination. How great is the usefulness of chicory and wormwood for treating the liver! How often do wormwood and mugwort divert certain death from women! But I shall cease this recounting.

The remedies against poisons are extraordinary, and in this kind the power of rue is evident; therefore it has great power in preventing the plague. Athenaeus writes that the tyrant of Pontus used to kill by poison the citizens invited to banquets. When this was noticed, they equipped themselves with rue in advance when they were about to go to his banquets, and ate the poison without injury [*Banquet of the Seven Sages*, III.85.b]. More astonishing is what he tells about the lemon, and he cites someone who was an eyewitness of the event. In Egypt, when some criminals were taken to the asps to be killed by their bites, by chance a young woman who was with the prison guard, moved by pity, gave the trembling and thirsty men a lemon, so that they could restore their forces. When they had eaten this and were led to the asps and wounded by their bite, the power of the poison was without effect, and they did not die when wounded. The magistrate was astonished by the strangeness of the event, and diligently searched for the reasons. When, among other things, he asked what they had eaten on that day, the lemon was mentioned. So the power of the lemon was tested: on the next day they were again taken to the asps, but one of them was commanded to chew a lemon beforehand, while the other was forbidden to do so. When they were both wounded, the one who had not had a lemon died, and the other, who had eaten it, remained unharmed [*ibid.*, III.84.e–f]. However, not only stories, but also everyday experience provide countless examples, which are sufficient testimonies to the power of remedies. Therefore, those who despise God's gifts from a heinousness of character attack God with invective.

I wanted to say these things in advance at the beginning, both about the merit of the discipline and its philosophy, and about the usefulness of memories, so that you would think that the art is to be loved and esteemed, and therefore think more highly also of the writers on this art, who employed their zeal in describing nature and in benefiting the life of men. Since, according to custom, something has to be spoken about, I have chosen to recite something about the life and praises of Galen, whom you know as the most prolific author on the art of medicine. I believe that the elders and the wise too will welcome the enumeration of this great man's studies, sagacity and diligence in teaching as well as in practising the art. In medical treatment it is truly most useful for the young to have excellent examples, which they can imitate both in learning and in making judgements.

Galen was born in Pergamum, and his father was an architect of the town, highly educated, as Galen states, in grammar, dialectics and mathematics. Galen himself narrates that it was of great benefit to him to have such a father, who not only loved these disciplines, so that in time he introduced his son to them, but who also taught him himself at home. He says that from this he learnt the basics of the arts, and when he had grasped those, when he was already fifteen years of age, he was taken to the teachers of philosophy. There he applied himself to dialectics and the rest of philosophy, for his father intended him not for medicine, but only for the philosophical profession, as it was then called. When the youth had been studying with the philosopher for two years, as he himself says, he was admonished most distinctly in a dream to learn the art of healing. Indeed, I do not doubt that by divine providence this discipline was presented to him and an impulse for this study given to him. In those times the art was dissipated and, as one can understand from Pliny, many impostors had arisen who depraved the art, not only in practising medicine, as it happens in all ages, but much more in teaching; they showed new tricks, and immersed feverish patients, and those suffering from any kind of disease, in water. Therefore God, willing to maintain the art and preserve it for coming generations, in order to give the world an outstanding craftsman, roused Galen's intellect to these studies. For God preserves the true arts in life; this is clear from the fact that there are no outstanding craftsmen without divine inspiration.

Thus, since he was already prepared in dialectics and the basics of philosophy by his youthful learning, he had a powerful intellect, and his mind burned with the desire to learn and with enthusiasm, he began to devote himself with equal zeal to philosophy and medicine. First he studied with a doctor by the name of Satyrus, who was a pupil of Quintus, the most famous among the teachers who had pupils before Galen's times and who were studiously engaged in expounding Hippocrates. After that he studied with the physician Pelops; although Galen censures some of his anatomical errors, he nevertheless applied himself diligently to anatomy while with him.[3] At the time there were great numbers of the most learned men in the Egyptian city of Alexandria, therefore he travelled there and investigated their studies and judgements. Then, he says, he gained access to and studied with all the most learned and most famous doctors of his time. Although he was so outstanding in intellect, he nevertheless severely chides those who believe that they can become craftsmen without teachers.

He travelled to Rome twice, first by his own decision and in order to listen to the doctors there and to furnish proof of his intellect among the famous and numerous doctors in Rome. However, he disagreed with the others now and then, and noticed that he incurred their hatred, and he says that because of that he gave up the discussions, particularly since he was able to gain more esteem and repute in public orations. He says that he had singular good fortune in the use of the art and in healing, as is credible, for he had been encouraged to medicine by a divine and heroic impulse, which is usually accompanied by singular good fortune. He came to Rome when he was thirty-four years old, and he wrote many things there, among these also philosophical writings on demonstrations, in order to refute the insanity of some impostors, who at that time asserted – in order to subvert

[3] For Satyrus, see Galen, *Anatomical Administrations*, II. 224f. and for Pelops, *De atra bile*, V.112.

the arts – that nothing was certain and weakened the precepts of all the arts by sophistic disputations. It appeared to those impostors to be a great commendation of their intellect not to explain what is true, but to subvert wantonly the received beliefs. They vexed Galen's intellect so much that he said that he, too, would have followed that doubt of the Pyrrhonians,[4] if he had not been accustomed to geometry and demonstrations as a boy. By that discipline he not only succeeded in distinguishing the certain from the uncertain, but also – and this is much greater – in loving truth more and in guiding his intellect with a bridle by directing his mind to the demonstrations. Euripides calls the wantonness of the tongue the vilest disease [*Orestes* 10], but this licentiousness in criticising – the *sophistomania*, to use a word of the ancient Greeks – and zeal in subverting true and useful opinions is vile in no one more than in the philosophers, who profess love for truth and its protection. Rightly Galen's purpose is to be praised therefore, that he harshly persecuted these Pyrrhonian tricks. He wrote many things at that time, which perished in the conflagration of Rome, when the fire spread widely and also consumed the Temple of Peace, where his writings had been deposited.

In his thirty-seventh year he left Rome and returned to Asia. I believe that on that journey he also sailed to Lemnos in order to examine in truth the nature of Lemnian earth, and one should consider his diligence in this matter. For since Dioscorides had written that goat's blood was mixed with Lemnian earth [*Materia Medica* v.lxxviii], of which great use was made in remedies, Galen himself went to the places where it was found in order to examine with certitude how it appeared, and he found out that its nature is metallic without the admixture of goat's blood. It is in use so much nowadays, and held in such admiration among the Thracians and the Turks, that the Turkish tyrant habitually gives Lemnian earth to the ambassadors among special gifts, for last year we saw some such seals (*sphragidas*) that had been given to Cornelius Scepperus.[5]

However, not long after his return to his country, he was called back to Italy by a letter from the emperors Verus and Marcus [Aurelius] Antoninus, with whom he was well acquainted, as is apparent from some

---

[4] Followers of Pyrrho of Elis (365–275 BC), who claimed that certain knowledge was unattainable and that one should therefore suspend judgement and strive to achieve mental quietude: see also note 3, oration 9, p. 85.

[5] Cornelius Duplicius Scepperus (*d.* 1555) was first in the service of King Christian II of Denmark whom he accompanied to Wittenberg in 1523. From 1526 he was in the service of the Emperor Charles V and in 1533 and 1534 he was on an embassy to Constantinople.

of his narrations. The emperor's judgement of Galen is most apparent in that he entrusted the health of his son Commodus Caesar particularly to him, when he set forth to Germany for the war against the Marcomanni. Galen says that at that time he wrote those divine anatomical books which are extant, and which should be in the hands not only of the students of medicine, but of all those who love philosophy. For certainly the teaching of the parts of the human body and their functions is a distinguished part of philosophy. While it is full of sweetness, it also brings great benefits, and it is enormously useful to individuals for the protection of health. It also guides behaviour, since it instructs one what the nature of each part requires. Furthermore, since it puts before us this admirable structure of human parts, it teaches that this nature does not exist by chance, but that it is created by an eternal mind, which did not engage in the shaping of man for nothing, but to demonstrate that it cares for humankind. Therefore Galen said most wisely that the knowledge of anatomy is the beginning of theology, and the path to the knowledge of God [*On the Use of the Parts* XVII], and these books should be loved all the more by those studying philosophy, because in them Galen has added what is lacking in Aristotle's anatomy; he has also learnedly corrected some things, and has shed light on many passages in Aristotle. Since in the good doctor faith is no less required than erudition and industry, Galen is to be greatly loved, who, as the facts show, was outstanding not only in industry and dexterity, but also in faith. For who is more diligent and productive in teaching? And he himself speaks of his faith in the third book of *On the Affected Parts*: 'I make God my witness therefore, that I shall declare what I have obtained after a long inquiry in the very practice of the art, and in disputations with the most learned men, and decide is the most true.'[6] Who would not consider worthy of perpetual praise such a spirit that loves truth and is desirous of helping humankind?

After the death of Antoninus the Philosopher – who died on that campaign – and since the young emperor Commodus was more delighted by the company of gladiators than by that of philosophers, Galen returned to Asia and spent the rest of his life in his country, teaching, practising the art and writing, and he said that he lengthened his life by diligence until late into his old age. Clearly, therefore, he did a service not only to the men of his age, but also to all posterity, and by instructing others and writing he embraced the entire art and left later generations a great help for life.

6 *On the Affected Parts*, VIII.143.6. Melanchthon has rendered Galen's plural gods in the singular.

Although later some Arabs and Greeks practised medicine with great renown, it is nevertheless well known that Galen was the source of both kinds, that is, the art of disputations, or the dogmatic kind, and remedies. Leaving out many other things, how profitable is the discipline that is called physics, which is transmitted nowhere else more learnedly and more abundantly than in several books by Galen? And yet he wrote many more, which have perished, partly because of the barbarity that prevailed in Asia and Greece, partly because of other reasons.

I would also repeat some of his divinations and admirable cures, if the brevity of time permitted it. When nerves are injured in the human body, mobility is lost and the limbs waste away; Galen was the first to find a way for healing injured nerves. How astute he was in finding remedies from the observation of the properties of things, can be judged from the following. When he returned home from Alexandria, he sojourned on the way at some rustic estate, where the master happened to be ill and was almost suffocating because of a swelling of the uvula and the tonsils. Since other remedies were lacking and the nuts were already ripening – the nature of the shells being considered sharp and astringent – he squeezed out the juice of the outside covering, added honey to it and immediately delivered the sick man by this remedy. He relates that after this he always made use of it with the greatest success, and so he found a great benefit in a base thing. I shall not add further examples here.

Furthermore, the students should realise that all posterity owes him much, since this writer has done great service to the life of men; he has described the nature of things eloquently; he has taught us many remedies; and he has collected what the ancient physicians found and added new things. They should love him in such a way that they also desire to know, for I feel that those who are engaged in philosophy cannot defend their function without Galen, for most of Aristotle cannot be understood without Galen's explanations. Furthermore, because of the most useful records which he left on nature and on remedies, Galen is most worthy, if anyone is, of the laudation by which Homer celebrates the son of Asclepius: 'A physician is a man worth many another' [*Iliad* XI.514]. I have spoken.

27 On the life of Avicenna (1549?)

CR XI, 826–32

Oration on the life of Avicenna, recited by Doctor Jakob Milich[1]

The entire nature of things is a theatre to be admired, in which God wills that he be beheld and that the distinct testimonies of His presence, wisdom and goodness be considered. Therefore the Architect of great wisdom has employed such a variety of skill in the building, arrangement, shapes, motions and powers that human minds would be forced to acknowledge that this most beautiful work was not blown together by chance, but that there is indeed a constructing mind. And they should conclude with the strongest approbation that men need to be subject to that constructing mind, and that our morals need to agree with that eternal precept which resides in the Maker Himself, who pours the rays of His light into us. And they need to conclude that the Maker is to be worshipped with true praises.

It is evident that the contemplation of nature is necessary for this important reason. Furthermore, we are also moved by our own benefit. Help for life has to be sought in this great variety of things, which are partly nourishment for our bodies, partly remedies. I commend the zeal and counsel of those who, in reciting the praises of the art of medicine, demonstrate in some way that the consideration of nature is pleasant and useful. Nevertheless, the scope of the argument is such that barely a few portions can be plucked from this multitude, and can be set out and demonstrated. And so I confess that I am discouraged by the greatness of the matter, so that I cannot provide an oration about the praise of the art, that is, about the contemplation of nature.

However, I deplore my sloth and that of us all; for we are all negligent in beholding nature, and in contemplating that theatre of God as it ought to be done – since, after all, God summons us to that study, nothing is sweeter than that reflection, and this diligence will be of great benefit for health and life. Although no one can be a sufficiently attentive spectator of nature, nevertheless all good minds are to be encouraged to that contemplation which is the most honourable for man. Indeed, since God Himself enjoins it, I pray to the Maker of nature Himself that He may incline the minds of many towards that study, and that He may rouse them to recognise, worship and praise Him in this contemplation.

[1] Jakob Milich was rector of the University in 1549; for Milich, see further note 6, oration 18, p. 147.

The diligence of the doctors is praiseworthy: although no one person is capable of disclosing all of nature, nevertheless they have shown many parts that they revealed, and they preserve the knowledge of them for humankind; it is profitable to read their works, not only those in Greek, but also those composed among other peoples and in other times. For the more recent Arabs have discovered many things in nature and in the art that had been unknown to the Greeks; in this they were also much helped by the nature of the regions in which they lived. For Syria, Arabia, Egypt, Cyrenaica, Africa and Spain are extremely rich in remedies. And indeed, all the Arab writers traversed these places, and the Arab people were of keen wit, and were committed to this one field of study which they had learnt from their oldest forefathers, that is, from Job and others. Although most added much that was corrupt, nevertheless no one among the Arabic writers taught the art more purely than Avicenna. So, in order to commend Avicenna to students, I have decided to speak about his life and studies.

Avicenna was born in the year of the Lord 1145 in the town of Edessa in Commagene – which lies by the Euphrates and is subject to the king of Persia – of a noble father whose name was Hali, and a mother called Cithara, the daughter of a Persian satrap.[2] Every time he remembered his father, he called him 'Prince', and later this title attached itself to the son. The boy was entrusted to a local teacher, who was distinguished in these lands by the renown of his intelligence and his teaching; when he realised that the youth's nature was appropriate for sciences, he taught him dialectic, geometry and astronomy soon after the first elements of writing. They say that Avicenna was exceedingly pleased by reading Euclid, so much so that he wrote a summary of that author. He continued in this course of studies with the private tutor until his eighteenth year. When Avicenna's father, who was also a man of great intelligence, noticed his son's powerful intelligence and his vigorous nature, he wanted to commit him to the court of the Persian king, where he would have the opportunity to practise his wit because of the variety and greatness of the duties. However, his son, who was already acquainted with the strife of the court, pleaded with his father to grant him leisure to learn. The father, who was also delighted by his son's talents, granted this, and commanded him to travel to Alexandria, furnished with supplies; there were still the remnants at Alexandria of the old and most famous school that had been distinguished by the concourse

---

[2] Commagene is the northern Province of Syria. There seem to be several confusions about the details of the life of Avicenna (980–1037): cf. S. M. Afnan, *Avicenna: His Life and Works* (London, 1958).

of teachers and students under the Egyptian kings and then in Roman times. Although, because of the reign of the Saracens, the use of the Greek languages was no longer widespread, and all the arts were taught in a neglected way, and many corruptions were mingled with the sciences, nevertheless studies were not yet utterly silenced. There still persisted some remnants there, particularly of those arts of which human life cannot be devoid, such as medicine and astrology, but each was miserably marred by the ill will of the Saracen people. For in place of medicine they taught an illiterate and miscellaneous mass of experiences.

In place of astronomy, which measures the heavenly motions with fixed computation, and searches for the causes and effects of heavenly appearances, they preferred some kind of prediction, indeed divinatory magic. From this one can see that people's great savagery together with its diabolical cunning: since they could not take away the arts in their entirety, they nevertheless marred them thus.

At that time there lived in Alexandria the physician Rhazes,[3] who prevailed over the others both in knowledge and in his success in healing; Avicenna turned to him. For when he saw that philosophy is certainly incomplete without the art of medicine, he directed his mind to the teaching of the physicians, so that he could comprehend nature disclosed in its entirety, as far as this can be done at all by human diligence. For in old times it was not dishonourable for princes to learn the art of medicine, as is shown by the examples of Peleus, Achilles, Alexander the Great and Pyrrhus,[4] but nowadays the studies of princes and of the mighty are greatly different. When Avicenna was a youth, he studied with Rhazes, who was older; although he found much lacking in that teacher, he nevertheless attended him as being better than nothing.

However, when he had strengthened his judgement by age and knowledge, he realised that Rhazes had greater empirical knowledge than rational knowledge. Since he had been drawn to these studies kindled by divine inspiration, he easily understood the weakness of his teacher, and what was true or false in his teaching. For since Rhazes had departed too far from the sources, Hippocrates and Galen, necessarily his treatments were not free from errors. Avicenna says so expressly in book four on the general cure for

---

[3] Rhazes (*c.* 854–925), who became the head of hospital in Baghdad, could not have met Avicenna.

[4] Achilles, son of Peleus and Thetis, was brought up by the centaur Chiron, renowned for his knowledge of music, medicine and shooting; Pyrrhus (*c.* 318–272 BC) was a renowned general. Alexander the Great showed interest in treatment given to wounded friends: see Plutarch, *Life of Alexander*, VIII.1 and XVI.

fevers. There he says that it would truly have been profitable for that man – here he means Rhazes – not to move too far away from the opinions of Galen and Hippocrates. That way there would be fewer contradictions and errors in his works.

After four years he left Alexandria and travelled to the Spanish town of Cordoba, where Averroes[5] was teaching; summoned by his fame, Avicenna betook himself to him. In those times Averroes' name was very famous, but Averroes was of a harsh, quarrelsome and conceited disposition, and he acquired his fame by finding fault with others – he was often lured away from truth by his zeal in contradicting others; he overthrew the rightly established arts by sophistic tricks; he took away the mixtures of temperaments; denied that some humours originate in the liver, and he contrived a new and absurd opinion concerning nutrition. But what need is there to enumerate individual points? He only did this so that, having removed the authority of the old authors, he could put himself in their place. His boastful utterances are relevant here, by which he indicated that he would cleanse philosophy, and would make known again the true and unspoilt philosophy, shorn of all blemishes. These utterances and these boastful promises struck his students with consternation, and procured renown and admiration for the teacher. But I shall return to the history of Avicenna.

When he had remained in Cordoba for some time, and had listened to Averroes' teaching, he left him and returned to Alexandria. For since he had been properly instructed from childhood, and accustomed to geometry and demonstrations, he could easily distinguish between those who taught the truth and those who taught what was false. In Alexandria he began to set up as his teachers Hippocrates and Galen, whose teaching he judged to agree most with truth. For although the Greek language had been expelled, and the ancient authors, too, were banished, nevertheless some scholars searched for the origins. Therefore several works of Hippocrates, Galen and Ptolemy had been translated into Arabic by Saracens; not much later they were translated into Latin by the generosity of our emperors Lothar and Frederick II,[6] and all schools have been using these translations up to these our own times.

Thus Avicenna turned to the true sources and, since he excelled in education and disposition, he could easily disclose and understand what

---

[5] Again, Averroes (1126–98), who was born in Cordoba, could not have taught Avicenna.

[6] Lothar III (1075–1137) was Duke of Saxony before becoming Emperor; for Frederick II, see note 3, oration 13, p. 114.

was unknown to others. When he had corroborated his medical knowledge in Alexandria and had travelled throughout Egypt, where he discovered several remedies that were unknown to other doctors, he returned to his country. When he had yielded the government to his brother, he dedicated himself to writing. For when he saw how much recent medicine had degenerated from ancient medicine, he wanted to recall it to its origins and to cleanse again what had become enveloped by mould and rust through the sloth of men.

Since Galen's books, in which the art is transmitted correctly, were not in the hands of those studying the art because of the imperfection of the times, and since furthermore Galen did not represent the entire art in one book, Avicenna himself provided a book in which he represents the entire art of medicine by a most learned and fitting method.[7] In this he gathered into one body everything that is said dispersedly in Galen – organising the art as a body (*sōmatopoiēsas tēn technēn*), as the Greeks say – and represented, without sophistry, what he judged to be most true, after a long examination, in the practice of the art and in disputations with most learned men. This work by Avicenna was received with such praise by all the learned that it has been expounded by teachers in all public universities for more or less four hundred years. Since he brought Galen's disputations back to light he changed the course of studies in his century by that work, not a mean feat, in particular as empirical medicine only was in use.

We cannot make judgements on Avicenna's eloquence, because he wrote in Arabic and found a translator, such as that century had to offer, who without doubt expressed indistinctly many outstanding sentences by his inelegant translation. It would not be difficult to produce examples for this, if we were not prevented by the shortness of time. He employed discrimination in his writing in order to select only the best things, which he arranged so accurately that the elegance of this order could both attract and engage the reader. For he describes the art from the first beginnings and elements, and then elaborates it through temperaments, humours and the individual parts of the human body, so that the order itself may shed great light on the matters. Then he explains the general and specific diseases, their causes, their way of development, their signs and treatment so clearly that the reader needs nothing else. For he uses the simplest and clearest

---

[7] The *al-Qanun* (codes of law) was translated in the Latin West by Gerard of Cremona and became known as the *Canon*. For its career as a textbook, see Nancy G. Siraisi, *Avicenna in Renaissance Italy: the Canon and Medical Teaching in Italian Universities after 1500* (Princeton, 1987).

method, like a thread to guide the reader, so that he never strays from the purpose, as one notices it happens in some places to the more inexperienced in reading Galen. However, he does not intend by his writings to hold back the learned from reading Galen, but he intends to attract them further – so that they may know where the individual parts that Galen explains in individual books are to be recounted.

Indeed, in what pertains to the treatment of diseases and to remedies, he prevails by far over all those who wrote before him, and he has this praise, without debate, from all those who are in their right minds – although nowadays some, who have not corroborated the precepts of the art by any use, do not cease from bawling against him. Nevertheless, they describe remedies taken word for word from his book, and they act exactly as is said in the story about wine: 'They find fault, and yet they drink.' Furthermore, no one can express to its full merit the greatness of Avicenna's service in pointing out how the juices of herbs boiled with sugar can be preserved for a long time; and in transmitting for the first time the boiling of sugar pressed from cane, as it is brought to us nowadays. This boiling process does not exist anywhere among the ancient Greeks, nor was it in use before Avicenna's time.

Avicenna was also the first to make use of cassia for fistulae, a truly blessed remedy, which because of its outstanding quality can safely be offered to both children and the elderly. He has also pointed out the use of the root of rhubarb. Those who use it know how pleasantly that root draws out bile, and at the same time also strengthens the inner organs, especially the liver. I shall say nothing here about tamarind or about the various types of behen-nuts. How long it would be to enumerate the composite remedies whose mixture he first taught, pointing out their use for various kinds of diseases. I shall furthermore not say anything about his cures, which he effected with extraordinary success. With marvellous diligence, he saved the son of the Persian king, who was afflicted by phrenitis, and he delivered countless others who were afflicted by pernicious diseases.

If those who in a war saved a citizen or protected an imperilled soldier with their shield were decorated by the state, some with a golden crown, some with a statue, and even their children were given an annual income of natural products, what prize is due to him who did not save some individual citizen or some single city, but a great multitude of any kind of people and nations, and for so many centuries? No man's oration, be he ever so skilled in speaking, can describe the greatness of his service. In truth, although I recognise my want of eloquence, nevertheless whenever this thought crosses my mind, I cannot restrain myself from praising him abundantly. And I would wish that God grant me such an oration by which I could drive out this lethargy from the minds of men and remove that extreme ingratitude, not only against men, but even more against God, who is the Maker of the remedies and the one who showed us the art. Since nevertheless the ill is so inveterate that it is utterly incurable, I, too, shall bear more patiently in my mind this fact of the times. Some time God will exact the penalty for this ingratitude with great severity.

But I urge you, young men, to keep inviolable the memory of the masters who did and endured much, in order to leave the arts to us more readily and more clearly. In this dotage of the world, there is not enough vigour left in men's minds to create anything new. Therefore you must cherish with respect what has been transmitted by the masters, God going ahead and showing the way; not only those of you who study medicine, but also those who stand in need of medicine. Since now, and by their own volition, human bodies become weaker than before, tending towards destruction, and are weakened by excessive drinking, which has now become a habit and is not at all considered bad, we all have to recognise the benefits of this art, and give thanks to God the Maker, as it is written: 'Honour the physician, for God created him for our need' [Sirach 38:1]. I have spoken.

28 On the life of Rudolf Agricola (1539)

CR XI, 438–46

Oration on the life of Rudolf Agricola, of Frisia, given in the
month of July by Johann Sachs of Holstein, when he conferred the
title of Master on some worthy and erudite young men, at the
University of Wittenberg[1]

It is most profitable for us to understand correctly the kind of life in which
we abide, and the obligation given to us by divine providence, that is, the
preservation and propagation of the true teaching about religion and other
worthy things. For even though other ranks and orders of life have more
magnificence, nevertheless, if we judge truly, the schools have the greatest
merit. The realms and all states should protect them in particular. For,
since men are made for the purpose that knowledge of God may shine in
this world, and since civil society is established by divine providence so that
there would be assemblies of teachers and students, and knowledge of God
be kindled and spread wide, it is sufficiently clear that it is the highest duty
of all rulers to preserve the Church and the schools. Consider, I entreat
you, how majestic and venerable the congregations of the angels are. The
assemblies of scholars must be their images on Earth; this is certainly an
obligation and a duty. They should in the same way profess what the angels
sing: 'Glory to God in the highest, and peace on Earth, and joy to men.'
Thus the schools must worship God and propagate the teaching that is
useful for the peace and harmony of the Church, and also what brings
about heavenly joy for men. If we consider this great dignity of our obligation,
and ponder it in our minds, we shall both love studies and the schools more,
and shall be greatly delighted by these scholarly rites and assemblies. If
there is anyone who is not moved by so weighty a reason to love schools,
then 'the hard Caucasus, bristling with rocks, has brought him forth, and
the Hyrcanean tigers suckled him' [Virgil, *Aeneid* IV.366f]. Therefore it
behoves us to preserve this custom of graduation, which we recognise as
an advantage to the order of learning.

Since it is the custom to have an oration on studies on this occasion, and
others who have more authority often show either which road is to be taken,

---

[1] For a comparison with other lives of Agricola, see James Michael Weiss, 'The Six Lives of Rudolph
Agricola: Forms and Functions of the Humanist Biography', *Humanistica Lovaniensia*, 30 (1981),
19–39.

or admonish you to strive for the knowledge of the best arts, I have decided
to speak about the life of Rudolf Agricola, as far as I could examine it. For
good examples have great power, and good dispositions are most greatly
roused and kindled by the consideration and admiration of virtue in excellent men. Furthermore, the life-stories of learned men shape the judgement
of the young on many things. It is well known that when Rudolf first
improved the style of speech and dialectic in Germany, and showed a better
method of learning, students were admonished in a useful way by many of
his utterances and discussions. Even though there is no one who does not
love Rudolf's name for his erudition and merits, nevertheless a private
sense of duty impels me to speak about him. For my home is not only near
Friesland, but also a colony of the Frisians, which even today retains the
name Frisia Minor in Holstein, and in the ruling of the state it preserves,
not without merit, the impartiality of the ancient law. Therefore I judge that
the praise of Rudolf in some way also pertains to my fellow-citizens, and
since that is the case, I hope that you will approve of my decision to speak
about Rudolf's life-story – although I myself also wish that it were gathered together more richly by others who have lived among those who knew
Rudolf's life and study better. We have gathered little, taken partly from
his own writings, and partly from those who remember the discussions of the
old men who were familiar with Rudolf at the University of Heidelberg.[2]
And I have decided not to give a eulogy, for, since he achieved great fame by
his eloquence, which can be judged from his writings, he does not need praise,
especially not that of one who is not eloquent. I weave only a historical
account, in which I truly enumerate what I inquired about his life, morals
and opinions, and I shall cite most eminent witnesses. Furthermore, this
mentioning of studies and opinions is no less profitable for students than it
is for a warrior to know the stratagems and counsels of ancient leaders.
Therefore I now come to the life-story.

Rudolf Agricola was born in Friesland, on a farm not far from the town
of Groningen, of honest parents whose means were not bad for the standards
there. Therefore they were able to supply their children generously with
funds for studying. Since I have not heard anything about his studies in his
early childhood, I did not think that I needed to invent anything. No one
can achieve outstanding virtue without great power of intellect and some

---

[2] Melanchthon was a student at Heidelberg and probably heard about Agricola from the latter's friends
and colleagues there: see Quirinus Breen, 'Melanchthon's sources for a Life of Agricola: the
Heidelberg Memories and the Writings', *Archiv für Reformationsgeschichte* 52 (1961), 49–74.

enthusiasm, and since this is a very sharp goad to good dispositions, without doubt Rudolf grasped the first elements of the arts quickly, as it is said about heroic nature: 'Before his years he achieved courage and manly concern.' For from his writings and counsels, too, the power and ardour of his intellect are evident.

When the Germans used a most corrupted kind of speech, and there was such ignorance of letters that our people could not even conjecture what it meant to speak correctly, while, on the contrary, even absurdity was admired, Rudolf alone first began to perceive these faults with his ears and his mind, and to desire a better manner of speech. This was the sign of an extraordinary sagacity – of the powers of intellect and of knowledge, because he fashioned a kind of speech that was pure, magnificent, sonorous, without awkwardness, and also appropriate to the weight and seriousness of the subject-matter. Nor was it only sagacity, but also a certain loftiness of mind and an admirable avidity to learn, because, having some means, he travelled to Italy in order to search for a better kind of teaching. If I am about to say much in praise of his intellect, I could also expand this by a commendation of my home country. For just as Friesland once flourished by the greatness of its exploits, so now, too, it brings forth intellects that are by no means base, but are suitable for letters as well as for the guidance of great things. As it seems to me, they are not only sagacious and rational, but also endowed with noble-mindedness and an extraordinary loftiness of mind. But, as I said, Rudolf's genius can be judged from his writings.

I hear that he first shook off his inexperience at Louvain, where, when he had become acquainted with some Frenchmen, he immediately studied French with them – either in order to avoid the carousing of the Germans, or because the French were more erudite. When he had quickly grasped what is taught in the schools on dialectic and philosophy, he himself used to search for better things in his mind and, hiding himself in libraries, he read good writers following his own counsel, debating much, in the meantime, with the more learned about more accomplished philosophy. But he had heard that the study of Greek and Latin was being renewed in Italy at the time. For after the fall of Byzantium many Greeks, driven from their country, came to Italy, and they renewed philosophy and eloquence there; after the collapse of the Roman Empire the study of these had utterly abated in Italy. He understood that philosophy could not be grasped without the Greek language. Therefore he decided to journey to Italy in order to improve the style of speech by the fellowship and examples of eloquent men, and to get to know the sources of philosophy.

He came to Ferrara, where at the time the study of philosophy and eloquence flourished more than at the other Italian universities. For Ercole, the Duke of Ferrara, perceived that concern for assisting matters of erudition belonged to a good ruler's duty, and he himself enjoyed the writings of learned men. Theodorus Gaza was in Ferrara, who surpassed all the Greeks who were in Italy then in erudition and eloquence. Guarini taught Greek and Latin there, a most diligent man. The poets Strozzi were there, with whom Rudolf appears to have been well acquainted.[3] The writings of mathematicians who then lived at Ercole's court also survive. In short, all the arts were taught most successfully there. What more desirable thing could happen to an intelligent man, who was aflame with the true love of knowledge and was avid to learn, than to live in such an assembly of learned men? There he contended with Guarini in prose, in verse with the Strozzis, and he debated about philosophy with Theodorus Gaza and the other excellent men. He heard teachers of all the arts. Since he trained his intellect equally by a variety of knowledge, and exerted himself in eloquence, he turned the mouths and eyes of all of Italy towards himself. With great success he discussed and explained authors of either language in that university, and he gave orations to the great approval of the learned.

Furthermore, it was a great success for a German to give satisfaction to the Italians – who judge in a capricious and haughty way – not only in erudition and manner of speech, but also in beauty of delivery. I do not believe that the Italians thought so highly of any German before him that they listened with admiration to him teaching in public, and were equally satisfied with his erudition, his manner of speech and his delivery. I hear that Erasmus was often asked in Italy to give an example of his erudition and eloquence by giving a public lecture. However, he could never be prevailed upon to do his friends' will in this matter, for fear that the Italians would ridicule a German's pronunciation. And Erasmus often extolled Rudolf's nature, which he asserted was capable of imitating the Italian beauty without absurdities.[4] Indeed, musical natures are more talented for pronunciation

---

[3] Agricola was organist to the court of Duke Ercole I d'Este (1471–1505) at Ferrara. Agricola could not have met Theodore Gaza (1400–76) at Ferrara, since the latter left by 1450. Here, Melanchthon is probably thinking of the Strozzi poets, Titus and Ercole, but Agricola only knew Titus. Battista Guarinus (1434–1513) succeeded his father, the humanist Guarino Veronese, at Ferrara.

[4] For Erasmus' interest in Agricola, see Lisa Jardine, *Erasmus, Man of Letters* (Princeton, 1993), pp. 83–98.

and delivery than others. It is well known that Rudolf excelled in music to such an extent that he composed songs; indeed, that he was very pleasing to the Italians, because he sometimes played the lute at banquets of learned men.

One can judge how much persistence he had from the fact that he copied all of Quintilian with his own hand. He himself indicates that while in Italy he read Pliny's *Natural History* diligently, perhaps spurred by the opportunity of inquiring into plants more easily there. Without doubt he saw Aristotle and Theophrastus in the translation by Gaza, and when he read those he decided that he needed to add Pliny, in order to observe from where Gaza had taken the Latin names. This comparison was most profitable to him for increasing both his knowledge of things and his wealth of words. Then, when he had improved himself among most learned men, he finally returned to his home-country, where he did not stay for long.

Some time after his return he was invited to Heidelberg by Dalberg, Bishop of Worms, and Pleninger, whom he calls Pliny.[5] For in Italy Rudolf had been very well acquainted with them, and later they both came to the court of the Count Palatine Philip, who was noble, and not ignorant of letters, and endowed with great affability, and wanted a court adorned with learned men. The chancellor Dalberg was then made Bishop of Worms. He called Rudolf to Heidelberg, either in order to train himself to write correctly by his company, or in order that the young might have someone to fashion their style. He made use of Dalberg's association as long as he lived. And although he was free to be idle, he nevertheless publicly taught Greek and Latin at the university for the benefit of the young. Nor did he consider it too dishonourable for himself to teach like a courtier – as, now, many who are only lightly imbued with erudition shrink from teaching; such is the arrogance of this most perverted century. He often undertook debates in all disciplines. In philosophy he corrected the absurd opinions of the Scholastics. There he also wrote books on dialectic, in order to cleanse the art, and by leading it from the dark into the light and into view, to show its use. Old men at Heidelberg tell that his morals were honourable and chaste, and most alien to spite, malevolence and wantonness. He did not have the habit of provoking the capricious by inopportune

---

[5] Johann von Dalberg (1455–1503) became the Bishop of Worms in 1482. He was highly esteemed by Philip, the Elector Palatine, and supported humanism. Through his efforts Agricola was called to the University of Heidelberg, of which Dalberg was chancellor. For Dietrich (*d.* 1520) and Johann von Pleningen (*d.* 1506), see Breen, 'Melanchthon's Sources', p. 53, and for Johann von Pleningen's biography of Agricola, see Weiss, 'Six Lives of Rudolf Agricola', pp. 34–7.

reprimands, so that he would not sow the seeds of strife in the school, and he often said that a guest had to conceal many things, as the Greek verse says: 'A stranger should keep silent rather than brawl' (*Xenon de sigan kreitton ē kekragenai*). He was often consulted by the learned, both in philosophy and in the other arts. He translated much of Aristotle and interpreted it for those who examined his opinions. At the time no one had seen Aristotle's books on animals. Thus his service was most agreeable to the learned, when at some time he quoted a remarkable passage from it; when they discussed what Aristotle thought of the immortality of the human soul, this sentence, taken from the book *On the Generation of Animals*, was received with great astonishment: 'the mind is added from outside; it is not born from the matter of the body'. Sometimes he imparted to the students something from Aratus about the position, rising and setting of the stars.[6]

He was not without service to the teachers of other disciplines. By chance a debate occurred between theologians and lawyers about the saying: 'He who does not serve the canons of the synods serves the Gospel in vain.' While some twisted this in order to strengthen superstition in ceremonies, and others lamented that the saying (*to rhēton*) was too hard and said that it had to be mitigated by some interpretation, Rudolf said that in general in the interpretation of the law a knowledge of history and antiquity was very profitable. In particular, all needed to know the history of the Church and its past disputes, in which an interpretation of old sayings could often be found. The ancient synods, he said, called 'canons' the points of doctrine decided upon in the synods only, and not instructions about ceremonies, and there was no doubt that the former was the meaning of this saying, but that it was later distorted by error. It is true that the Gospel is not served by those who spurn the decrees against the Samosatene, or Arius, or the deeds of the Macedonians;[7] for the most ancient synods were called together because of conflicts of dogma, and not because of increasing ceremonies. What an unworthy utterance would it be to say that faith in Christ is useless and inane without the observation of all human rites? Or that the light and eternal life in the mind would be extinguished if some ridiculous ceremony were neglected? He added that such rites could often be omitted without any sin. By this very skilful interpretation he gave satisfaction to all.

[6] Aratus, ancient Greek poet and author of the poem, *Phaenomena*.

[7] The Samosatene are Paul of Samosata and his followers: see note 3 oration 23, p. 185. Arius (*c.* 250–336) put forth a heretical view that denied the divinity of Christ. Macedonians are the followers of Macedonius (*d.* 362), who defended a semi-Arian view.

Often he also explained, to those who asked him, what could be sought from history in civil law, such as the passage about interests. In the same way, he explained what was an undefended action (*erēmē dikē*) [Thucydides, *History*, VI.61], and then what were the degrees of ancient Roman trials. As for what he wished for in theology, I remember that Josquin of Groningen,[8] an old man of outstanding piety and seriousness, wrote that in his youth he was present at the sermons of Rudolf and Wessel,[9] in which they lamented the darkness of the Church, and reproved the profanation of the mass and of celibacy. In the same way they also discussed the justice of faith, why it is that Paul repeats so many times that men are justified through faith and not through deeds. Josquin wrote that they openly rejected the belief of the monks which claims that men are just through works. He also writes that they thought, with regard to human traditions, that those are mistaken who devise for themselves the esteem of veneration, and judge that they cannot be violated. I am not inventing any of this, for Josquin wrote these things almost literally.

And it is sufficiently credible that Agricola debated assiduously about Christian doctrine, in particular since he was acquainted with Wessel, who had the highest intellect, to which he added the greatest erudition in all disciplines, as well as the knowledge of Greek and Hebrew. In addition to that he was experienced in religious disputes. Expelled from Paris for having reproached superstitions, he came to Basle; there they called him Basil of Groningen instead of Wessel. Capnio relates that at the same time he taught theology, Greek and Hebrew to the students, if any wanted to study with him.[10] When he had returned to Belgium from there, Rudolf often looked more like an older man though he was younger, but more learned in Latin and Greek, and glowing with enthusiasm for Christian doctrine. He himself often proclaimed that he was to devote what years he had left to the Holy Scriptures; if he had lived longer, he would without doubt have accomplished outstanding work for the Church. However, the studies he actually made were also profitable to the Church, because he

---

[8] Goswin van Halen (*c.* 1477–1530) was a *famulus* to Wessel Gansfort and studied under Alexander Hegius, both of whom were close friends of Agricola; see Weiss, 'Six Lives of Rudolph Agricola', pp. 24–7.

[9] Wessel Gansfort (1419–89), born in Groningen, was accomplished in Latin, Greek and Hebrew. After taking his BA and MA at the University of Cologne, he travelled and stayed in Louvain, Paris, Cologne, Heidelberg, Zwolle, Rome, Venice and Paris. During his travels he met several humanists, including Agricola and Alexander Hegius.

[10] For Johann Reuchlin (1454/5–1522), see note 8 oration 4, p. 35. He arrived in Heidelberg only after Agricola's death, however.

called back our men to a better method of learning. That service is not to be rated lightly. But I return to the story of his life.

When he lived in Heidelberg in such a way that he was most dear to all those who were learned and good, he not only came to be known to the Duke Palatine Philip, but the prince also enjoyed his company, and often summoned him to weighty deliberations. When, as happened, ancient empires were mentioned, and Rudolf called to mind now Greek, now Roman, history, the prince commanded him to translate many things, not only from the histories, but also from the poets. He asked him to put together for him a complete sequence of four monarchies, in order that he could see the order of things better, and consider their growth and changes, and the causes of these; for these examples in particular can instruct princes in many things. Therefore Rudolf put together a most learned epitome from the Bible and Herodotus, about the empire of the Assyrians and the Persians, about the civic dissensions of the Greek cities, from Thucydides and Xenophon, and about Philip and Alexander and the latter's successors, from Diodorus and Polybius. Then he selected some most excellent passages from Roman history. Finally he gathered the principal facts about the German empire. In this work he not only took pains to narrate these great things clearly, but also to instruct the prince about many things, in passing, as he was reading it; it was manifest in this matter that he excelled not only in erudition, but also in civic sagacity. However, when his age had advanced, and he had already begun theological lucubrations, not long after his fortieth year, he was released from human concerns. I hope that immortal joy has been given to him, since we read that he thought piously about Christ, and devoted his studies to the glory of God, and we hear that his conduct was pious and honourable. There you have the story of Rudolf's life.

Now it remains for you to preserve the memory of this great man gratefully. Consider what an ornament he was for Germany, and what a service he has done for erudition. For he was the first in Germany to correct the manner of speech, and he kindled the study of Latin and Greek; therefore we all owe him much. Also, admonished by his examples and sayings, the young should learn to judge more sagaciously on studies, and imitate his diligence and application, of which weaker intellects have much more need than those heroic natures, for whom many things come to pass, so to speak, without effort (*anērota*). They should also learn to heed his counsel in studying, that is, that he did not separate arts joined together by nature, but in either kind he strove with the greatest effort of his mind and intellect, and I encourage you all, as much as I can, to do so as well. And for that purpose the scholarly exercises have been established, so that we may strive in either kind, as we need to do in order to be of use for the Church and the state. For neither can knowledge of things be obtained in the right way without practice in speaking, nor are those who are without the knowledge of things suitable for expounding serious matters. Furthermore, if we do our duty diligently, God will honour us with rewards: God will preserve the Church as well as the schools, which are an important part of the Church, even though they are neglected by those who are in charge, who certainly go far astray. Because of the Church and the schools they themselves and the states are protected. Therefore they in turn should be thanking us; if they do not do so, God will punish them, and will nevertheless show some haven to the Church, the schools and our rank, as he promised that he would not abandon those who strive to propagate and honour knowledge useful to the Church. I have spoken.

29 On Johannes Regiomontanus (1549)

CR XI, 817–26

Oration on the mathematician Johannes Regiomontanus, given by
Erasmus Reinhold, of Saalfeld, professor of mathematics, at the
proclamation of the degree of Master of Philosophy[1]

To begin with, I give thanks to the eternal God, Father of our Lord Jesus
Christ, the Maker of Heaven and Earth and of His angelic and human
Church, together with His Son, our Lord Jesus Christ and His Holy Spirit,
for not allowing studies of this subject to perish. And I pray to Him with
all my heart that He may guide us and sustain our studies, and assemble
among us a following for His Son, our Lord Jesus Christ, who was crucified
for us and was resurrected; a following which may delight in His goodness
for all eternity and worship Him. It is proper for you all to beg for this with
fervent prayers – for in these scholarly assemblies, too, prayers should be
mingled with admonitions about knowledge.

But it is the custom occasionally to declaim here the stories of famous
men, especially of learned ones, because these stories teach us much about
the arts which they rendered illustrious, and because the commemoration
of such men is agreeable to worthy minds. Therefore I have now put together
an account of Johannes Regiomontanus, partly from his own writings, partly
from the oration of that most learned man, Johannes Schöner.[2] Although
it is rather short and will not fulfil your expectations, it nevertheless needs
to be handed on to the young, so that they may come to know and admire
this great man, and may strive after these arts whose seeds he sowed.
Admittedly the power and sharpness of his intelligence, his erudition and
the correctness of his judgement can be seen especially in his writings, but
this realisation is limited to the masters. Although this account of his zeal,
of the works he published, his struggles with the masters, his travels and

---

[1] In 1549 Erasmus Reinhold (1511–53) was Dean of the arts faculty. This is the oldest extant biography
of Regiomontanus, for whose life see E. Zinner, *Regiomontanus: His Life and Work*, trans. E. Brown,
Studies in the History and Philosophy of Mathematics (Amsterdam, New York, Oxford, Tokyo,
1990). For his achievement, see Menso Folkerts, 'Regiomontanus' Rôle in the Transmission and
Transformation of Greek Mathematics' in *Tradition, Transmission, Transformation: Proceedings of
Two Conferences on Pre-modern Science Held at the University of Oklahoma*, ed. F. Jamil Ragep and
Sally R. Ragep, with S. Livesey (Leiden, 1996), pp. 89–113.

[2] Johann Schöner (1477–1547) of Nuremberg had access to several works of Regiomontanus and
printed them. Schöner's own oration of Regiomontanus, however, on which this oration was based,
is no longer extant.

his friendships with the greatest men show that he had many other virtues, it also shows that he had a powerful intellect and an enthusiasm, implanted by divine providence, for rendering illustrious the arts. Indeed, I admire the brilliance of his mind as much as I am delighted by the subtlety of his books. At the same time as his mind flits through the entire nature of things, and measures the heavens and the spaces of the Earth, his body travels through Germany, Italy and Hungary; he learns Greek, and even that peculiar language particular to the geometers, and he compares his ideas with other learned men. He not only wrote much that would be of use for future generations, but he also fashioned machines by his own hand, and he built a printing-press. A slothful nature neither undertakes such a variety of toils, nor can it support it. But whatever trace of his virtues can be shown in such a narrative, I hope that this account will be agreeable to you.

Johannes Regiomontanus was born in a town of Franconia called Königsberg, which because of its closeness is known to most of you. I hear that his parents were worthy people of some means, as things go in our towns, so that they were able to bring up and educate their children in any way they desired. I know that some men born in that family were also known to some of our colleagues. And since it is a matter of fact that dispositions take on some impetus from heavenly causes, I shall also recount the time at which he was born and the position of the stars which shone at his birth. He was born in the year 1436, according to the customary way of counting, on the sixth of June, at the fourth hour and fortieth minute after noon.[3] I would wish that the complete positions of the celestial signs at birth were preserved in all histories for those who either excelled by their natural goodness or were of monstrous perversity. Nevertheless, I shall now recount the horoscope and the position of the planets so that the entire position of celestial signs can be the better judged by the eyes. The horoscope was the fifteenth degree of Scorpio, with the sun, the moon, Mars and Mercury together in Gemini – a sign that portends very little wildness, but a moderate and docile nature suitable for discipline; and since the sun and moon and Mars and Mercury came together in it, it was a disposition that was neither dull nor sluggish. Jupiter in Libra and Venus in Cancer increase the goodness of the temperament. I shall not add a longer explanation, but I leave it to

---

[3] It was then customary to use unequal hours (dividing the period between sun-up and sun-down into twelve equal hours): Zinner, *Regiomontanus*, p. 1. It was unusual to give the exact minute of birth, but it may have had astrological significance.

the learned to consider, who see what threatens the disposition of life. But the signs of disposition and character will not be discovered to be absurd. The seeds of his nature were sufficiently propitious, and his disposition was docile and keen; nevertheless, without divine inspiration he could not have thoroughly grasped so many and such varied arts, learnt so many languages, supported simultaneously so many toils in studying, teaching, fashioning machines, observing the positions of the stars, writing most learned explanations, disclosing so many mazes, publishing his own tables and those of others, and also *Ephemerides*, especially in the course of such a short life, if God had not kindled and assisted the fire of his mind and heart. In that way, in His great goodness, He is wont continually to encourage and help masters in every field in order to restore and protect the arts that are necessary for life. For truly the preservation of arts and sciences among humankind is the favour of the eternal God, who is the fount of wisdom. Therefore let us give thanks to Him, who repeatedly restores the light of the sciences, and let us pray that He will not let it be extinguished. However, He wants some diligence and zeal in us to be added to His generosity; and He does not want His gifts cast away with disgust and contempt, as it is expressed in a more weighty argument in the parable about the traders. And it is not incongruous that Plato says in book four of the *Laws*: 'That the god and opportunity steer all human matters, it is more civilised to agree that art has to follow these as a third' [709b].[4] That is, a god and opportunity rule all affairs, but it is nevertheless more civil to grant that art is to be added, as on a ship: even if a storm has the upper hand, nevertheless the oars should not be idle. In this way let us also accept the divine gifts with respect, delight in them assiduously, and protect them for the glory of God and for the common good, as much as we can with our mediocre diligence, as it is written. This is demanded of us, in order that we be faithful, and imitate Regiomontanus in this matter. When God had given him the powers of the intellect and the body necessary for learning, an excellent teacher and books as companions for his studies, he did not neglect these opportunities; he did not, like many others, prefer pleasures or money, but attached himself to these studies with all the powers of his intellect and his mind. He searched everywhere for learned men by whose wisdom he could be instructed, and in turn he adorned the arts by his works as much as he could. Let us therefore give thanks to God, who does not allow these His gifts to perish utterly, and let us praise the will, effort and assiduity of

4 The quotation is slightly shortened to omit the word 'chance'.

Regiomontanus. In order that you may better behold his virtues, you should know his ways.

After studying grammar in his home-town, he came, still a boy, to the University of Leipzig, where he seized eagerly upon dialectic and the elements of the science of celestial motions. But burning, by disposition, with the desire to learn, he needed guides in this study as well as companions in this most beautiful toil, and he heard that Vienna was a particular home to this philosophy. Therefore he travelled to Austria when still a youth. There he encountered the Bavarian Peuerbach, a most ingenious man, in the prime of his age and reputation.[5] The latter valued Regiomontanus, when he had examined the power of the youth's nature and his will, and became not only his encourager, but also his guide to the most sacred sanctuary of these arts. When I think of their companionship, studies and struggles I also see in my mind's eye the ancient schools by whose diligence these arts were propagated. Thus the Egyptian priests taught Theletes, Meton and Eudoxus, and Eudoxus taught Plato. In that way it is said that Atlas taught this knowledge to Orion; indeed, as I believe, in that way those long-lived men in the first ages of the world, Adam, Noah, Shem and Joseph, passed on this knowledge to coming generations, and its possession was preserved in Egypt from the time of Joseph to the age of Ptolemy, and somewhat longer, for over two thousand years. For such a long time God bestowed upon this knowledge a stable and fixed abode, among the changes of the various monarchies. But then the wisdom of the principal monarchs was such that they knew that they ought to wage war against the enemies and not against the arts, and in the midst of wars they protected the abodes of erudition and the assemblies of the learned. Now, oh grief, that knowledge roams without protectors and without a fixed abode, so that one must fear the ruin of these arts. But let us pray to God the Maker not to allow His gifts to perish.

Since there was the greatest friendship between him and Peuerbach, and an assiduous comparison of ideas for about a decade, they shed light on many obscure matters and, as they say, the two beginning together (*synte dyō archomenō*) they observed the motion and detected that the motion of Mars did not correspond to the tables, but that there was an error of about two degrees. Therefore they began the correction of the tables. By chance

---

[5] Georg Peuerbach (1423–61) attended the University of Vienna, obtaining his BA in 1448 and MA in 1453. He lectured on astronomy and poetry at Vienna: see Zinner, *Regiomontanus*, p. 8. Regiomontanus matriculated at the University of Vienna in 1450.

Bessarion, a Greek, who excelled in knowledge, was at the time ambassador to the emperor Frederick, since he was a cardinal.[6] When he had inquired much about the knowledge of Ptolemy from Peuerbach, and had admired his skill in expounding, he asked him to compose a *résumé* of the book entitled *Megalē Syntaxis* (the *Almagest*). Regiomontanus completed that work that was interrupted by the death of Peuerbach, because – as he himself relates – the dying Peuerbach had asked him on the point of death. In this matter it is much to be marvelled at that at the time they were able, without the Greek sources, to pluck the meaning from those Arabic translations. This could in no way have been done if the demonstrations had not been obvious and easily penetrable to them because of their great practice in that entire circle of arts. But nevertheless later Regiomontanus corrected that work in Rome, when he had learnt Greek and compared it with Theon. There survives a letter by Regiomontanus full of honesty, in which he deplores the death of his teacher and proclaims his genius, saying that he preferred him to all the mathematicians of his day.[7]

The desire to go to Italy struck both Peuerbach and Regiomontanus, in order to listen to learned men in Italy – for Bianchini's renown[8] was being praised – as well as to apply themselves to the Greek language, in which they knew the sources of these arts to be contained, and they wanted to read Ptolemy speaking his own language. And Bessarion encouraged them to travel with him. Regiomontanus also relates that he was much aggrieved that he could not examine the sources when, as a youth, he saw two most ingenious men, Peuerbach and Franciscus Mantuanus,[9] at a loss in the translations of the geography of Ptolemy because of their ignorance of Greek. There were no teachers for the Greek language, and because of that he decided at some time to travel to Italy. The youth took it ill that there were so many errors in the translation of the description of the Danube. For when the text had *ektropē*, which is passage, where another stream flows into it, such as the Inn flowing into the Danube at Passau, the translator

---

[6] See note 4, oration 12, p. 108.

[7] See Regiomontanus, *Rudimenta Astronomica Alfragani. Item Albategnius Astronomus Peritissimus de Motu Stellarum . . . Item Oratio Introductoria in Omnes Scientias Mathematicas* (Nuremberg: J. Petreius, 1537). This contains a preface by Melanchthon addressed to the Senate of Nuremberg.

[8] Giovanni Bianchini had no formal university training and was in the service of Nicolò d'Este at Ferrara. He published several large astronomical tables, which were used by Peuerbach and Regiomontanus to provide the *Ephemerides*.

[9] Franciscus Mantuanus: Regiomontanus is here probably referring to Francesco Berlinghieri, who was an orator at the Este court in Mantua. For Berlinghieri's translation of Ptolemy's *Geographica*, see Jerry Brotton, *Trading Territories: Mapping the Early Modern World* (London, 1997), pp. 87–99.

had translated it as divisions in many places, as though the other rivers were arms of the Danube. The description of the Po is obscured by a similar wandering of the mind.

However, Peuerbach's untimely death cut short his plan for this journey. After his death, sorrow also influenced Regiomontanus to leave Vienna more easily. He therefore accompanied Bessarion who was returning in Italy, when he was not far from his thirtieth year. In Rome Regiomontanus often met with Trebizond. He also explored the libraries, which spurred him even more to give attention to the Greek language. Therefore, burning with this desire, he copied many things by his own hand, and made himself familiar with the books of Ptolemy. Then he also wrote the dialogue against the *Theorica* of Gerard of Cremona.[10] Some time later he went to Ferrara, where Blanchinus and Theodorus Gaza were at the time, and Guarinus taught there in Greek.[11] There he accomplished with zeal an excellent work in Greek, in more than a year; and he studied so much that he was also able to write verse in Greek, which is still extant, and to busy himself with the Greek philosophers without difficulty. There he already began to compare the commentaries of Ptolemy and Theon. Some time later he left Ferrara and went to the University of Padua, where, upon request by the students of philosophy, he gave a public lecture on Alfraganus.[12] The introductory address given there still exists, in which he not only extols the subjects, but also, with great brilliance, praises the mathematicians, who were famous in Italy at the time, and whom he had attached to himself by friendship because of their fellowship of studies and virtues. When Alfraganus' lecture had finished, and Bessarion had already returned from Greece, Regiomontanus betook himself to Venice, in the year 1464. There he composed the book on triangles with great diligence, and the refutations of the quadrature of the circle, which[13] Nicolas Cusanus was believed to have demonstrated.[14] Then he returned to Rome, where he copied some

[10] The *Theorica Planetarum* is usually attributed to Gerard of Cremona (1114–87). For Regiomontanus' criticism of it, see his *Contra Cremonensia in Planetarum Theroicas Deliramenta ... Disputationes*, which underwent several editions since 1483.

[11] Theodore Gaza (1400–76) taught Greek at the University of Ferrara between 1447 and 1449. For Guarinus, see note 3, oration 28, p. 230.

[12] *Oratio Iohannis de Monteregio quam habuit ipse Patavij in praelectione Alfragani* (Wittenberg: V. Creutzer, 1549), with this oration by Reinhold attached.

[13] Reading *quam* for *quas*.

[14] Nicholas Cusanus' (1401–64) attempt to square the circle appears in the *De Quadratura Circuli* (1450), a copy of which was sent by Cusanus to Peuerbach, who in turn indicated corrections to Regiomontanus. See his *De Triangulis Omnimodis. Libri quinque ... Accesserunt huc Incalce Deque Recti ac Curvi Commensuratione ...* (Nuremberg: J. Petreius, 1533).

Greek and Latin books by his own hand – for he drew the shapes of the letters with great skill and ease – and had some of them copied at great expense. There he also had the most vehement disputes with Trebizond,[15] whose reveries in criticising Theon he refuted ingenuously.

After having travelled through Italy he returned to Vienna, where he began to teach, but was summoned by King Matthias and by the bishop of Esztergom, and was given great rewards by both.[16] The king also decreed for him an annual pension of 200 Hungarian gold coins. There he also constructed instruments for observing the motions of the heavens for both the king and the bishop. For the bishop had great learning in these subjects. And although no other prince of that time was more warlike, the king was nevertheless not uneducated in the knowledge of the celestial motions. It is said that he was also saved from a very serious illness by the counsel of a mathematician. For when the doctors found no cause for the illness in the humours, and noticed only that the faintness of the heart was strange, a mathematician advised that this feebleness of the vital powers was because of an eclipse which had threatened the king's life, and that the cause was not to be sought in the humours,[17] but the powers of the heart could only be assisted by pleasant things. Thus the king recovered.

At that time Regiomontanus also composed for the bishop the tables of directions. Although he had taken over their foundations from others, a great part of the work is nevertheless his own. And this imparting of works is proper and most worthy of praise – for preceding generations to pass on the seeds of the arts to following generations, and for the following generations to preserve them faithfully and render them illustrious.

At the same time the king of Hungary, Matthias, waged war against the Bohemians, a fact that troubled the peace of many regions nearby. Some of the Bohemians invited Casimir, the king of Poland, some attempted to surrender the kingship to Albert Duke of Saxony, and others invited Matthias, who, since he was the most spirited, preceded the

---

[15] In 1451, George of Trebizond (1395–1484) was commissioned by Pope Nicholas V to produce a Latin translation of Ptolemy's *Almagest* from a Greek manuscript borrowed from Bessarion. Trebizond criticised the corrections made by Theon of Alexandria in his edition, for which see John Monfasani, *Collectanea Trapezuntina: Texts, Documents and Bibliographies of George of Trebizond* (Binghamton, NY, 1984), pp. 671–87. Bessarion objected to Trebizond's criticism and defended Theon's commentary on Ptolemy's *Almagest*.

[16] Matthias Corvinus I (1443–90), King of Hungary, book-collector and patron for scholars and artists. Johannes Vitez, Archbishop of Gran (Esztergom) was also a patron of arts.

[17] Reading *humoribus* for *honoribus*.

others.[18] Since, therefore, Hungary, Austria and all the regions nearby were in great commotion, Regiomontanus looked for a quiet place for his studies and, in 1471, he betook himself to Nuremberg. He himself said that he would like to spend the rest of his life in that town, because there were craftsmen there who were capable of constructing machines necessary for this art, and, furthermore, because he could easily send letters from there to other regions by merchants. For, when he was already famously learned in the subject, had examined the judgements of others, and equipped himself for making mathematics illustrious and promoting it as much as he could, he determined to edit also the ancient writers, and to publish his interpretations.

For that purpose he fitted out a printing-house and set up a list – which still exists[19] – of the books he was about to publish, and he began at a fortunate moment with the publication of the *Ephemerides* covering thirty years. The work was so pleasing at the time that single copies of it sold for twelve Hungarian gold coins, and they were desired eagerly by men of all nations. No Italian, Frenchman, Hungarian, Pole or German had ever seen a similar calendar. The Venetians also brought it to Greece. You know that it is also the will of God that the years are divided, and that learned distinctions are a great pleasure to all those in their right mind. Therefore we should abhor the ravings of the Cyclopes, who either hate or scorn the study of these arts.

The expense of setting up the printing-house was borne mainly by Bernhard Walter[20] – the members of whose family are not unknown in these regions – who had very great means as well as cherishing the study of the knowledge of the heavens. He also attracted the good will of many other citizens, so that they began to acquaint themselves with, and come to know, these subjects. These 'nurseries' of the subject were first spread in Nuremberg. Therefore up to now the study of these arts flourishes more

[18] There seems to be some confusion of names here: Vladislav II (1456–1516), who was elected King of Bohemia in 1471, was the eldest son of Casimir IV Jagiello and brother of Sigismund I of Poland. Territorial agreements were reached in 1478 and 1479 after a protracted military conflict between Vladislav II and Matthias Corvinus I. Albrecht, Duke of Saxony (1443–1500) had married the daughter of Georg, King of Bohemia, whom he tried to succeed (in vain) after the latter's death in 1471.

[19] For a description of the trade-list, see Zinner, *Regiomontanus*, pp. 112–17; and for a photograph of a surviving copy, see L. Jardine, *Worldly Goods* (London 1996), p. 348.

[20] Bernard Walter (*d.* 1504), a citizen of Nuremberg, was a student of Regiomontanus and had built an observatory in his own house. He purchased books and instruments of Regiomontanus after the latter's death, but there seems to be no positive proof that he financially assisted Regiomontanus' printing enterprise.

in that city than in most universities. And by decree of the most wise senate there is a certain income for the arts, so that they introduce the young to the knowledge of them. In recent times the learned and most worthy man Johannes Schöner had encouraged many to study. You can see what a great thing Regiomontanus had set in motion.

He established new translations of the *Almagest* and the *Geography* of Ptolemy, and he also provided verifications for his corrections. In passing he also examined and disclosed other workings of nature. He researched how high vapours are raised up above the earth, and he discovered with admirable dexterity that they are no further away than 12 German miles.

We read that at the time two comets burned in two consecutive years, namely in 1471 and again in 1472. Such drought ensued that the courses of rivers and springs dried up. They also tell expressly that fires in many towns ensued. Also, the Hungarians and the Poles fought among themselves about Bohemia; and the Turkish tyrant Muhammad occupied Walachia in Europe and the kingdom of Trebizond in Asia,[21] to leave out much else. Since Regiomontanus knew that comets do not often burn in two consecutive years, and was impressed by the magnitude of the events that had followed, he published an admirable work about the true location and size of comets.[22]

At the same time there was a man in Erfurt who was very learned in these subjects, Master Christianus.[23] How much Regiomontanus set store by him is apparent from his letter, in which he writes that working on the publication of useful writers, he would therefore like to move to Nuremberg, so that he would not be far away from him, since he desired greatly to be helped by him, and to make use of his judgement and criticism in many matters. I praise the openness of the most excellent master, that he was a stranger to disparagement and envy towards the teachers of his art, and I believe that he sought in earnest for companions in this most beautiful toil and for the criticism of a great master.

The edition of the *Ephemerides* was particularly popular in Rome, and learned men, who knew his intelligence and erudition, desired to recall him

---

[21] For the struggle between Hungarians and Poles around 1472, see note 18 above. Turks occupied Walachia in Europe in 1393 after the battle of Kossowo (1389) and Trebizond, the last Greek state, fell in 1461.

[22] *De Cometae Magnitudine, Longitudine ac de Loco eius Vero Problemata* (Nuremberg, 1544).

[23] Christian Roder was a professor of mathematics at the University of Erfurt. Regiomontanus' letters to him are edited in M. Curtze, *Urkunden zur Geschichte der Mathematik in Mittelalter und der Renaissance* (2 vols., Leipzig, 1902), vol. 1, pp. 324–36.

to Italy, so that they could profit from his teaching. These encouraged Pope Sixtus to invite him to Rome, and as a justification it was put forth that there would be deliberations on the emendation of the calendar. Regiomontanus bore it ill that he had to tear himself away from the printing-house and the edition of Ptolemy, and he had a presentiment of his death, and, as they relate it, he complained that he undertook the journey unwillingly; nevertheless the pope's authority won. Also a reason had been proposed which moved a man who desired to serve the public good. For you know how useful it is to have a computation of the year that is properly ordered and corrected. He did not want to be absent from such a great and useful venture. It is also possible that he shrank less from the journey, because he looked forward to conversations with the learned, and the libraries attracted him. He returned to Rome therefore, where he died in the year 1476.[24] That was the year in which the king of Hungary, Matthias, defeated Muhammad in a great battle at Smederevo, in which Muhammad is also said to have been wounded.

Who would not grieve that a longer life was not given to such a man of genius, especially as he was undertaking the most useful things? For he was cut off when he had only entered his forty-first year. The rumour is that poison was given to him by the sons of Trebizond, because he had criticised the latter's translation of Ptolemy and refuted the errors in his commentary and his criticism of Theon.[25] His horoscope not only announced a man who would die a violent death (*biothanaton*), but also one who was upright and combative. Therefore perhaps the liberty of his tongue was harmful to him. But whatever way he was cut off, it was an untimely death and one that even now is to be mourned, because we lack those works which he was yet to begin. It should not be disregarded that to such erudition and his other virtues he added piety towards God, and in order to worship Him by true recognition and invocation he copied the entire New Testament in Greek most elegantly by his own hand; Schöner has shown me that book along with his other memorials. And it is fitting that such great men, who everywhere see the marks of divinity engraved upon the nature of things and consider them attentively for the sake of knowledge, are greatly moved by these tokens of evidence. And they declare much more firmly that this world is made and ruled by

[24] Reading *1476* for *1470*.
[25] The rumour of poisoning was first mentioned in 1482 by Jacobus Sentinus: Zinner, *Regiomontanus*, p. 152.

an eternal constructing mind than do other men who are strangers to this study of contemplating so many and such excellent marks of God in nature. Indeed, I often shudder throughout my body to think that when God shows most truly by so much evidence that He is nearby, and that He is the observer and judge of all our actions, our hearts nevertheless feebly fear Him and do not burn with trust in Him. Wherever you turn in this entire nature of things, whether you contemplate the shape of the heavens, their motions and harmony with the elements, or observe wonderful skill in the construction of our body or the fertility of the earth, the order in all things cries out that there is an eternal constructing mind. And it is to be recognised as it discloses itself in the Church. Since Regiomontanus did that, let us consider that he now sees the idea of the entire world in God Himself, and the causes of the way[26] in which everything is made, that he beholds in person the heavenly bodies, and that he converses most pleasantly with the first fathers about the invention of their arts and their observations, as with fellow philosophers (*symphilosophois*), and worships God the Creator.

The library of Regiomontanus was bought by Walter, the citizen of Nuremberg of whom I spoke earlier; when he had died, the senate took charge of preserving his effects. That most learned man, Schöner, published some useful writings from among those; but we would have many other, and by far more useful, writings, had the author not been cut off before his time by a tragic destiny.

I have surveyed briefly the history of the most learned man Regiomontanus, which is beneficial for students to know. For although natural excellence cannot be transferred to others, nevertheless others can in some way imitate will-power and assiduity. First, however, let us give thanks to God when thinking about this history, for preserving the arts, and for rousing some worthy minds to study and adorn them; and let us pray to Him that He may not allow such studies to be exhausted now. Then let us also praise in gratitude the memory of Regiomontanus himself, and let us strive to profit from his teaching. Let us also imitate, as much as we can, his studies and assiduity, and let us furthermore love and esteem the arts which he adorned. Let us not reckon that the wonderful sight of the motions of the heavens is put before the eyes of men in vain, or that such a knowledge is useless, but let us truly realise that the order of the motions and its knowledge itself are admonitions from God, and that this knowledge is profitable for

[26] Reading *quo* for *hoc*.

the life of men in many ways, as it is shown clearly in measuring, in the computation of the year and in the knowledge of the position of countries. I have spoken.

30 On Erasmus of Rotterdam (1557)

CR XI, 264–71

Oration on Erasmus of Rotterdam; given by Master Bartholomaeus Calkreuter of Cross, 1557

Our minds should always give attention to God, and, thinking of his continuous favours, recognise Him as their Maker, worship Him and be stirred up, full of lamentation because of our unworthiness. And let us plead with ardent prayers that we be guided by the light of the Son of God, our Lord Jesus Christ, and the Holy Spirit, and that we be protected and preserved. God said that He would carry the Church, just as the shepherd carries young lambs.

The expression of our gratitude and invocation must be shown most in public assemblies. Therefore, recite with me at the beginning with pious minds this first and principal part of the oration.

We thank you, almighty God, everlasting Father of our Lord Jesus Christ, Creator of heaven and earth and of men, together with your coeternal Son, our Lord Jesus Christ, and the Holy Spirit, that in your great goodness you both show us other countless favours and truly set up the eternal Church among us by the voice of the Gospel, and that you preserve among us assemblies of those who teach and study your doctrine. These great goods are not distributed by chance, but they are truly God's works and gifts. We acknowledge that we are unworthy of such great beneficence, but for the sake of your glory let there be a Church that unites, worships you duly and invokes you. Let there be proper studies of doctrine, and let us be the lambs you carry in your bosom. We plead for this with ardent prayers, which we humbly pray you will grant for the sake of your Son the Mediator.

It is a worthy custom in these gatherings to speak about a part of erudition, or to call to mind examples that are useful for the students. Even though, because of my insignificance, I should have chosen a less difficult topic, having these days heard a discussion among friends about the studies of those times in which Erasmus of Rotterdam was mentioned, I nevertheless decided to bring chiefly that man's history here. I am not doing this in order to make a public proclamation of my stupidity through inept ostentation in praising him, as if I wanted to praise Hercules or Cyrus, but in order to admonish the young to read his useful writings and consider his particular virtues. Along with such a greatness of intellect with which he was equipped by God, he had many and outstanding virtues: keenness in inventing, and sagacity and circumspection in choosing arguments and opinions; in speaking he had facility of speech, as well as splendour of figures of speech, beauty and charm, in which he excelled to such an extent that it may seem as if the Graces themselves had strewn his speech with flowers everywhere.

We need to read the greatest masters, such as Homer, Isocrates, Cicero and others, not because we could imitate all of them, but in order that we take from them what we can convey to ourselves. Let us imitate his language, the knowledge of things, counsel in arranging matters, and if nature assists us let us follow in one way or another his traces in speaking. For let us understand that dispositions are different and that nevertheless the weaker ones need to be helped by art, good examples and some practice – as happens with painters. Therefore I shall speak about the history of Erasmus, and we shall respectfully add something about his language and his writings – not like Midas judging Apollo [Ovid, *Metamorphoses* XI.157–93], but in order that the young love more, and read, Erasmus' useful writings, of which there are many.

His life, too, contains examples of many virtues, namely of assiduity, endurance of labours, modesty and kindness. For that reason I shall speak about the entire course of his life, as much as I have heard from trustworthy men.

The Batavii are mentioned in many histories; now they are called the Dutch. A renowned city of theirs is Rotterdam, where Erasmus was born; his parents' small house can still be seen today. He was born in the year 1467, on the twenty-eighth of October, in the fourth hour before sunrise. In the position of the stars there are clear indications of intelligence, eloquence and charm.[1]

He studied Latin and Greek at Deventer, at the school of Alexander Hegius,[2] who was acquainted with Rudolf Agricola. Erasmus himself used to tell about Rudolf Agricola's prophecy on the young man's study. By chance Hegius had shown the writings of the boys to Rudolf who had come to the school as a guest. While he approved of all the attempts and rejoiced

---

[1] For the life of Erasmus, I have followed Cornelius Augustijn, *Erasmus, His Life, Works and Influence*, trans. J. C. Grayson (Toronto, 1991). Further details of people mentioned in this oration may be found in *Contemporaries of Erasmus: A Biographical Register of the Renaissance and Reformation*, ed. P. B. Bietenholz (3 vols., Toronto, 1985–7).
[2] Alexander Hegius (*d.* 1498) studied Greek with Rudolf Agricola (1444–85) in Emmerich before becoming rector of St. Lebuin's School at Deventer between 1483 and 1498. Erasmus met Agricola at this school before leaving in 1484. For references to them, see Erasmus, *Adages*, I.iv.39 and II.ii.81.

at their studies, he nevertheless preferred Erasmus' written work to the others because of the keenness of invention, the purity of the language and the figures scattered suitably like flowers. He was so delighted by that piece of writing that he wanted to draw conclusions on his disposition from his features as well. He therefore ordered Erasmus to be called, and when he had inquired about a few things, he observed the shape of his head and his bright eyes, admonished him to study and said: 'One day you will be a great man.'

And so he continued successfully in his studies, and the death of his parents did not interrupt the studies he had begun. For in Holland and Belgium there are fraternities in monasteries, more of them and more devoted to education than in this our Germany, which willingly assist scholars. Therefore the members of the fraternity at the monastery of Deventer invited Erasmus, who had lost his parents, and gave the orphan the hope that they would send him to Paris, which was done shortly thereafter. In that university he not only studied, but since his writings opened the way for him to learned and noble men, his behaviour was modest and his courteousness admirable, some noblemen took him into their company and he instructed them.

He narrates in a letter that the assiduity of the students was such that at lunches and dinners, too, they used to summon readers for reading out the Latin writers. When an unclear passage occurred in these, he either requested an interpretation from the others or provided it himself when necessary.

His exercises in style were also such that he not only changed a few words in someone else's writings, but wove entire orations anew, so that the students could see what was lacking in the entire construction. The fame of his intellect and eloquence quickly reached the Belgian court. When Jacob Batt[3] recommended him to the rulers there, he was assisted by the generosity of the court.

However, the English took him with them from France back to their country.[4] He travelled there willingly, both because of the quantity of Greek books which was already great there at the time, and because there were several outstandingly erudite bishops in England then. Since both the power of his intellect was great, and his erudition in Latin

---

[3] Jacob Batt (*c.* 1466–1502) of Bergen was a loyal friend of Erasmus and probably used his influence with the bishop to free Erasmus for study in Paris.

[4] Erasmus visited England twice, between 1499 and 1500, and in 1509 and 1514 at the invitation of William Blount, Lord Mountjoy.

and Greek was extraordinary, the learned and wise bishops – the one at Canterbury[5] and others – straightaway began to honour him generously, in particular since already his manly age lent him some authority. There he translated two tragedies by Euripides,[6] and it can be understood how he felt about them from the fact that, when Longueil[7] said in his presence that his language was humble and submissive and lacked splendour and grandeur, Erasmus commanded him to attempt whether he could turn a tragedy by Euripides or Sophocles into Latin with similar splendour.

He was then given a position for teaching Greek and Latin publicly at the University of Cambridge, which he accepted willingly so that he could make use of Greek books. Some time later he was sent to Italy with the sons of the king's physician; there he listened more to the lectures of the doctors than to those of the theologians or lawyers, although he listened to their lectures as well. He did not listen to professors of Latin, because there was no other professor there except Baptista Pius, an inept man. The language of Baptista was monstrous, imitating not the speech that was customary in Rome from the time of Terence to the age of Augustus, but that used by the Volscian rustics before the Decemvirs. He was therefore scorned in stage-plays. When, having heard Baptista once, Erasmus was asked by a friend what he thought of him, he replied: 'He has outstripped my imagination by far.' 'What?' asked the friend. Erasmus said: 'Before I considered him inept, but now I have understood that he is utterly mad.'

Since there was a large number of books in Bologna, he undertook the larger work of the *Proverbs*, which he later published, extended and embellished, at the printing-house of Aldus in Venice.[8] In Bologna he enjoyed the company of a well-spoken man, Paulus Bombasius.[9] When he lived at Aldus' house in Venice, he was known and dear to all accomplished men, but in particular to Marcus Musurus,[10] a most learned man from Crete,

---

[5] William Warham (c. 1456–1532) was Archbishop of Canterbury from 1503; he met Erasmus in 1506.

[6] Erasmus translated Euripides' *Hecuba* and *Iphigenia in Aulis* and dedicated them to Warham.

[7] Christophe de Longueil (c. 1488–1522) considered Budé superior to Erasmus.

[8] The collection of proverbs, the *Adagiorum Collectanea*, was first published in 1500 in Paris. Aldus Manutius printed the 1508 edition. For subsequent expansions, see M. Mann Phillips, *The 'Adages' of Erasmus, a Study with Translations* (Cambridge, 1964). For Aldus, see Martin Lowry, *The World of Aldus Manutius: Business and Scholarship in Renaissance Venice* (Oxford, 1979).

[9] Paolo Bombace (1476–1527) welcomed Erasmus to Bologna and helped him with Greek studies.

[10] Marcus Musurus (c. 1470–1517) studied with Janus Lascaris and Demetrius Chalcondyles in Florence and joined the circle of Aldus Manutius. He was made professor of Greek at the Unversity of Padua in 1503.

who was later summoned by Pope Leo to Rome for the promotion of the Greek language. At the University of Siena he also taught the son of James king of the Scots, Alexander, whose death he laments in the saying: 'You have reached Sparta, adorn it.'[11]

When he had published the *Proverbs*, he returned to England. And since many wise and learned men admired him more because of that publication, princes and bishops sought his acquaintance even more. However, he always shunned the courts; and after being supported by the generosity of Warham and Mountjoy, whose wisdom and virtue were outstanding, he returned to Italy in order to enjoy the company of learned men in Rome. There he became acquainted with the Venetian Cardinal Grimani,[12] whose house was like a university, because he himself, too, surpassed the other cardinals in erudition and modesty.

At that time, because he had seen the misfortunes of Italy and France which were caused by the war that Pope Julius had started against Louis king of France, he wrote a lament for peace. When outstanding men who were afflicted with unnecessary wars being waged had read it, rumours about Erasmus and about people's judgements of him were brought to Julius. Enraged, Julius summoned Erasmus. Although Erasmus knew the tyrant and was thoroughly frightened, nevertheless, contrary to everyone's expectation, Julius admonished him gently not to write about the business of kings. 'You,' he said, 'do not understand such things, as Phalaris said to Simonides: "You should concern yourself with the famous labours of the Muses".'[13]

Having returned to Belgium from Italy, he wrote a eulogy for Philip king of Spain, which is worth reading both because of the memory of King Philip, who had the elements of many virtues, and because of the brilliance of the oration.[14]

On so many travels he had contemplated many cities as well as many thoughts and beliefs, his judgement on many important things had been strengthened, the fame of his erudition, and his age, added authority and he had seen the great wounds of the Church. He therefore decided to publish

[11] Erasmus, *Adages*, II.v.1. Alexander Stewart (c.1493–1513), the son of James IV and Marian Boyd, and his half-brother, James Stewart (1499–1544/5), were tutored by Erasmus in Siena in 1508–9.
[12] Domenico Grimani (1461–1523), son of a Venetian Patrician who had studied at the University of Padua, met Erasmus in 1509 in Rome. Grimani was papal secretary and had a famous library and Erasmus often asked for the loan of books and manuscripts from it.
[13] There is no evidence that Erasmus met Julius II (1443–1513) either in Bologna or in Rome. Perhaps this is an oblique reference to Erasmus' alleged authorship of *Julius exclusus*.
[14] It is unclear which work was meant to have been dedicated by Erasmus to Philip II.

a mainly grammatical interpretation of the New Testament, and to add suggestions regarding vocabulary and diction.[15] By that work he judged that he would do two important and useful things; studies would be improved and more people would study Latin and Greek, and with the light of truth dawning little by little, darkness would vanish and the vanity of many errors would be revealed.

It was a successful undertaking, and I certainly believe that his studies as well as his counsels were guided by divine providence towards that work. Because of the excellence of the contents as well as the pleasantness of the language, the published book attracted the young towards the study of languages and grammar, and it accused the older generation of many errors. Just as this labour was pleasing to good men, on the other hand hypocritical monks of all nations, fearing for their authority and their stomachs, attempted both to suppress these new studies and to destroy the author himself. They fought in the courts, in the women's quarters (*gynaeceis*) and in congregations that Erasmus be destroyed. They invented crimes and stories that were pleasing to their theatre, as at all times the hypocrites oppose the truth in the Church. However, God had armed Erasmus with his Gorgo,[16] that is, his eloquence, by which he bravely fought back the enemy.

Later the entire body of Church doctrine was cleansed again by the voice of the reverend Doctor Luther; the fact that the Apostolic books and the old histories were already in people's hands was a preparation for this. Although it appears that, regarding some controversies, there was some difference in judgement between Luther and Erasmus, there is nevertheless no doubt that Erasmus was pleased with that entire part of the correction which censured the errors of human ceremonies in the Church. It is also well known that he often said that in the interpretation of the Holy Scriptures all old and recent interpreters were vanquished by Luther, and that not even the exegetic (*exēgētica*) writings were better than the explanations of Luther expounding the prophets, which Erasmus himself commanded to be read to him at dinner. But Erasmus said of Luther that here and there he exaggerated terribly in his disputatious writings, so that he would not appear to yield in any disputed question.

[15] *Paraphrasis in Novum Testamentum.*
[16] Gorgo's head was depicted on shields to terrify opponents. Gorgo had a horrible face, with serpents for hair and glaring eyes whose gaze was believed to turn anything into stone.

Also well known is the conversation between the good prince, Duke Frederick, who excelled in wisdom, and Erasmus.[17] For since debates about doctrine had been set in motion recently, Duke Frederick foresaw what a great storm was imminent, and he was neither going to allow those spurious facts to be circulated, nor did he want true and necessary corrections to be suppressed out of fear of the dangers. He consulted Erasmus on such an important matter. Duke Frederick had asked before the beginning of the meeting, so that some merriment should be visible in the first meeting: 'For what reasons are the monks so angry with Luther?' Erasmus answered: 'He has committed two great sins: he assaulted the Pope's crown and the stomachs of the monks.'

Then there followed a serious debate in which Erasmus said this kind of doctrine was pious, but that he wished to side-step some unnecessary and more terrible questions, and to discuss matters in a more peaceful way. Erasmus died in prayer to God; and he wanted to be a member of the Church of Basle.[18]

It is indeed not surprising that, amidst such a great number of controversies, somewhere even among good men a difference of judgements comes to pass. But I shall leave out this discussion. There are many signs of a modest mind in Erasmus. He could have received great rewards for flattery from the bishops, if he had placed ambition before studies. And it is evident that his labours for encouraging the study of Latin and Greek were useful. He will also live on in these useful works, in the interpretation of the New Testament, and that book that is like a cornucopia, in which there is such a varied and pleasant interpretation of proverbs – a book which I urge you strongly to read often and in depth.

You will also be able to appropriate the style and many examples of figures of speech from his language. For although some critics say that the charms are unrestrained, and that here and there the figures of speech are inopportune, and censure negligence in composition, they nevertheless threaten[19] what is good, the quantity of good words. That very fecundity that is censured is a praise of his genius; something should also be allowed

---

[17] Frederick III, Elector of Saxony, called 'the Wise' (1463–1525). He received humanist education and became patron of arts. He founded the University of Wittenberg in 1502 and was the first to respond positively to calls for curricular reform led by Luther. The personal meeting with Erasmus took place on 5 November 1520 at Cologne. Erasmus advised Frederick the Wise not to send Luther to Rome for trial then: Augustijn, *Erasmus*, p. 124.

[18] Erasmus was buried in the Cathedral of Basle, and a funeral oration was delivered by the head of the reformed church in Basle, Oswald Myconius: Augustijn, *Erasmus*, p. 183.

[19] Reading *eminent* for *minent*.

to the nation, and to his early education in France, where the native language has many charms.

The language of Demetrius of Phaleron was pleasant, and he did not drop the form of Attic speech, even though it is said that his language had somewhat more charms.[20] In the same way the language of Erasmus should also be pleasant, and acknowledged as Latin, even though the flowers are rather thickly set, as in a meadow. I speak rather briefly about this form of language, because I want you to experience for yourselves the sweetness of his works by frequent reading. Certainly some of the sap will also be drawn off into your language, if you read them often.

Therefore, since Erasmus had great powers of intellect, as well as many outstanding virtues, and since he did much for the study of the languages that are necessary for the Church and for civic life, let us preserve his memory with grateful minds, read his works and honour him gratefully. At the same time, let us give thanks to God for providing the Church with the knowledge of languages, and granting us the light of His doctrine, and let us make pious use of these favours of God. I have spoken.

[20] Demetrius of Phaleron, disciple of Theophrastus. He was elected decennial archon because of his eloquence and purity of manners: see Cicero, *Brutus*, ix.37f. and lxxxii.285.

31 At Luther's funeral (1546)

CR XI, 726–34

Oration on occasion of the funeral of Doctor Martin Luther (given by Melanchthon on the twenty-second of February)[1]

Although amidst this public mourning my voice is choked by grief and tears, nevertheless something had to be said amidst such a numerous attendance – not, as it was done by the pagans, in praise of the deceased, but rather in order to admonish this assembly about the wonderful guidance and the perils of the Church, so that they may ponder which things they need to be distressed about, for which things they need to strive in particular, and towards which examples they need to direct their life. For although impious men believe, amidst such disorder in life, that everything is brought about at random and by chance, nevertheless, strengthened by God's testimonies, let us sever the Church from the impious multitude. Let us acknowledge that it is truly guided and preserved by divine providence; let us contemplate properly its state, recognise its true governors and consider their career, and choose appropriate leaders and teachers, and let us follow and revere them piously. One needs to think and speak of these great things every time the reverend Doctor Martin Luther, our dearest father and teacher, is mentioned. Although many impious men hated him most bitterly, let us, who know that he was a minister of the Gospel called forth by divine providence, love and esteem him, and collect evidence that his teaching does not consist of mutinous beliefs spread by blind impulse, as the Epicureans judge it, but a demonstration of the will and the true veneration of God, an explanation of the Holy Scriptures and a proclamation of the word of God, that is, of the Gospel of Jesus Christ.

Therefore, although in the orations given on such an occasion much is usually said about the private honours of those who are praised, I shall nevertheless leave out that part of the oration and speak only about the most important topic, that is, his office within the Church. For thus worthy minds will always judge: if he explained a teaching that was beneficial and necessary for the Church, God must be thanked for calling him forth; and

---

[1] Luther died on 18 February 1546. This oration by Melanchthon was by far the most influential oration on Luther. Melanchthon's criticism of Luther's personality was toned down in the printed edition, compared to the oration Melanchthon actually delivered on 22 February. For an excellent analysis of this oration, see James Michael Weiss, 'Erasmus at Luther's Funeral: Melanchthon's Commemorations of Luther in 1546', *Sixteenth Century Journal* 16 (1985), 91–114.

his labours, faith, constancy and other virtues must be praised; and his memory must be most dear to all who are good.

Therefore, let this be the beginning of our oration. As Paul says [Colossians 3:1], the Son of God is seated at the right hand of the eternal Father, and He bestows blessings upon men, that is, the word of the Gospel and the Holy Spirit. In order to impart these He calls forth prophets, the Apostles, teachers and ministers – and He chooses them from this our assembly, that is, the assembly of those who study – who read, listen to and love the prophetic and Apostolic writings. Nor does He call only those to that warfare who have customary power, but often He wages war against them through teachers chosen from other ranks. It is a pleasant and useful sight to behold the Church of all ages, and to contemplate the goodness of God who has repeatedly sent salutary teachers in a continuous sequence in such a way that – similar to the line of battle – as the first ones died, others soon stepped into their footsteps.

The sequence of the first fathers is well known: Adam, Seth, Enoch, Methuselah, Noah and Shem; while the latter was still alive and living in the vicinity of the Sodomites, when already the tribes had forgotten the teaching of Noah and Shem and worshipped idols indiscriminately, Abraham was called forth to be Shem's companion and his associate in that greatest task, in propagating the true teaching. He was followed by Isaac, Jacob and Joseph who kindled the light of the true teaching in all of Egypt, which was then the most prosperous realm in all the world. Then followed Moses, Joshua, Samuel, David, Elias, Elijah whom Isaiah heard; Jeremiah heard Isaiah, Daniel heard Jeremiah and Zachariah Daniel. Then Ezra and Onias. After the latter, the Maccabees. Then Simeon, Zachariah, John the Baptist, Christ and the Apostles. It is of use to contemplate this continuous sequence which is an evident testimony of the presence of God in the Church.

After the Apostles there follows a multitude which, although it was weaker, is nevertheless honoured with God's testimonies: Polycarp, Irenaeus, Gregory of Nyssa, Basil, Augustine, Prosper, Maximus, Hugo, Bernard, Taulerus and some others. Although this last dotage of the world is more obscure, God nevertheless always preserved some remnants. And it is clear that a more brilliant light of the Gospel was lit by the voice of Luther.

Therefore he is to be included in that most beautiful multitude of excellent men whom God sent to unite and restore the Church, and whom we should understand to be the distinguished flower of humankind. Solon, Themistocles, Scipio, Augustus and the like were by all means great men who established or ruled great empires; nevertheless they are by far inferior to our leaders – Isaiah, John the Baptist, Paul, Augustine and Luther. It behoves us in the Church to understand these distinctions.

Then, what great and true things have been brought to light by Luther, which show that his career is to be praised? For many complain that he has thrown the Church into disorder and spread inextricable quarrels. I reply here that such is the governing of the Church. When the Holy Spirit reproves the world, discord arises because of the obstinacy of the impious, and the fault lies with those who do not want to listen to the Son of God, of whom the heavenly Father said: 'Hear Him' [Matthew 17:5]. Luther brought to light the true and necessary doctrine. For it is evident that there was the thickest and most impenetrable darkness in the doctrine on penitence. Having dispersed that, he showed what is true penitence, what is the haven and what is the firm consolation for the mind greatly terrified by the idea of the wrath of God. He explained Paul's teaching that says that man is justified by faith. He showed the distinction between the Law and the Gospel – the justice of the Holy Spirit and that of the state. He also showed the true invocation of God, and called back the Church from its pagan madness which pretends to invoke God, even though minds overwhelmed by Academic doubts flee God. He commanded that the invocation be made with faith and a good conscience, and he brought us to the one Mediator, the Son of God who is seated at the right hand of the eternal Father, and who intercedes for us; he did not bring us to statues or dead men, as impious men in their terrible madness invoke statues and dead men.

He also showed other true duties pleasing to God, and he adorned and defended civic life as it has never been adorned and defended by anyone else's writings. Furthermore he distinguished between necessary tasks and the childish drilling of human ceremonies and the rites and laws that hinder the true invocation of God. And in order that the illustrious heavenly doctrine be transmitted to posterity, he translated into German the prophetic and Apostolic writings, with such clarity that his translation brings more light for the reader than most commentaries.

He himself also added many explanations of which Erasmus, too, used to declare that they surpassed by far all the existing explanations. And just as it is written about those who erected Jerusalem that with the one hand they built it and with the other they held the sword, so he struggled with the enemies of the true doctrine, and at the same time he composed explanations full of the heavenly teaching and brought support to the conscience of many by pious advice.

Since a great part of doctrine is set beyond the ken of men, such as the doctrine on the forgiveness of sins and on faith, one needs to acknowledge that he was instructed by God; and many among us saw the distress among those whom he taught that it needs to be acknowledged by faith that we are received and heard by God.

Therefore always and for all eternity worthy minds will praise the gifts that God has given to the Church through Luther. And first they will thank God. Then they will declare that they also owe much to man's own labours, even though godless men, who mock the entire Church, judge that these virtuous actions (*katorthōmata*) are a silly game or madness.

Neither have quarrels been set in motion, nor – as some say falsely – has the apple of strife[2] been thrown at the Church, nor have the riddles of the sphinx (*sphingos*) been set forth. For to the sound-minded and pious, and those who do not judge in bad faith, it is easy to see, by comparing opinions, what agrees with heavenly doctrine and what does not. Indeed, there is no doubt that in the minds of all the pious these questions have already been decided. For, since God willed Himself and His will to be beheld in the prophetic and Apostolic language in which He disclosed Himself, one must not assume that this language is obscure, like the leaves of the Sibyl.[3] These fly away whirling, the sport of the rapid winds.

However, some who are not evil have nevertheless complained that Luther was harsher than he needed to be. I do not argue for either side, but I reply with words that Erasmus often said: 'Because of the greatness of its diseases God gave this final age a severe physician.' Since He had called forth such a great instrument against the proud and impudent enemies of truth – as He said to Jeremiah: 'Behold, I have put my words in thy mouth . . . I have set thee over the nations . . . to throw down, to build' [Jeremiah 1:9–10] – and He had wanted to oppose them with that Gorgo,[4] so to speak, they dispute with God in vain. God neither rules the Church by human counsel, nor does He want His instruments to be utterly similar. But it is common that mediocre and moderate intellects approve less of

---

[2] In German, *Zankapfel* referring to the apple which the goddess of discord, Eris, tossed into the assembly of Gods. A competition over this apple which had an inscription 'to the fairest', led to the judgement of Paris, and to the ruin of Troy.
[3] Sibyl wrote her oracles on leaves, which were disturbed in her cave by a wind: see Virgil, *Aeneid*, III.444–50.
[4] For Gorgo, see note 16, oration 30, p. 253.

more passionate impulses, be they good or bad. Aristides saw Themistocles undertake great things with a prodigious impulse of his mind and conduct them successfully; but although he rejoiced in the success of the state, he nevertheless strove to call back Themistocles' excited mind from that course.

Nor do I deny that now and then the more violent impulses go amiss; for amidst this weakness of nature no one is utterly without blemish. However, if there is still someone who is as the ancients described Hercules, Cimon and others – unadorned, but for the most part, good (*akompsos men, alla ta megista agathos*) [Plutarch, *Life of Cimon* IV.4] – he is a good man and worthy of praise. And if he serves properly as a soldier in the Church, as Paul says, keeping his faith and good conscience, he pleases God and is to be revered by us.

We know that Luther was such a man. For he both steadfastly defended the purity of doctrine and kept the integrity of his conscience. Moreover, who is there who knew him who does not know with how much humanity he was endowed, how great his kindness was in gatherings with friends and how little disputatious or quarrelsome he was? And nevertheless everything had an added gravity, as there needs to be in such a man, for in that 'a character without deceit, and a courteous mouth' (*apseudes ēthos, euprosēgoros stoma*).

Or rather everything was, according to Paul, most true (*hosa alēthē*), honest (*hosa semna*), just (*hosa dikaia*), pure (*hosa hagna*), lovely (*hosa prosphilē*) and of good repute (*hosa euphēma*), so that it is evident that his harshness was zeal (*zēlou*) for truth, and not for ambition (*eritheias*) or harshness [Philippians 4:8]. All of us, and many outside, are witnesses to these things: if I undertook a laudation of the man regarding the rest of his life which he led, until the age of sixty-three, in the greatest and harshest study of piety and all good things and arts, what a distinguished and splendid oration could I have! Never were any doubtful desires noticed in him, nor any quarrelsome counsels; rather he was the one who advised, several times, that weapons should be laid down; he did not mingle affairs of the Church with any cunning for the increase of his power or that of his followers. I reckon that this wisdom and virtue is such that it should not appear that it was possible to obtain it by mere human diligence; but it is also necessary for the mind to be curbed by divine providence, in particular those that are severe, excellent and passionate – and the facts show Luther to have been utterly so.

What shall I say of his other virtues? Often I myself came upon him as, in tears, he said his prayers for the entire Church. For almost daily he took a certain time for reciting the Psalms, with which he mingled his prayers, lamenting and weeping; and often he said that he was angry with those who – either from ignorance or because of their interest – say that it is sufficient to pray only with lamentation. He said that the forms of prayer are prescribed to us by divine counsel so that the saying of prayers rouse the mind; indeed so that the voice also acknowledge whom we invoke as God.

In like manner, when many weighty decisions on public dangers often came to pass, we noticed that he was endowed with prodigious strength of spirit, not in the least timid (*psophodeē*) or ever weakened by any fears. For he relied on the sacred anchor, as it is called, that is, the help of God, and he did not allow his faith to be driven out.

Otherwise he was also of such keenness of mind that in obscure matters he alone saw best of all what would be useful. Nor was he, as many believe, negligent in considering the state or in comprehending the wishes of others, but he both knew the state and accurately perceived the frame of mind and wishes of all those with whom he lived. And although the power of his intellect was most sharp, he nevertheless read most avidly ancient and recent ecclesiastical writings and all works of history, relating their examples to the present business with outstanding dexterity.

Certainly eternal monuments exist of his eloquence, in which without doubt he was equal to those in whom one considers the power of oratory to have been greatest.

We justly grieve for our own sake that such a man – endowed with the greatest powers of intellect, versed in doctrine, trained by long practice, adorned with many outstanding and heroic virtues, chosen by God for the renewal of the Church, and who furthermore embraced us all in his fatherly heart – has been called from among us. For we closely resemble orphans who have lost an outstanding and faithful father. But since it is necessary to obey God, let us nevertheless not allow the memory of his virtues and services to perish among us. For Luther himself, however, let us rejoice that he is already in the friendly and most sweet fellowship of God and His Son, our Lord Jesus Christ, and of the prophets and Apostles, a fellowship which he always sought and longed for. There he not only hears that the labours he endured in spreading the Gospel are esteemed by the sign of God and the testimonies of the entire heavenly Church, but – having already been led forth from his mortal body as from a prison, and entered into a much more erudite school – he beholds nearby the essence of God, the two natures joined in the Son, and the whole purpose of the created and redeemed Church. These greatest things which he pondered in faith here when they were hidden and set forth in brief prophecies, he now sees before his eyes, and is now filled with the greatest joy and is already thanking God ardently with all his heart for such a great favour.

There he learns why the Son of God is called the word and image (*logos kai eikōn*) of the eternal Father, and in which way the Holy Spirit is the bond of mutual love, not only between the Father and the Son, but also between Them and the Church. He had grasped the first elements and rudiments of that doctrine in this mortal life, and he often used to speak most weightily and wisely about these highest things – about distinguishing between true and false invocation, about the true knowledge of God through understanding the divine revelations, and about distinguishing the true God from imaginary deities.

Many in this assembly heard him once expound the saying: 'you will see heaven opened and the angels of God ascending and descending upon the Son of man' [John 1:51]. On that occasion he first enjoined the listeners to fasten in their hearts this immense consolation which confirms that heaven is open, that is, it is opened for us towards God, that for those who take refuge with the Son the restraints of divine wrath are removed, that God is already dwelling close to us, and that by invoking Him we are received, guided and saved by Him.

He admonished us that this ordinance of God – which godless men clamour is fanciful – is to be set against human doubt and the fears which deter fleeing minds so that they dare all the less to invoke God, and do not rest in God. Furthermore, he said that the angels ascending and descending in Christ's body were the preachers of the Gospel who first, led by Christ, ascend to God and receive from Him the light of the Gospel and the Holy Spirit. After that they descend, however; that is, they perform the ministry of teaching among men.

He also added the explanation that even these heavenly spirits themselves, whom we usually call angels, in beholding the Son, are instructed and gladdened in that wonderful joining of the two natures; and that, since they are the Lord's soldiers in the defence of the Church, they are, so to speak, ruled by His hand.

Now he himself is a spectator of all these best things, and just as before he ascended and descended among the preachers of the Gospel, led by

Christ, so now he sees the angels being sent by Him, and together with them he delights in the contemplation of divine wisdom and the divine works.

We remember with what great pleasure he used to recount the polity, the councils, the perils and the liberation of the prophets, and with what great erudition he used to compare all the ages of the Church, in order to express his unique and burning desire to meet these most excellent men. Now he is embracing them, and rejoicing in listening and speaking to them face to face. They are now gladly greeting their fellow student (*symphoitētēn*), and together thanking God who unites and preserves the Church.

Let us therefore not doubt that Luther himself is happy. However, let us be distressed about our loss; and although it is necessary to obey the will of God – since He called him there – we should realise that God willed it, too, that we keep the memory of his virtues and services. Let us then perform this duty. Let us acknowledge that he was a salutary instrument of God, and let us study his teaching assiduously. Let us also imitate the virtues necessary to us for the benefit of our mediocrity: fear of God, faith and ardour in praying, integrity in the ministry, morality, diligence in avoiding quarrelsome counsel and desire to learn. And just as one needs to think often and much about the other pious leaders of the Church whose histories have come down to us, such as Jeremiah, John the Baptist and Paul, so let us also often consider this man's teaching and career, and let us add to this thanksgiving and praise – which it behoves us to utter now in this assembly as well. Therefore, say it with me with true piety of the heart.

We thank you, all-powerful God, eternal Father of our Lord Jesus Christ, Maker of your Church, together with your coeternal Son, our Lord Jesus Christ, and the Holy Spirit, who are wise, good, compassionate, a true judge, strong and most generous, for uniting to your Son the inheritance from humankind, for protecting the ministry of the Gospel and for having renewed it now through Luther. We pray with ardent prayers that you will continue to protect and guide the Church and seal up in us the true doctrine – just as Isaiah asks of his disciples – and kindle our minds by your Holy Spirit, so that we may invoke you properly and guide our behaviour piously.

Furthermore, since the death of great leaders often announces hardship for posterity, we beseech you, and all those to whom the office of teaching is entrusted, to think of the dangers of the world. In some parts the Turks are roaming, in others other enemies are threatening with civil wars, and everywhere the wantonness of people's minds is great which – particularly since they no longer fear Luther's criticism – corrupts with greater audacity the properly taught doctrine.

In order that God may avert these evils, let us be more diligent in guiding our behaviour and studies, and let us always keep this sentence imprinted in our hearts, that as long as we keep, take heed of, study and love the pure teaching of the Gospel, we will have a home with God, and the Church, as the Son of God said: 'If anyone loves me, he will preserve my word, and my Father will love him, we will come to him and make our home with him.' Let us encourage ourselves with this great promise to study the heavenly doctrine, and let us realise that humankind and the states are preserved for the sake of the Church, and let us perceive with our minds that future eternity to which God has called us. Certainly He did not disclose Himself in vain by such clear testimonies, nor did He send His Son in vain, but He truly loves, and cares for, those who praise these gifts. I have spoken.

Index

Biblical Citations

Cambridge texts in the history of philosophy

Titles published in the series thus far

Arnauld and Nicole *Logic or the Art of Thinking* (edited by Jill Vance Buroker)

Boyle *A Free Enquiry into the Vulgarly Received Notion of Nature* (edited by Edward B. Davis and Michael Hunter)

Bruno *Cause, Principle and Unity and Essays on Magic* (edited by Richard Blackwell and Robert de Lucca with an introduction by Alfonso Ingegno)

Clarke *A Demonstration of the Being and Attributes of God and Other Writings* (edited by Ezio Vailati)

Conway *The Principles of the Most Ancient and Modern Philosophy* (edited by Allison P. Coudert and Taylor Corse)

Cudworth *A Treatise Concerning Eternal and Immutable Morality* with *A Treatise of Freewill* (edited by Sarah Hutton)

Descartes *Meditations on First Philosophy*, with selections from the *Objections and Replies* (edited with an introduction by John Cottingham)

Descartes *The World and Other Writings* (edited by Stephen Gaukroger)

Hobbes and Bramhall on Liberty and Necessity (edited by Vere Chappell)

Kant *Critique of Practical Reason* (edited by Mary Gregor with an introduction by Andrews Reath)

Kant *Groundwork of the Metaphysics of Morals* (edited by Mary Gregor with an introduction by Christine M. Korsgaard)

Kant *The Metaphysics of Morals* (edited by Mary Gregor with an introduction by Roger Sullivan)

Kant *Prolegomena to any Future Metaphysics* (edited by Gary Hatfield)

Kant *Religion within the Boundaries of Mere Reason and Other Writings* (edited by Allen Wood and George di Giovanni with an introduction by Robert Merrihew Adams)

La Mettrie *Machine Man and Other Writings* (edited by Ann Thomson)

Leibniz *New Essays on Human Understanding* (edited by Peter Remnant and Jonathan Bennett)

Malebranche *Dialogues on Metaphysics and on Religion* (edited by Nicholas Jolley and David Scott)

Malebranche *The Search after Truth* (edited by Thomas M. Lennon and Paul J. Olscamp)

Melanchthon *Orations on Philosophy and Education* (edited by Sachiko Kusukawa, translated by Christine F. Salazar)

Mendelssohn *Philosophical Writings* (edited by Daniel O. Dahlstrom)

Nietzsche *The Birth of Tragedy and Other Writings* (edited by Raymond Geuss and Ronald Speirs)

Nietzsche *Daybreak* (edited by Maudemarie Clark and Brian Leiter, translated by R.J. Hollingdale)

Nietzsche *Human, All Too Human* (translated by R.J. Hollingdale with an introduction by Richard Schacht)

Nietzsche *Untimely Meditations* (edited by Daniel Breazeale, translated by R.J. Hollingdale)

Schleiermacher *Hermeneutics and Criticism* (edited by Andrew Bowie)

Schleiermacher *On Religion: Speeches to its Cultured Despisers* (edited by Richard Crouter)

Schopenhauer *Prize Essay on the Freedom of the Will* (edited by Günter Zöller)